FROM RATTLE TO RADIO

Dedicated to the past and present staff of the
Metropolitan Police Communications Branch

FROM RATTLE
TO RADIO

by

John Bunker

K.A.F. BREWIN BOOKS. 1988

First published November 1988 by
K.A.F. Brewin Books, Doric House,
Church Street, Studley, Warwickshire.

ISBN 0 947731 28 8

Typeset in 11pt. Baskerville
and made and printed in Great Britain
by Supaprint (Redditch)Ltd.,
Redditch, Worcestershire.

CONTENTS

ACKNOWLEDGEMENTS

The author acknowledges with thanks the assistance given in preparing this book by the staffs of the Public Record Office, Kew, The Science Museum, South Kensington, The British Newspaper Library, Colindale, The Post Office Archives, St Martin Le Grand, Hammersmith and Fulham Libraries and the Hillingdon Library Service.

Also appreciated are — Roy Bertauche, British Telecom; E.T. Birch, British Telecom Museum, Oxford; Fred Geeves and Tony Elwood, Telecom Showcase, Blackfriars; Roy Rodwell, The Marconi Company; Ute Lammers, Siemens Museum, Munich; M.W. Hopson and Arthur Bishop, Modern Alarms; Ray Le Monde, ADT Systems; Stan Groom, Chubb Alarms; Mr. James Luxton, Home Office Directorate of Telecommunications; Mrs. C. Constantinides, the Post Office Archives, St Martin's Le Grand; Wendy Morris and the staff of the London Fire Brigade Library; Mark Hayball, Police History Society.

The following members of the Metrpolitan Police Civil Staff provided much valued assistance — Paul Williams, Ken Stone and Richard Sharp of the Metropolitan Police Museum; John Back, Carmen Donaldson and Sheila Bywater (retired) of the Metropolitan Police Archives; Norman Fairfax MBE (retired) of the Metropolitan Police History Society; Roy Kepple of the Photographic Library; Pat Plank (retired) and the staff of the Metropolitan Police Library, New Scotland Yard; Peter Walton (retired), Dennis Wildey and Lyell Herdman (retired) of the Chief Engineers Department; Bill Waddell, Curator of the Black Museum; Brian Blacklock (retired) of General Registry Noting Index, NSY. Beverley Sparrow, Toni Mead (nee Gowler), Dawn Lillywhite, John Collings and Iris Barnes also provided help without which this book would not have been possible.

The following police officers with an interest in police history also provided useful information or support — Ch. Supt. Edward Gleeson, TO25 Branch, Ch.Supt. Peter Galley, M.B.E.TO25 Branch (retired), Inspector Eddie George, Command and Control Group, Sergeant Ray Seal, Met. Police Traffic Museum, Sergeant Bernard Brown, Battersea Police Station, Constable Bryn Elliot, Waltham Abbey Police Station and Constable Daniel Lines, Thames Division Museum. Chief Inspector Tony Tyrrell of MS21 Branch provided endless encouragement throughout the project.

Particularly appreciated were the experiences of retired police officers — ex Superintendent John Trendall, ex Inspector Thomas George Cole and ex Constable Harold Langton.

INTRODUCTION

Telecommunications are today an integral part of efficient and effective policing. That the earliest officers were required to perform all aspects of their duties without proper facilities is difficult to imagine in these days of computerised systems. This operational policeman's view (without the benefit of technical knowledge) of the important events in Force communications may place a different emphasis to that of the engineer.

Before arriving at Cannon Row Police Station on 23 April 1957 to start my first day of duty I had been instructed to blow three short sharp blasts on my whistle to summon assistance in an emergency or, at night, to avoid attracting attention, the torch could be flashed three times towards the direction in which another constable may be patrolling. Once out on my beat the Police Box was to be my sole means of communicating directly with the police station and 'Charlie-one' Area Car provided 'A' Division's two way radio link with Information Room to respond to '999' emergencies. As I progressed through my service the personal radio was to replace the Police Box and the computer screen has now had considerable impact on the paper message.

My involvement in commissioning the new Command and Control system, introduced in 1984, sparked an interest in the history of communications. In the many histories of the Metropolitan Police Force produced over the years only passing reference has been made to this very important subject.

The years from 1829 to 1937 cover the times when there was little or no 'telecommunications' apart from the rattle, through the development of the electric telegraph, telephone and by the 1920s the birth of wireless albeit mainly Morse Code. November 1987 marked the fiftieth anniversary of the introduction of the '999' system into Information Room which provided a suitable landmark to complete the detailed research.

It has to be conceded that the Force was slow to realise the value of rapid communication in its early years and in many instances there was solid opposition to new technology. Although the electric telegraph was well established by the middle of the century it was not until 1867 that the internal Force system was introduced. Public telephone exchanges for example had been operating for many years before the Force, as a result of public pressure, agreed to be connected to the network. Other police forces were often ahead of the Metropolitan Police in adapting to new technology.

This book contains no historical analysis of events or technical descriptions of equipment. It is intended to be a detailed account of the development of Metropolitan Police communications and the difficulties of policing without adequate equipment. Suppliers of apparatus have been identified along with specific dates of implementation where these can be verified.   The details of the pioneers of wireless and Information Room up to 1937 purposely includes the names of those lower ranks who actually performed the tasks.   The writer apologises for any exclusions but it has been necessary to rely on occasions upon incomplete records and fading memories.

The basic ingredients for successfully preventing and detecting crime have differed little over the centuries.   John Fielding suggested in his plan for his 'thief takers' in 1753 'quick notice and sudden pursuit' and the Commissioner of the late 1920s, Viscount Byng of Vimy, observed, 'Time is always on the side of the criminal.   We must give the criminal less time!'   Improved communications have played an essential role in the Force's successful challenge to the criminal.

This book has brought the previously rather fragmented and sketchy accounts of Metropolitan Police communications prior to World War II into some sort of order.   In addition to its general interest, future historians, who wish to study particular aspects in more detail, should find it a sound base for their research.

Although considerable care has been taken in compiling and verifying information contained in this publication the author accepts full responsibility for any errors or omissions which may occur.   As a serving police officer I must also emphasise that any views expressed are personal and do not reflect the policy of the Metropolitan Police.

John Bunker

T.O.25 Branch
New Scotland Yard
July, 1988

CHAPTER I

COMMUNICATING IN THE EARLY DAYS –
RATTLES, ROUTES AND ELECTRIC TELEGRAPH

On 29th September, 1829 the first Constables of the Metropolitan Police Force paraded for duty at 4 Whitehall Place, Westminster (known as Scotland Yard) and at five old watch houses. The Force initially comprised of about 1,000 men policing the six divisional areas nearest Westminster north of the Thames and under the command of the two Commissioners, Richard Mayne and Charles Rowan. Each company or division consisted of 164 men, although this standard strength did not remain for long. In February, 1830 a further five divisions were formed and, as more men were recruited, the number increased to seventeen covering the City of Westminster and specified parts of Middlesex, Surrey and Kent (roughly the limits of the Bow Street Foot Patrols) with a total strength of about 3,350 men.

The area was enlarged in 1840 to incorporate the County Borough of Croydon and parts of the counties of Hertfordshire and Essex the establishment then being increased to 4,300. The boundary now extended to approximately the distance covered by the Bow Street Horse Patrols, about 15 to 16 miles from Charing Cross. These patrols, formed in 1805, were incorporated into the Metropolitan Police in October, 1836.

The divisions, each under the overall command of a Superintendent, were divided into measured beats varying according to local conditions and an officer would normally be able to cover the whole of his beat on foot at two or three miles per hour in ten to fifteen minutes. His instructions were to see every part of his beat within the alotted time on a regular basis. In this way any member of the public requiring to communicate with the officer for assistance would merely have to remain in the same spot for a short time and would thereby meet the constable.

A Commissioner's Order of 30th November, 1829 drew notice to the manner in which constables on duty were to make their rounds and that they 'should more ordinarily be at about 3 miles per hour and ensure constant observation of all parts of their beat'. The constable was not to stop or loiter unnecessarily.

In the early days the constable on his beat would act as an 'alarm clock' for some of 'his residents' providing their early morning call. Requesting payment for this service, however, was clearly against Force regulations. During an enquiry into the Force in 1868 Superintendent Kittle of the Executive Branch at Scotland Yard when asked, in reference to such calls, 'Do you think that it tends to take a man away from certain parts of his beat, to the part that pays him best?', agreed that there may be such a tendency, but was of the view that a constable did not normally neglect any part of his beat for another.

The 1830s and 1840s were to be turbulent times and from the first

1

day the officers on the beat were policing a large area of the crime ridden city with minimum means of communication. Forty years on a Force-wide telegraph system was to be introduced and many years later a telephone network. Robbery and burglary were widespread as they are in modern times and these formative years were to witness much civil unrest in the Metropolis.

By 11 a.m. on the first day Mr Parker of Holborn had supplied one thousand rattles, which were to remain the only means of rapid personal communication for the man on the beat for many years. The rattle, which was carried in his coat tail pocket, was the constable's main means of summoning help and had been used by the Watchmen or 'Charleys' long before the Force had been instituted. The Watchman also resorted to his bell or tapped his staff to communicate; methods which do not appear to have been undertaken by the Metropolitan Force.

The Instruction Book of 1836 included in the duties of a police constable, 'He is not to call the hour; and if at any time he requires immediate assistance, and cannot in any other way obtain it, he must spring his rattle, but this is to be done as seldom as possible, for although he is provided with one, and may sometimes find it necessary to use it, such alarm often creates the inconvenience which it is intended to prevent, by assembling a crowd. He is required to report to the Sergeant of his party every occasion of using the rattle'. The Watchmen had been responsible for calling the hour a practice not transferred to the new Force.

A Police Order of 3rd October, 1829 states 'When Police Constables are sent up on Special duty amongst the crowd or to clear away a mob of persons they will always have in addition to the staff which they must have upon all occasions when on duty each a pair of handcuffs and a rattle, neither of these however will be made use of except in cases of necessity'.

The rattle was in due course marked with the divisional letter and number of the officer to whom issued and had to be shown to the Inspector by him when parading for duty. On 10th February, 1838 a report was called for in respect of damaged rattles in order that an assessment of the number could be made and constables charged for any damage found to the equipment.

One of the responsibilities of the new police — to preserve life and protect property — meant that fire was a matter of great concern to the Victorian policeman who co-operated as far as possible with the various fire brigades and escape stations. The fact that he often received a reward for his assistance at the scene of a fire may have aided the co-operation. The constable was instructed as early as 1830 that he must 'learn the residence of any firemen on his beat and call him up as soon as possible after the alarm is given.' However, the officer was not always popular with firemen and his instructions were not to direct or control the proceedings of the regular firemen at the scene of a fire, although he was to avoid sending for the brigade if he could extinguish the fire himself.

A 'Charlie', Charles Rouse, equipped with rattle and lantern at his
Box in Brixton Road.

3

It is claimed that prior to 1833 a third of all fires were extinguished by police prior to the arrival of the brigade.

The London Fire Engine Establishment, formed on 1 January, 1833 for 'the prevention and better extinction of fire', incorporated a number of the old insurance company brigades with a total of nineteen stations and eighty four men. Details of stations, locations of engines and addresses of turncocks were recorded in Police Orders for the information of the divisions.

The rattle played a very important role for a constable who discovered a fire, his first duty being to arouse the inmates of the stricken premises by 'springing his rattle', ringing bells and knocking the doors. In addition to assisting the occupants' escape the policeman had to send messages to the fire officer, the engine keeper, the turncock and obtain further police aid; a busy man without any technical means of communication.

At 12.20 a.m. on 5th January, 1870, Sergeant Dolphin saw flames coming from the kitchen at 37 Gloucester Place, London, W2. He sprang his rattle and violently rang the house bell causing the residents to appear at one of the upstairs windows. This prompt action be the sergeant and his rattle saved the lives of the threatened occupants. At a similar incident on 6th January PC Thomas Leach, on patrol at 2.45 in the morning, saw smoke coming from the shop shutters at 86 Harrow Road. Two officers came to his assistance after he raised the alarm with his rattle. Between them they rescued the residents after breaking down the door.

Specific references to springing the rattle in the event of fire are made in the instructions dealing with the policing of exhibitions attracting large crowds of people; such an event was the International Exhibition of 1862.

James Braidwood, the Superintendent of the Fire Engine Establishment, issued cards to police containing information regarding the methods of dealing with fires. The cards, initially issued in 1842, were carefully preserved by each constable and replaced from time to time with up to date details of the Establishment's stations. In addition to summoning the fire engines the constable was responsible for ensuring that there was no delay in calling the independently organised fire escapes although in a Police Order of May, 1857, the Commissioner declined to give an instruction that the nearest fire escape station should be notified before the brigade. An Order of April, 1858 requested reports on whether it would be practical or advisable for the second constable arriving at a fire to give an alarm to the conductor of the nearest escape before sending for the fire engines. Sergeants were instructed to frequently question their constables ensuring that they knew the nearest escapes to their beats and the sergeant himself was required to know the location of all such equipment on his section.

The brigades often relied upon watch towers to locate fires with firemen taking turns as lookouts; runners were used to raise the alarm and call out firemen from their homes. Between 1860 and 1869, police attended a total of 6,782 fires in the Metropolis.

In January, 1841 divisional Superintendents, at a briefing by the Commissioner, were told that officers discovering a fire and reporting it to the fire brigade stations would receive ten shillings reward from the Fire Establishment, providing that no lives were lost. Any gratuities granted to constables for assistance had to be approved by the Commissioner and were published in Police Orders. Expenses incurred by the officer in giving information to the brigade, including the cost of cab hire, were reclaimed from the Superintendent of the Establishment.

Operating in many areas were the volunteer fire brigades and officers were instructed by a Police Order of February, 1864 to 'give notice of all fires south of the Thames within a moderate distance' to the Surrey Volunteer Brigade at 30 Hill Street, Peckham. Similar instructions were given in respect of the Kentish and Camden Fire Brigade. Mr Hodges' Fire Engine Station at the Distillery, Lambeth was to be notified when a fire occurred on L, M, P or R Divisions by an Order of 14th February, 1862. By the 1860s many of the fire escape stations employed a conductor in attendance during the night from whom police were to obtain assistance. Such stations were operating at Stratford-le-Bow, The Broadway, Kentish Town, Coburg Street and Trinity Street, Rother-hithe, Shadwell, Kilburn, West Ham and many other areas.

On 5th August, 1868 a Police Order was published consolidating the instructions to officers attending fires. As the telegraph and telephone were introduced these facilities began to play a more important part in passing information (described in the following chapters).

The Enfield Royal Small Arms factory was policed by Metropolitan officers who also operated the fire engine. In the case of fire a constable was to spring his rattle and inform the sergeant who would take charge of the engine. A similar system operated after the Force took over policing the dockyards.

Although the rattle was for the officer's benefit in obtaining assist-ance it could be used against him as PC 205K was to discover when he disturbed three men committing a burglary at Lower Shadwell on 19th December, 1872. A struggle ensued as he arrested one of the burglars and he took his rattle out to spring for assistance. The instrument was wrenched away from him and one of the criminals struck him violently on the head with it. The constable was then dragged down the stairs at Bell Wharf to the River where two of the men climbed into a boat pulling the constable's prisoner behind them. PC 205 did not give up but held on to his man until, up to his neck in water, he was forced to release him. Fortunately another constable came to his aid and one of the men was subsequently detained.

During the Fenian troubles an Order of 1868 directed that, in the event of any sudden emergency requiring the attendance of officers from their beats 'the Inspector or Sergeant is to cause the rattle to be sprung at the Station House door continuously until the Constables are assembled.'

As early as 5 February, 1845 the replacement of rattles by whistles was being considered. However, this did not occur and in 1865 one hundred new pattern rattles were distributed on a number of divisions for evaluation; the list of appointments supplied by the contractor indicates that in 1873 two patterns were in use. Rattles continued unhindered until in 1883 tests carried out compared their effectiveness with that of whistles. The findings were that a rattle could be heard well up to 400 yards and very indistinctly up to 700 yards whereas a whistle was distinct up to 900 yards and could still be heard at 1,000 yards. 'Punch', describing the earlier experiment with the whistle, even suggested that it would be attached to the truncheon fearing more use of the weapon by constables.

The magazine showed considerable interest in the whistle in 1883, with the verse 'The Whistling Bobby'.

> WHEN bold burglarious BILL
> In suburbs loiters late,
> His whistle low and shrill
> Is signal to his mate.
> Who-ee! Who-ee! Who-ee!
> "BOBBY!" the wise ones said,
> "Come! this will never do.
> The whistling thief to equal, you
> Must have a whistle too—
> A loud shrill whistle too!
>
> "You've lived a long time, BOBBY,
> In danger, if not fear;
> Now you shall have a whistle,
> That all around may hear."
> Brave BOBBY mutters "Fiddle!"
> And tips his mate the wink.
> Says he to himself— "Old bloke, you are
> A snide one, I don't think,—
> A cute one, I don't think!"
>
> "BOBBY, the Public seems
> Uneasy in its mind;
> But a pistol's an awkward thing,
> Which needless you will find."
> "That's true enough, by day,
> But perhaps I may remark,
> Through a truncheon may do in a city fray,
> It's a different thing in the dark;
> In suburban lanes in the dark!

"Say SIKES is on his lay,
On a night with ne'er a moon,
Must I out with my whistle and play
A sort of a lively tune?
What if BILL hears my tune?
A thundering lot he'll mind.
He outs with his 'barky' shart and soon;
And you can't charm bullets with wind,
Charm pistol-bullets with wind.

"BILL's not such a fool as you think;
He'll 'cop' my truncheon, pat,
Jam the whistle into my mouth,
And stretch the Peeler flat.
No, no! on a lonely beat,
I'd like more comrades near,
And—something to reach the Cracksman's head
As well as the public ear,—
As well as the neighbouring ear!"

'Punch' also prepared some New Police Regulations — 'to accompany the Presentation of the latest arm of the Force; a whistle.'

1.   SHOULD you notice a Housebreaker entering a mansion at midnight by a cut-out window, you will ask him politely what business brings him to the place in so unconventional a manner and at so inconvenient an hour.

2.   Should the Housebreaker refuse to answer you, or reply rudely, with an oath, that "You had better mind your own concerns, and leave him alone," you will produce a text-book upon the Criminal Law, and explain to him in what manner he may be guilty of a felony.

3.   Should he treat your lecture with contempt, you will assure him that you are a Constable, and produce your credentials for his examination.

4.   Should the Housebreaker be still unreasonable, you will call upon him to distinguish the difference existing between the status of one of the Public and that of an Officer of the Law.

5.   Should the Housebreaker still turn a deaf ear to your admonitions, you will warn him that if he enters the mansion with felonious intent, it will be your duty, in discharge of your official position, to arrest him.

6.   Should the Housebreaker after this enter the mansion, seize all the plate, slaughter the larger part of the family, and fire with a revolver half a dozen shots at yourself, you will instantly produce the substitute you have recently received for your rattle, and — whistle for the thief!

Initial opposition to the abolition of the rattle in favour of the whistle resulted from not only its value as an alarm but the service it gave

7

for defensive purposes along with the truncheon. On 7th February, 1884 whistles were provided to police serving on outer districts and approval given for the issue of 7,175 of the pattern used by the Manchester Police. The Force were 'not to issue superior officers with a different class of whistle'.

On 10th February, 1885 each officer was issued with a whistle in place of a rattle. Night duty sergeants and constables were still required to carry rattles from stocks kept in the station; however, evidence taken from a number of constables led to the recommendation that rattles should be abolished completely as they were considered too cumbersome. Soon only whistles were carried and on 16th April, 1887 a direction required that all rattles be collected and returned to the Receiver's Store. Instructions were that police summoning assistance or raising alarm must sound a very long and a very short blast alternately. In this way it would be recognised as a police whistle.

REAL PRESENCE OF MIND

Policeman X 24, drunk and almost incapable, is just able to blow his whistle for help!

Although residents of a neighbourhood wishing to obtain the assistance of police often used a rattle clearly some doubt existed about the authority of the public to possess a police whistle. Mr Crosbie of Leytonstone wrote to the Commissioner in 1885 after purchasing two whistles, with Metropolitan Police thereon, through the Illustrated London News from Baxter and Co, Eland Street, Wandsworth and asked whether they could be used by the public for 'legitimate alarm'. He was asked to forward them to Scotland Yard for examination, and his attention was drawn to an act of parliament, although it was not made clear whether their use was illegal.

Bent and Parker of Birmingham wrote to the Receiver in April, 1885 stating that the company had 2,000 whistles in stock and asked if they could be taken off their hands at ten pence halfpenny each by the Metropolitan Police.

The original whistle chain, 15 inches long, was fastened to the second buttonhole of the tunic or greatcoat. Not until the 1920s were whistle pockets introduced in the uniform and the chain reduced to a 12 inch length.

The constables of the five dockyard divisions (described later) used whistles from the time of their formation although rattles were also provided. Wooden summonsing whistles were carried on Thames Division skiffs to attract the attention of watermen and it is claimed that officers on the River, like their counterparts ashore in the dockyards, also carried a whistle and chain by 1872 (this has not been confirmed). A short silver plated brass driver's whistle was used in the 1890s on the early launches. Dockyard police used a naval 'flute' pattern whistle.

The London Dock Company Regulations included instructions that, upon the alarm of fire being received from any part of the docks, 'the Police Constable stationed at Wapping Basin is to ring the Bells over Trench Street Gate to alarm the officers resident on the Pier Head'.

The whistle continued as the main instrument for obtaining assistance on the beat until the introduction of the personal radio in the mid 1960s; still carried for use in an emergency it is arguably more reliable, but whether all officers would always appreciate the significance of such an alarm is doubtful. Instructions are today that officers should blow three sharp blasts. Until very recent years whistles were inscribed with an identifying serial number, also noted on the constable's records. Whistles have changed little in the one hundred years that have passed being supplied almost exclusively by J. Hudson & Co., 131 Barr Street, Birmingham.

During his night patrols, normally commencing at 6 p.m., the officer on the beat would carry an oil lantern or 'lanthorn' as it is described in early Police Orders. Although there are no specific references to the use of the 'lanthorn' for communicating after dark in Victorian times, in modern days a constable who requires assistance may flash his torch three times in the direction in which another officer is likely to be patrolling. No doubt the man on the beat made similar use of this

9

equipment in the last century.

The initial 'lanthorns', supplied by a Mr Joyce, were ready for issue to the night duty officers on the day the Force was formed. Thomas Joyce and Son still supplied the famous 'bulls eye' lanterns to the service in 1843 and were required 'to clean and trim them daily with good burning oil and keep them in a thorough state of repair'. The contract with the Joyce company was cancelled in June, 1844. The cost to the Force of five pence halfpenny per lantern per week amounted to considerable expenditure. This was raised as a matter of concern as early as 1832 when the Commissioner questioned the considerable number of lamps in use and directed that Superintendents investigate the necessity of having so many issued. Recommendations as to those which could be dispensed with by constables or sergeants were requested from the Superintendents.

There was even a worry about fuel consumption when an Order of 1833 stated, "It has been reported that constables after their lamps are extinguished in the morning are in the habit ot taking out what oil is left considering it to be their own property. This practice is immediately to be put a stop to by the Superintendent". An interesting Order of May, 1840 states that officers were not to turn the lanterns suddenly on persons on horseback for fear of frightening the horses.

The divisional winter requirement for 'lanthorns' in 1847 was 1,601 an increase of seventy over the previous year. The largest allocation was to 'P' Division where two hundred and thirty were held compared with only eight on 'A' Division. The lanterns of the officers dismissed from their beats by the sergeant at the end of their tour of duty were gathered together and either taken to the station by the sergeant, or by a nominated constable.

Lanterns were only issued to a portion of the night duty shift during the winter months and in 1858 Superintendents were asked for their views as to whether all sergeants and constables should be supplied with one.

The bull's eye lamp supplied by Hiatt and Co, Birmingham was used by the Force from the 1840s followed in 1860 by an improved pattern. Examples of lamps marked Christie patent, Birmingham have been examined but references to their use have not been found. The Hiatt lantern it appears was issued to Thames Division in 1841 prior to which oil hurricane lamps were presumably used.

The contract with W Nunn and Co., 204 George Street, London Docks for supplying lamps and lanterns to the Force in 1877 required that those in use by constables were to be prepared by 6 p.m. each day by the contractor for the officers who would carry them on night duty. By this time the Force were using a total of 4,050 lanterns; 139 were allocated to Bow Street far in excess of any other station.

Certainly the lantern continued as a major expenditure as far as the Force was concerned. The cost of lanterns for officers on night duty in 1833 was £1,225.16s.9d. which included oil, trimming and repairs. This expenditure far exceeded that of the Force telegraph system for many years after its introduction in 1867. For example, in the financial year

Bulls eye lanterns — (i) Hiatt, (ii) Christie (iv) Nunn

Thames Police — signal to the shore

1872/3 £1,300.17s.6d. was spent on the telegraph and £6,103.2s.6d on lanterns. By 1899 the number of lanterns in use had risen to 6,463.

In 1885 the 'Crescent Lamp' supplied by Dolan and Co. of Vauxhall was approved for use by the Force. In that year a 'leather guard' issued for attachment to a constable's belt, was worn to avoid oil from the lamps soaking into the uniform.

The first electric lantern for police use, developed by George Wootton, subsequently the Force Engineer, was in operation early in the 1920s. His four volt model replaced the oil lamp followed in 1924 by the Wootton two volt accumulator on which a narrow or wide angle beam could be produced.

The twentieth century's increase in motor vehicles and their obvious danger to police on traffic point duty led to a short experiment in Brixton in 1915 where constables on such duties wore bullseye lanterns, displaying a red light, on their backs. White gloves, for constables employed on traffic duties, were introduced in 1921 thereby making signals more easily distinguishable and seven years later the local authorities agreed to provide spotlight to illuminate traffic pointsmen. White coats soon followed providing even more safety.

In 1839 the River Police, which had been established by Dr Patrick Colquhoun in 1798-1800, were incorporated into the Force. Thames Division officers made more use of lamps as signals than those on foot duty; when they required assistance from, or wished to communicate with Police on duty beside the river, they would show a red signal light towards the shore. On 13th April, 1841 'R' Division of the Force took over the responsibility for policing Deptford and Woolwich Dockyards from the Old Dockyard Police. Instructions were given that Inspectors on Thames Division boats, which were rowing boats at that time, had to pass the dockyard within 'hail' and render any assistance required.

Megaphones of hard leather would have been used on occasions to aid in passing messages from a boat to shore during the 19th century, although specific references have not been found. Signalling flags were available during the last century but more research is necessary to establish whether police actually used them. Yellow/red quadrant flags were, during the Second World War, a method of passing messages during radio silence.

The police on duty in the dockyard were instructed that on requiring the aid of a police boat they were to turn their light to the river and a signal would be returned by the red light from any boat within sight. The duties of the crews were arranged so that boats on patrol between Wapping and Greenwich were constantly in the vicinity of the Deptford Dockyard. Similarly Woolwich Dockyard was covered by a boat from Blackwall Station. In 1907 Thames Division replaced their oil lamps with acetylene lamps and continued to use these until the early 1930s after which the Aldis lamp was introduced.

There is evidence of signalling devices used on land from the trial recorded in Police Orders of 1st May, 1858 when the Superintendents of

A,B,D,G,H,M.P and T Divisions were instructed to attend Marble Arch to witness an experiment with a signal light. No further information has been found concerning the purpose of this signal. The street crossing signal installed in 1868 at Bridge Street near the Houses of Parliament incorporated semaphore arms and a green and red light to control traffic. An explosion of gas in the light put an end to this equipment the forerunner of the traffic light which is beyond the scope of this book.

No account was taken of their lack of communication facilities when dealing with officers for breaches of discipline. As early as 11th December, 1829 Sergeant Thomas Wright and Constable Isaac Crutherton were suspended from duty for lack of vigilence in preventing a burglary. Absence from his beat was an offence for which an officer would normally be dismissed and on 15th December, 1829 men took advantage of the dense fog to leave their beats unattended. The failure to discover a burglary, in an incident where a ladder had been placed against a wall, resulted in the dismissal of PC Betts in January, 1830. There are many other examples of harsh discipline in the early days.

In some instances, however, constables were encouraged to use initiative in the absence of good communication facilities. A Police Order of 16th October, 1829 instructed that a constable was permitted, on seeing a Hackney Coach pass in suspicious circumstances, between the hours of 12.30 a.m. and daylight, 'to quit his beat for the moment and jump up behind it if he cannot get the number otherwise and see where it goes to'. He had to tell the first constable he passed what he was doing in order that it could be arranged for another man to cover his beat until he returned.

Complaints that officers in uniform did not always respond to requests for assistance from the public led to a blue and white striped armlet being introduced shortly after the Force was formed. The armlet, worn by the sergeants and constables, communicated to the public and other officers that they were on duty. When the officer went off duty the armlet was removed; this remained a part of the uniform until 1968.

Divisional letters and numbers were a feature of the uniform providing a means of personal identification. They were embroidered on the collar surrounded by a crows foot pattern: sergeants were allocated the lower numbers between 1 and 16. Each sergeant and constable in today's Force still wears this form of identification.

Superintendents, Inspectors and sergeants were ordered in January, 1840 to pay more attention to teaching the men to be alert and intelligent in the performance of their duty and 'to make greater use of their eyes'. The Order went on to say 'If a man thinks he is doing his duty by loitering along the street without looking to the right or left he is much mistaken and cannot expect to remain in the service long'.

It was obviously important that the location of the police station should be communicated to the public. The origins of the Blue Lamp, now found outside the majority of police stations, are rather vague but in the early nineteenth century Westminster City Council made a ruling that all the police houses in the area were to carry lights to distinguish them from other premises. Eventually when gas lights were introduced blue glass was placed around the lamp in order that the police station could be easily identified to the public. A Police Order of February 1861 directs divisional Superintendents to requisition for three squares of glass for each lamp outside their stations.

Queen Victoria, attending the Royal Opera House, objected to the blue lamp above the door of Bow Street Police Station; this royal objection resulted in its removal. The Queen's distaste did not deter the Force and the 1940s film 'The Blue Lamp' starring Jack Warner immortalised Paddington Green's lamp.

In 1862, due to the number of street robberies and garrotting, a total of 17 sergeants and 176 constables were taken from beat duty and employed in plain clothes from 10 p.m. until 2 a.m. throughout the Force area. The largest number totalling 25 officers were employed on 'G' Division but attempts to secure assistance in the event of a violent arrest would probably have been in vain without the advantages of telephone or wireless.

Communicating information to the public was generally by the posting of notices, a method still used today. Police Orders of 1st November, 1831, instruct Superintendents to employ a 'Bill sticker' to

Blue Lamp

post up the 'Police Cautions' in the most public part of their division. Shopkeepers were requested to place police notices in their windows for the information of the public and references are made, in Commissioner's Orders of October, 1850, to the circulation of 'Caution to Households' bills 1,870 of which were sent out to divisions for distribution.

Notices offering rewards for information leading to the apprehension of murderers were printed by W Clowes and Sons, 14 Charing Cross on behalf of the Metropolitan Police. In many cases an accomplice, who had not actually committed the murder, was offered the grant of Her Majesty's Pardon if he gave evidence leading to a conviction. Advice provided by police officers personally was sometimes more appropriate as with warnings to watchmakers, jewellers and silversmiths about the possibility of breakings between Saturday night and Monday morning.

By the middle of the century it was becoming impossible to provide adequate coverage on all beats and as Superintendent Kittle of the Executive Branch was to report to a Committee in 1868, 'Another continuous complaint on the part of the Superintendents is their not having sufficient men to give proper protection to beats in new neighbourhoods'. One Superintendent reported that the number of houses on one beat on his division had increased from 100 to 1000. Officers were also taken away from beat duty to perform duty at theatres and other places of entertainment which attracted large crowds. The original guarantee that the member of the public remaining in one location in the street for a short time would be certain to see a constable was no longer achievable. An answer was found with the establishment of Fixed Points on 3rd December, 1870.

In 1871 the public were assisted when printed notices detailing the fixed points on a division were distributed to respectable householders in the area and also displayed at police stations. This made it essential that a constable was always on duty at the point at the agreed times in case his services were required by the inhabitants of the area. Details of the location of fixed points were published in Police Orders.

By the end of the year there were a total of 207 approved fixed points throughout the Force which, although a monotonous duty for the constable, were widely praised by the public and Superintendents in charge of divisions. In these early days there were some fixed point boxes but generally the constable was merely posted to a specified location and on hearing a rattle sounded or the 'persistent ringing of a bell' would proceed at once to render assistance.

It was said that increases in the number of fixed points would make the common phrase 'never being able to find a policeman when he is wanted' a thing of the past. Complaints from residents were reduced as a direct result of the system and the Superintendent of M Division reported in 1872 the general satisfaction of the public who 'were easily able to obtain the services of a Constable'.

Long before the Force was formed publications were used to circulate information concerning suspects of crime. Sir John Fielding the

£50 Reward.

MURDER.

WHEREAS a Warrant has been granted for the Apprehension of FREDERICK GEORGE MANNING, late of No. 3, Minerva Place, New Weston Street, Bermondsey, charged with the MURDER and ROBBERY of Mr. PATRICK O'CONNOR, Custom House Officer, on the 9th day of August.

DESCRIPTION.

FREDERICK GEORGE MANNING, 35 years old, 5 feet 8 or 9 inches high, stout, very fair and florid complexion, full bloated face, light hair, small sandy whiskers, light blue eyes, and a peculiar fall of the eyelids at the corners, and large mouth. Was dressed in an invisible green overcoat, brown trowsers, black hat, and wore a small plaited linen shirt front. He was formerly a Guard on the Great Western Railway, and kept an Inn at Taunton, in Somersetshire, in the latter part of last year. Since then he kept a Public-house in the neighbourhood of the Kingsland Road, and has resided in Minerva Place since Midsummer last, out of Business.

A Reward of Fifty Pounds

Will be paid by Her Majesty's Government for the apprehension of the said FREDERICK GEORGE MANNING.

And the Secretary of State will advise the grant of Her Majesty's gracious Pardon to any accomplice, not being the Person who actually fired the shot, or inflicted the mortal wound, who shall give such information and evidence as shall lead to the Discovery and Conviction of the Murderer or Murderers of the before-named PATRICK O'CONNOR.

Information to be given to any of the Police Stations in the Metropolitan Police District.

Metropolitan Police Office,
August 22nd, 1849.

Printed by W. CLOWES and SONS, 14, Charing Cross.

POLICE CAUTION.

BURGLARIES OR LARCENIES IN HOUSES

Attempted in any of the following ways may be most effectually prevented if due precautions are taken by the inmates.

1st. By entering with false or skeleton keys in the absence of the family, especially on Saturday and Sunday evenings.

2nd. By passing through an empty house in the neighbourhood, and entering from the roof through the attic windows.

3rd. By window shutters insecurely fastened, which can be instantly removed, and property stolen by the hand, or passing any instrument through the window.

4th. By calling at houses under pretence of having messages or parcels to deliver, and, during the absence of the servant, stealing articles from the passage.

5th. By *climbing up the portico*, and entering through upper windows.

Metropolitan Police Office.

(3865.) — Z. 638—50,000—3/69

Bow Street Magistrate used his 'Quarterly Pursuit' and 'Weekly Pursuit', later renamed 'Public Hue and Cry', to circulate information in the 18th Century. As is the case today much of the communication in the early days of the Force was in the form of written or printed documents. An Instruction Book, issued to each constable soon after the formation of the Force, was his 'bible' containing orders on how the various duties were to be carried out.

The main documents, published for the circulation of information in respect of crime suspects and property lost or stolen in the last century, remain in being today still providing a valuable service to the Force. Most important is probably Police Gazette (previously entitled Hue and Cry) which, from 1828, under its new name, was edited by the Chief Clerk at Bow Street and published once each week and in due course circulated to every police force in the country. Publication was taken over many years later in 1883 by Scotland Yard and after 1914 produced more frequently. More recent years have seen the development of special supplements giving information concerning expert criminals, deserters, aliens and stolen motor vehicles.

The authorised circulation of Gazette in 1852 was two copies for each Inspector station, one for each sergeant station and one for each section. There were eight copies for the detectives at Scotland Yard. Distribution of 486 copies was as follows —

A Div. — 15	G Div. — 20	P Div. — 33
B Div. — 21	H Div. — 14	R Div. — 50
C Div. — 16	K Div. — 46	S Div. — 41
D Div. — 24	L Div. — 18	T Div. — 35
E Div. — 14	M Div. — 23	V Div. — 39
F Div. — 10	N Div. — 45	Thames Div. — 6
		Commissioner Office — 16

Police Orders were originally issued daily to the Force and, in addition to containing information regarding police resignations, dismissals, fines and punishments, gave instructions which were to be 'strictly and rigidly' obeyed by all ranks. These instructions were often consolidated into General Orders. Prior to 1857, when Harrison and Co. of St Martins Lane were contracted to print them, Police Orders were handwritten. In 1864 the printing moved to premises at the rear of 4 Whitehall Place and in 1891 the Receiver purchased the printing plant from the then contractor, James Truscott and Son, and employed his own printing staff.

Initially Informations relating to crime, property lost, stolen or found or animals lost, found or wanted were circulated six times in each twenty four hours. From September, 1857 they were printed and in due course issue was reduced to four times each weekday and twice on Sunday. The printer would continue to add information right up to the moment of despatch.

Pawnbrokers Lists gave details of identifiable articles stolen and were

POLICE GAZETTE; OR, HUE AND CRY.

Published by Authority.

CONTAINING

The Substance of all informations received in Cases of Felony and of Misdemeanors of an aggravated nature, and against Receivers of Stolen Goods, reputed Thieves, and Offenders escaped from Custody, with the time, the place, and the circumstances of the Offence. The Names of Persons charged with Offences, who are known but not in Custody, and a Description of those who are not known, their Appearance, Dress, and other marks of identity. The Names of Accomplices and Accessories, with every Particular which may lead to their Apprehension. Also, a Description, as accurate as possible, of Property that has been Stolen and a minute description of Stolen Horses, with every useful Information, for the purpose of tracing and recovering them.

No. 1048.] WEDNESDAY, JANUARY 31, 1838.

**** It is requested that all Communications for the purpose of obtaining, or giving, information respecting supposed offenders, or stolen property, especially stolen horses, may be addressed to Mr. Burnaby, the Editor, Public Office, Bow-street.*

As no charge is made for the insertion of Articles relating to Stolen Property in the Police Gazette and Hue and Cry, all Letters addressed to the Editor upon that subject, are requested to be post-paid, otherwise the insertion requested will not take place; and Letters transmitted in any other way than by the post will not be noticed, as a penalty of £5 for each Letter so sent is incurred.

MURDER AND MALICIOUSLY STABBING.

On Wednesday evening, the 17th instant, about six o'clock, as Mr. Rumboll, of Lyneham Court Farm, in the parish of Lyneham, Wilts, was returning home from Calne Market, whilst passing through a Gap at the top of the first field leading from the Turnpike-road to his house, was shot at, and dangerously wounded in the arm.—Whoever will give such information as may lead to the discovery and conviction of the offender or offenders, shall, on such conviction, receive £200 Reward—£100 from the said Mr. Rumboll, and a further reward of £100 offered by Her Majesty's Government, who have also been pleased to promise a free Pardon to an accomplice making a full disclosure, except the actual perpetrator of the deed: the accomplice making such disclosure will also be entitled to the Reward.

ROBBERY FROM THE PERSON.

On Thursday evening, the 4th instant, John Jackson, of the Cross Houses, near Shrewsbury, on his return home, near Springfields, was stopped, by two Men, and robbed of a silver Watch, maker's name 'Robert Morris, Shrewsbury, No. 1639.'—They were about twenty years of age, five feet five inches high, slender made; one had on a fustian coat and trousers, the other a fustian stable-jacket.—Information to be given to Zachariah Price, police-officer, Shrewsbury.

On Wednesday night, the 6th ultimo, about half-past six o'clock, William Taylor, of Mill-hill, Hendon, Middlesex, was stopped at the end of Hendon Wood-lane, and robbed of twenty-two Sovereigns, two Half-sovereigns, and five-and-sixpence in silver, by four men, two of them tall, in long smock-frocks, one short and thin, in a fustian stable-jacket, who put a pistol to Mr. Taylor's head, the other was short and stout, with a ragged fustian coat. Five Pounds Reward will be paid by the said William Taylor, to any person that will give such information as will lead to the conviction of the offenders. Information to be given to Isaac Pye, superintendent of police, Barnet.

HOUSE-BREAKING.

JAMES JOHNSON, alias JENKINSON, stands charged with having broken into the dwelling-house of Miss Moore, at Parkstone, in the town and county of Poole, and stolen therefrom a variety of articles. He is a native of Lancashire, has a strong provincial dialect, and is supposed to have a wife and family residing at or in the vicinity of Manchester, from whom he has been absent about four or five years: he is apparently about thirty-five years of age, and five feet seven or eight inches in height, and wore, when he left Parkstone, a sleeve-waistcoat, canvas trousers, and a black glazed hat with a low crown and broad brim.—Information to be given to T. L. Whitt, constable, Parkstone, who holds a warrant for his apprehension.

On the night of the 25th instant, about six o'clock, the shop-window of Mr. Costar, watch and clock maker, of Maidenhead, was broken, and the following new silver Watches stolen therefrom, viz.: one double-bottomed Hunting-watch; one single-cased engine-turned Watch; one double-cased ditto, maker's name 'Marshall'; one ditto ditto, maker's name 'Hibbenline'; one second-hand small double-bottomed engine-turned Casewatch; one second-hand plain hunter, winds up on dial; two ditto double-cased, Italian figures; and one metal hunter, case recently re-gilt, with Italian figures.—Information to be given to Daniel Sexton, chief constable, Maidenhead, Berks.

On the night of Tuesday the 23d instant, or early the following morning, the workshop of Mr. John Money, at Little Coxwell, near Faringdon, Berks, was broken and entered, and three Hand-saws, one Tenant-saw, one Dovetail-saw, four small Hammers, two broad Axes, one Jack-plane, one Smoothing-plane, two Spoke-shaves, one large pair of Pincers, and a Bench-brush, were stolen therefrom. The handles of all the above articles (except the pincers) are marked "J. Money," with a small punch.—Whoever will give such information as may be the means of convicting the offender or offenders, shall be rewarded, on application to Mr. Money, or to Mr. R. W. Crowdy, solicitor, Faringdon, Berks.

On Saturday night, the 27th instant, the Shop of Messrs. William and Thomas Atwood, Grocers, Sutton-at-Hone, near Dartford, was broken and entered, and the following articles stolen, viz.—Half a sack of Flour, in a sack, marked on one side 'I. T.' on the other 'Thorp, Greatness'; 10 round Dutch Cheeses, 10 lbs. Derby, 14 lbs. Cheshire, 7 lbs. Currants, 7 lbs. Raisins, 30 lbs. Bacon, 28 lbs. Sugar, 3 lbs. Tea, and other articles.—Five Pounds Reward will be paid by Messrs. Atwood, on conviction of the offenders; information to be given to W. L. Pearce, high constable, Dartford.

On Wednesday night, the 17th instant, the Hall House, at Ladbrooke, Warwickshire, the seat of William Palmer Morewood, Esq., was broken and entered, and a pair of silver-mounted Spectacles much tarnished, a counterfeit Sovereign, a silver Caddy-spoon, a pair of cotton Stockings, and other articles, stolen therefrom.—The same night the House of Mr. Mann, of the same place, was broken and entered, and a Sugar-basin, a pair of Lady's Snow Boots tanned leather and buttoned on the side, a pair of Lady's Slippers, a rifle-barrelled Pistol (maker's name 'Bond, London'), a pack of Cards with yellow backs, and two green baize Table-cloths, were stolen.—Foot-marks of four or five Men were left in the snow about the houses; one a large right foot turned inwards: and there is no doubt the robbery was committed by five Men who were seen in a Barn on the morning after the robbery, and who left the boots and slippers behind them. These five Men were seen at Dunchurch on the 21st instant: one is a slim-made man, about five feet eight inches high, well dressed with light drab coat, bright metal buttons, three down the pockets, and drab trousers; another a stout man, about six feet high, wore a short dirty white smock-frock, cotton cord trousers; another stout man, with very long white smock-frock, white leggings, large striped shawl round his neck; the other two had on light coloured fustian jackets. They are all apparently about thirty years of age, had decent black hats on, and were much wrapped up about their necks.—They left behind them a small pocket-knife and part of a flail, also a stick with a string at the end as if for a horses twitch.—Whoever will apprehend the offenders who committed the first robbery, shall, on conviction, receive Forty Pounds Reward; and whoever will give information to the Police-officer at Southam, as shall lead to the apprehension and conviction of the offenders, shall receive Twenty-five Pounds Reward, by applying to Mr. Francis Smith, Treasurer to the General Association for the protection of Property, Southam.

On Wednesday night, the 24th instant, or early the following morning, the Storehouse of William Marshall, at Littlewick Green, near Maidenhead, was broken and entered, and eight Flitches of Bacon, six Cheeses (weighing about 25 lbs. each, marked 'W. M.' and a private mark), part of a Cask of Sugar, several Hats value 7s. 6d. each, and three fresh Belly-pieces of Pork, stolen therefrom. The thieves left behind them a horses nose-bag, marked 'Jones' on one side and 'F. I.' on the other.—Information to be given to Mr. W. Marshall, aforesaid; and Five Pounds Reward will be paid by him, on conviction of the offender or offenders and recovery of the property.

On the night of the 15th instant, the Warehouse of Mr. Edward Fellows, 63, Old Broad-street, City, was entered by means of false keys, and the following parcels of thrown Silk stolen therefrom, viz.: about 200 lbs. Italian two-thread Tram, made up in small heads, or North-country work, with tickets on each bundle, printed 'Italian Tram, No. 235,' and 'Italian Tram, H;' about 90 lbs. Italian two-thread Tram, made up in large heads, or West-country work, with small card tickets, printed 'Italian Tram, No. 40;' about 140 lbs. Italian Organzine, made up in usual Organzine bundles, with tickets on each, written, 'Italian Organzine,' each bundle tied round with three bands of white lay cord; also, about 100 lbs. of 'Piedmont' Thrown Organzine; it is supposed a hackney-coach was engaged to convey the property away.—Two Hundred Pounds Reward will be paid on conviction of the offender or offenders and recovery of the property, or One Hundred Pounds will be given upon the apprehension and conviction of the offender or offenders.—Information to be given to J. or D. Forrester, at the Mansion-house; or to Mr. E. Fellows, 63, Old Broad-street, City.

On Wednesday night, the 10th instant, the House of the Rev. Mr. Richards, at Icklesham, near Rye, Sussex, was entered, and the following articles stolen therefrom, viz.—One black and gold japan Writing-box, lined with red velvet; a rosewood Work-box, inlaid with mother-o'-pearl, and 'A. R.' on the lid, containing a pair of silver embossed Scissars, a gold Thimble and Bodkin, Russia Needle-case, brass Knitting-hook, ivory Bodkins, and a carved ivory yard Measure; a cut Decanter, the stopper broken; a handsome (red blue and gold pattern on white) real China quart Jug; pair of plated Candlesticks, Stand and steel Snuffers; a blue pocket Handkerchief, marked 'T. R. 8'; a calico Night-shirt, 'T. R. 4, 1834'; a Macintosh Coat, full size, dark blue, with green plaid lining; three wicker Baskets, two with lids, and 'R.' painted in black on the bottom: Books—Marmion, Lady of the Lake, and the Lay of the last Minstrel, in three vols. (one vol. each), in vellum binding; Aikin's Queen Elizabeth, two vols., in Russia binding; 1st and 2nd vols. of Guy Mannering, ditto; Debrett's Peerage, 1st vol., and Baronetage, 2nd vol., half-bound: nine Tea-spoons, fiddle-pattern, not marked; mother-o'-pearl Box, about the size of a crown-piece, with heart's-ease on the lid and gold rim: five old silver Coins—a Shilling of Chas. I., a Sixpence of Chas. II., a Ditto of Queen Anne with a hole in it, a Shilling of Geo. I., and a Ditto of Geo. II., perfect.—Whoever will give such information that may lead to the apprehension and conviction of the offender or offenders, shall receive Ten Pounds Reward, by applying to Thomas Fancett, superintendent of police, Maidstone.

On Wednesday night, the 17th instant, the Infant Poor-House, Barnet-hill, was broken and entered, and two large Coppers were Stolen. Also, the same night, Under-Hill House, Barnet, was broken and entered, and one large Brewing Copper was Stolen; the property of Mr. Jinkins.—Information to be given to Isaac Pye, superintendent of police, Barnet.

On Tuesday night, the 9th instant, the House of Mr. John Williams, at Abbot's Bromley, in the county of Stafford, was broken and entered, and the following property stolen therefrom, viz.—Three Great Coats (one dark green, one brown, and one dark drab), a blue Coat with gilt buttons, a red spun silk Shawl, a pair of drab Gaiters, a long calico Night-gown, plaid Cloak and Shawl, two black Veils, a brown silk Umbrella, six or more silk Handkerchiefs, a quantity of Gloves, two pairs Irish cloth Sheets marked 'I. W.', several damask Table-cloths, Pillow-cases, Chamber-towels, Wine, a large Cake, some Tea, a tortoise-shell Tea-caddy, twelve silver Tea-spoons, four ditto Table-spoons, six ditto Salt-spoons, two pairs Sugar-tongs, (some of the Spoons marked 'I. W.'), a Drinking-cup with silver rim marked 'I. W.'; and some Wearing Apparel.—The Thieves are supposed to be two or three in number, and to have had a cart with them: one of them wears a new broad-brimmed hat.—Whoever will give information that may lead to conviction of the offender or offenders, shall receive Twenty Pounds Reward, by applying to Mr. Lees, Treasurer of the Abbot's Bromley Police, to whom, as also to Mr. Adlard Welby, Solicitor, Uttoxeter, or Mr. John Williams, at Abbot's Bromley, information is to be given.

HORSE AND CATTLE STEALING.

THOMAS MEYRICK, a native of Bishop's Castle, or neighbourhood, did on the 30th December last, steal from off a hill called Berfield, in the parish of Clun, in the county of Salop, two Ponies, the property of William Francis, which have been recovered. The said THOMAS MEYRICK is about twenty years of age, five feet six inches high, fair hair and whiskers, stoops forward, rather awkward in his gait, his knees bend forward in walking, and his arm was in a sling.—A Reward of Five Pounds will be paid on his apprehension and conviction, by William Francis, of Berfield, aforesaid.—The said THOMAS MEYRICK, also did on Thursday the 25th instant, steal from the same hill two other Ponies, the property of Roger Bryan, Esq., of Little Hall, in the county of Salop, for which offence he was apprehended near Wenlock, and took to Mr. Bryan's residence on the 27th, and escaped from the man who had him in custody on Sunday night the 28th instant; had on when he escaped, a pair of trousers made to fit tight up, but rather large at bottom, and a smock-frock over them; had also a bandage round one wrist; has lived at the 'Oak Inn,' in Leominster, as Boots; has been working of late in the neighbourhood of West Bromwich and Birmingham, sometimes on the rail-road, and sometimes as ostler.—Whoever will apprehend the said THOMAS MEYRICK, and lodge him in any of Her Majesty's gaols, shall, on conviction, receive a further Reward of Five Pounds, by applying to Roger Bryan, Esq., Little Hall, aforesaid.

Stolen or Strayed, on the 6th instant, from Woking Common, Surrey, a Black Mare, aged, about twelve hands high, a star in the forehead, and marked 'P. E.' on near shoulder.—Also a scue-ball coloured Filly, about thirteen hands high, a long tail, white face and legs and also under the belly.—If stolen, Two Guineas Reward will be paid, on conviction of the offender or offenders and recovery of the horses, by applying to Joseph Spooner, Woking, Surrey.

Stolen, on Friday night, the 5th instant, or early the following morning, from a Field, called North Mill, in the parish of Aston Clinton, a Tag Sheep.—Seven Guineas Reward will be paid to any person giving such information that may lead to conviction of the offender or offenders, by applying to the Aston Clinton Society for the Protection of Property; or to John Gates, Aston Clinton, aforesaid.

delivered to pawnbrokers and dealers each morning by constables to assist in identifying such property which may have been offered to them. Another independent publication, Pawnbroker's Gazette, was paying constables two shillings for information provided for advertisement in the circular. This reward was stopped by a Police Order of July, 1851 requiring it to be paid into the Force for use in a reward fund.

The gathering and preparation of information for the various publications required considerable organisation as did dissemination throughout the Force.

The seventeen divisions of the Force operating in 1832 consisted of a total of forty nine separate police stations, not including a number of detached offices. It is necessary to consider the location of these divisions and stations in order that the problem of circulation of information can be appreciated.

Division	Police Stations — Where situated
A	Great Scotland Yard.
	Gardners Lane, Westminster.
B	New Way, Westminster.
	Elizabeth Street, Pimlico.
C	Little Vine Street, Piccadilly.
	6 Dean Street, Soho.
D	Mary-le-bone Lane.
	Harcourt Street, Marylebone.
E	George Street, St. Giles.
	Kings Cross Battle Bridge.
F	Covent Garden.
G	Rosoman Street, Clerkenwell.
	Bunhill Row, St. Lukes.
H	29 Church Street, Spitalfields.
	Denmark Street, St. Georges East.
	Church Street, Whitechapel.
K	Mile End Road, M E Old Town.
	Devons Lane, Bromley St. Leon.
	Bethnal Green.
	Newby Place, Poplar.
	Green Bank, Wapping.
L	Waterloo Road, Lambeth.
	High Street, Lambeth.
	Christchurch Blackfriars Road.
M	Southwark Bridge Road.
N	High Street, Kingsland Road.
	Islington Road.
	Robert Street, Shoreditch.
	Church Street, Hackney.
	Red Lion Lane, Stoke Newington.

P	Park House, East House, Walworth.
	Camberwell Green.
	Brixton Washway, Brixton.
R	Rose Cottage, Greenwich Road.
	Lucas Street, Rotherhithe.
S	Albany St. Regents Park.
	Phoenix Street, Somers Town.
	Junction Place, Kentish Town.
	52 Salisbury Street.
	Holly Place, Hampstead.
T	1 Church Street, Kensington.
	Church Place, Paddington.
	Turnham Green.
	Old Brentford near the Cage.
	Hammersmith.
	Acton.
V	The Plain Wandsworth.
	Clapham Common.
	Millmans Row, Chelsea.

From the earliest days of 1829 the Superintendents of the five divisions existing at that time would prepare their Morning Reports and record on the back occurrences of the previous night. At 11 a.m. each day they attended Scotland Yard with these reports for the Commissioner and, in fact, an Order of October, 1829 directs that they arrive more punctually. On 17th May, 1830, by which time there had been an increase of divisions, a memorandum from a Commissioner instructed that the morning reports of first six companies (divisions) were to be at Scotland Yard by 10 O'Clock and the remaining companies by 11 O'Clock. The further increase in divisions to seventeen, as shown above, resulted in the first six divisions being ready to answer their reports at 11 O'Clock, the next six at 12 O'Clock and the last five at 1 O'Clock.

Variations were made over the years in the times of attending with reports and if the Superintendent was unable to attend, due to urgent duty, an Inspector went in his place with the ability to answer any questions asked of him by the Commissioner regarding occurrences. However, in June, 1834, orders were that Superintendents were to attend not less than three times each week in person which, after February, 1863, was reduced to Monday and Wednesday only. No doubt the Superintendents of Westminster, Lambeth, Finsbury and Whitechapel were delighted in August, 1830 when a horse was supplied to each. They were however, to wait until 1870 before being provided with carts on outer divisions leading one Superintendent to write, 'It enables us to visit our several stations with much less fatigue to both man and horse.' Superintendents of divisions found that a great amount of their time was wasted travelling to and from the Commissioner's Office particularly those from the outer divisions. Additionally, they were required to write many reports personally.

Superintendent Kittle reported in 1868, "There is a standing griev- ance with officers who come to Commissioner's Office, that there is no accommodation for them there; there is no provision for the Superin- tendents being able to write a Report or even to sit down at the Commissioners Office; the accommodation is very bad. The stabling for horses is also insufficient". Business was normally carried out in former kitchens and stables at the back of Whitehall Place and often officers attending had a long wait.

Morning Reports included accurate particulars of occurrences, accidents, fires, felonies, offences of a serious nature and a description of articles stolen. They also gave details of police defaulters and those wishing to resign. In later years Superintendents could recommend suitable crime cases for publication in Police Gazette providing that a warrant of apprehension had been issued.

Before printing began in 1857 selected items of information con- tained in the Morning Reports, along with other matters, were prepared in manuscript as Police Orders by the Executive Branch at Scotland Yard on behalf of the Commissioner. Every afternoon (except Sundays) the sergeant-clerk or assistant clerk from each division attended Scotland Yard and received the Commissioner's Orders. The Inspector of the Executive Department read out these Orders and the sergeant-clerk wrote them into order books for delivery to their respective Superintendents. At the divisional station they would be read to the constables parading for duty, copied by the reserve officer and the copies circulated to the nearest stations by hand. There they would be copied again and the process repeated to nearby stations. By this method the whole Force would receive the circulation.

Obviously travelling to and from Whitehall Place took the sergeants away from their other work for a considerable time and an Order of April, 1834 states that 'the Superintendents of G, H, K, N, P, R, T, V may send a man (not the regular clerks) to Scotland Yard for Orders on Tuesdays, Wednesdays and Fridays. Regular clerks will attend on Mondays, Thursdays and Saturdays'. Constables entrusted with the delivery of letters were required to sign in the Registry against an entry showing the number recorded on the envelope (Police Orders 22.9.1831).

Circulating information throughout the Force area in respect of crimes was addressed from the first months by the Commissioners. An Order of 5th October, 1829 states 'The moment a robbery of any kind comes to the knowledge of the Superintendent or Inspectors a list of the articles will be distributed amongst the men and sent to all the neigh- bouring pawnbroker's shops and a memorandum made up of the hour at which the communication was made to the pawnbrokers on that subject'. The Inspectors and sergeants during their patrols received reports from the sections nearest to their station (Police Orders 18.10.1839).

In a Commissioner's memorandum to Superintendents on 16th October, 1829 they were directed to send off to Mr May (the Superin- tendent in charge of the Executive Branch) at 13 Crown Street a report containing brief information about the burglaries and property stolen. Mr May incorporated the information into a more detailed report which was forwarded as soon as was possible to all stations.

In November, 1831 instructions were given that information provided to any officer regarding persons absconding or missing was to be communicated immediately to the nearest police station where the officer on duty was to take necessary steps for circulating it through divisions 'in such a manner as may lead to the discovery of the party'.

The method used for dissemination of Informations was by way of despatch routes known as 'Routes'. Each divisional station displayed a copy of their Routes in order that the men became familiar with them.

A typical example of Routes are detailed below in respect of Rotherhithe on 'M' Division.

1st Route	Rotherhithe to Tower Street 'L' Division, then to Gardners Lane, 'A' Division, to New Way, 'B' Division to Millmans Row, 'V' Division to Kensington, 'T' Division.
2nd Route	Rotherhithe to Greenwich, 'R' Division.
3rd Route	Rotherhithe to Bow Street, 'F' Division, then to Vine Street, 'C' Division, to Marylebone Lane, 'D' Division, to Albany Street, 'S' Division, Bow Street also forwarded to George Street, 'E' Division.
4th Route	Rotherhithe to Roseman Street, 'G' Division, then to Islington, 'N' Division.
5th Route	Rotherhithe to Spitalfields, 'H' Division, then to Mile End, 'K' Division.

By this method it can be seen that messages were disseminated throughout the existing land divisions of the Force by passing them from one to another by hand. This was a time consuming and manpower intensive process. In the case of any burglary or robbery taking place in any division between the hours of 9 a.m. to 5 p.m. (P.O. 19.10. 1831) the information was sent immediately to the Commissioner's Office from where it was circulated to the whole Force. After 5 p.m. the information was despatched to other divisions via their specified 'Routes'.

Instructions issued in 1842 were that details of 'trifling articles' stolen were not to be circulated by Routes. A Police Order of 16th February, 1847 went even further and directed that only information where a beneficial result was likely should be passed in this way. The Bow Street Runners had been disbanded in 1839, and three years later the first Detective Force was formed by the Commissioners with two Inspectors and six sergeants occupying an office at Scotland Yard and obviously their views had influence upon the type of information circulated in respect of crime.

A description of his work as a constable on reserve duty at Stone's End Police Station on 'M' Division in 1855 is given by Ex-Chief Inspector

T.A. Cavanagh in his book 'Scotland Yard Past and Present' which was published in 1893 — 'Tom was the gaoler, I took to him at once. "Can you write?" he asked. "A little," I replied. "Sit down and copy this." I was glad to sit down, and gladder still when I got hold of the pen, for I felt at home at once, and soon forgot all my troubles. The paper he handed me was termed a "route" paper. I must here explain that in 55 no printing was done in the Metropolitan Police. Neither was there any telegraphic communication existing between the different stations as at present. It was not until about 1858 that printing was practised in the service, and this was mainly due to the ability and energy of ex-Superintendent Kittle, of the Executive Department, Great Scotland Yard. Consequently, business was transacted in this wise, viz., the sergeant-clerk or assistant-clerk of each division attended every afternoon (Sundays excepted) at Scotland Yard for "orders". These consisted of information respecting burglaries, robberies of all kinds, &c., &c., &c., reported each morning by the various superintendents to the commissioners at head-quarters. The sergeant-clerk was supplied with an order book, and, as the inspector of the Executive Department read out all appertaining to above, the sergeants entered the particulars to take to their superintendents, who were in readiness to receive them. These were, after being read out on parade, as before stated, handed over to the gaoler, and by him given to the men on reserve to copy. This having been done in our case at Stone's End, my two companions were sent with them to the nearest stations of other divisions to be re-copied, and forwarded on to the next division, and so on throughout the Metropolis. This is how things were done thirty-seven years ago'.

Superintendents were liable to minimise the seriousness of crimes occurring on their divisions and in 1859 a Police Order drew attention to this stating that Morning Reports of cases of felony were to contain an accurate description of the crime and a lesser crime was not to be shown.

There are many early references to the circulation of information by hand. On 23rd July, 1832 Superintendents were ordered to send messages each morning for reports of cholera cases from any place where there had been previously reported incidents of the disease. Constables from a number of divisions attended the residences of 'medical gentlemen' for their reports which were delivered by the Inspector to Scotland Yard from where they were forwarded to the Council Office in Downing Street.

Each major station had stables and, although the main function of the mounted men was to patrol the highways in outer areas to protect the public, some would be involved in despatch duties. John Fielding in the previous century had used the mounted messengers to protect the suburbs where residents provided them with information about stolen property and descriptions of suspects which were conveyed to Bow Street for circulation. These men on horseback, whose expenses were met by the residents, would also pass the information to turnpikes and public houses on their route, thus raising the 'hue and cry'.

24

In 1858 a book was introduced and carried in the leather cases along with Police Orders and Informations which the Sergeant Back Hall signed indicating the time that the documents had been transmitted. The officer at the receiving station checked that the documents were correct, then signed and dated the entry. Similarly any documents sent to the Commissioner's Office would be entered in the book and receipt certified. Losses of documents by messengers resulted in a Police Order of November, 1859 directing that the cases be used. Officers bringing letters to the Commissioner or Assistant Commissioner were instructed by a Police Order in 1862 to await an answer before returning to their station.

Informations were being conveyed from C.O. to the headquarters stations of A, C, F and L and the City Police (Fleet Street), for onward transmission, via agreed Routes, to other divisions when, on 1st April, 1869, a more efficient method of despatch was introduced. This new system involved mounted constables, supplied from certain outer divisions, conveying, in holsters designed for the purpose, Morning Reports, Returns and other correspondence each day (Mondays and Wednesdays excepted) for the Force as follows:—

Divisions from which to start.	Name of Police Station and Hour at which Messenger to leave.	Police Stations at which to call.	Hour of		Arrival at Commissioner's Office.	Remarks
			Arrival	Dep		
K	Arbour-square, 12 noon ..	Leman-street (H) ..	12.15	12.18	}1 p.m.	The Superintendent of Thames Division is to send his papers to Leman-street Station (H), to meet the K Messenger.
		Bow-street (F) ..	12.45	12.48		
R	Blackheath-road, 12 noon.	Stones-end (M) ..	12.40	12.43	1 p.m.	
T	Hammersmith, 12 noon ..	Rochester-row (B) ..	12.30	12.33	}1 p.m.	
		King-street (A) ..	12.48	12.52		
V	Wandsworth, 11.45 a.m. ..	Brixton (W)	12.20	12.22	}1.15 p.m.	
		Carter-street (P) ..	12.45	12.47		
		Kennington-lane (L)	12.57	1.0		
X	Paddington, 12 noon ..	Albany-street (S) ..	12.15	12.18	}1 p.m.	The Superintendent of N Division is to send his papers to Islington Station to meet Y Messenger.
		Marylebone-lane (D)	12.35	12.38		
		Vine-street (C) ..	12.45	12.48		
Y	Kentish-town, 12 noon ..	Islington (N)	12.20	12.23	}1 p.m.	
		King's-cross-road (G)	12.32	12.35		
		Clark's-buildings (E)	12.44	12.47		

An ordinary despatch bag service was by this time operating for less immediate correspondence sent to and from the inner divisions. Authority had been given in 1865 for a reserve constable on duty at the principal station of each outer division, namely K, N, P, R, S, T and V to attend at 6 p.m. each weekday to collect Orders and letters. He was permitted to travel by 'omnibus, steamboat or rail'.

On 1st October, 1869 a more organised service was formed when three constables from R, T, V, W and Y Divisions were selected for daily mounted despatch duty. The Route Table for the new system, which allowed the procedure of sending reserve constables to Scotland Yard from exterior divisions to collect Police Orders to be discontinued, is detailed below.

Table of Routes for Mounted Messengers.

Division	Station from which to start.	Hour to commence journeys.				Intermediate Stations at which to call.	Arrival at intermediate Stations on journeys.				Departure from intermediate Stations on journeys.				Arrival at Scotland-yard on journeys.				REMARKS
		1	2	3	4		1	2	3	4	1	2	3	4	1	2	3	4	
		a.m.	p.m.	p.m.	p.m.		a.m.	p.m.	p.m.	p.m.	a.m.	p.m.	p.m.	p.m.	a.m.	p.m.	p.m.	p.m.	
R. Blackheath ..		8.15	12.15	5.15	9.15	Stones-end	8.55	12.55	5.55	9.55	8.58	12.58	5.58	9.58	9.15	1.15	6.15	10.15	S Division to send papers to Marylebone-lane (D) to meet T Messenger (on his way to Scotland-yard; and on the return journeys, D Division to transmit S Papers to Albany-street without delay.
T. Hammersmith ..		8.0	12.0 (noon)	5.0	9.0	Paddington...	8.35	12.35	5.35	9.35	8.38	12.38	5.38	9.38	9.15	1.15	6.15	10.15	
						Marylebone-lane	8.53	12.53	5.53	9.53	8.56	12.56	5.56	9.56					
						Vine-street	9.2	1.2	6.2	10.2	9.5	1.8	6.8	10.8					
V. Wandsworth ..		8.15	12.15	5.15	9.15	Rochester-row ..	8.55	12.55	5.55	9.55	8.55	12.58	5.58	9.58	9.15	1.15	6.15	10.15	
						King-street	9.5	1.5	6.5	10.5	9.8	1.8	6.8	10.8					
W. Brixton		8.25	12.25	5.25	9.25	Carter-street ..	8.50	12.50	5.50	9.50	8.53	12.53	5.53	9.53	9.15	1.15	6.15	10.15	
						Kennington-lane	9.0	1.0	6.0	10.0	9.3	1.3	6.3	10.3					
Y. Kentish-town ..		8.15	12.15	5.15	9.15	Islington	8.35	12.35	5.35	9.35	8.38	12.38	5.38	9.38	9.15	1.15	6.15	10.15	N Division Papers to be sent to Islington Station to meet Y Messenger, at which Station Papers will also be left on return journey.
						King's-cross-road	8.48	12.48	5.48	9.48	8.51	12.51	5.51	9.51					
						Clark's-buildings	9.1	1.1	6.1	10.1	9.4	1.4	6.4	10.4					

The time above allowed for reaching the various Stations and this Office is to be observed on the return journey, the Messengers leaving Scotland-yard at 9.30 a.m., 1.30 p.m., 6.30 p.m., and 10.30 p.m.

The Superintendents of H and K Divisions are to send their papers and matter for printing to the Wapping Station of Thames Division in sufficient time for the Superintendent of that Division to arrange to dispatch them with his own so as to arrive at Scotland-yard at 9.15 a.m., 1.15 p.m., 6.15 p.m., and 10.15 p.m.; the Printed Informations and other documents for H, K, and Thames Divisions, will be conveyed back to Wapping, from whence they are to be fetched by a Reserve Constable.

New pattern despatch bags were issued the following month to handle the increased work and the despatch was collected from Scotland Yard at 9.30 a.m., 1.30 p.m., 6.30 p.m. and 10.30 p.m. (A 'Holdfast' leather bag supplied by H. Mitchell and Co., London was a design in use at some stage during the last century). Informations were sent out by all despatches and those received from divisions in one despatch were returned printed by the second subsequent despatch. Morning Reports were conveyed to the Commissioner's Office by the second despatch (1.30 p.m.) thereby ensuring that any relevant matters could be printed in Police Orders which were circulated by the third despatch (6.30 p.m.) Police Gazette was sent by various despatches and Pawnbroker's Lists by the second.

Additionally a Police Order of the 18th July, 1869 directed that Superintendents were to send details of all their known thieves and receivers of stolen property on the division to the Detective Office at Scotland Yard where a Register of Habitual Criminals was to be kept. The Convict Supervision Office originally carried out the work of criminal identification, and not until 1913 was Criminal Record Office (CRO) formalised. A direction to Superintendents in 1870, instructed them to keep a register of thieves and suspected persons at each sub-divisional station which was to be open for inspection by the constables. A divisional register was also kept. Over one hundred years were to pass before criminal names were to be placed on the Police National Computer (PNC) with easy access by all police forces in the country.

The conveyance of the despatch by river from Wapping was by police rowing or sailing boats prior to 1885 when steam launches were first introduced. It was not unitl 1912 that the first internal combustion engined boat was acquired by Thames Division.

In 1860, five dockyard divisions of the Metropolitan Police were formed at Woolwich, Portsmouth, Devonport, Chatham and Sheerness, and Pembroke with a total establishment by 1868 of 710 men. Prior to 1869 the dockyard despatch bags were generally sent and received by rail. Those arriving were collected from the station and, in respect of Chatham and Woolwich, they would arrive at Charing Cross for collection at 10.30 a.m. by a constable who conveyed them to Scotland Yard. In later years the postal service was used for sending in the Superintendents' reports which would be made up at 6 p.m. each evening for the previous 24 hours. Reports from Woolwich were conveyed by messenger to Blackheath Station and then to Commissioner's Office.

By 1870 far less manpower was tied up with the conveyance of correspondence and reliance on the despatch for internal Force communication became less important with the introduction of the internal telegraph system. On 24th October, 1872 the first despatch cart was used on 'T' Division which replaced the mounted despatch riders. Three horses and three constables were detailed for this duty and they followed the same timetable as that of the mounted despatch. Carts continued to be used until 1908, when two 6 hp Siddeleys were purchased as despatch vans.   The service continues today in a form not unlike the system of the last century albeit in motor vans driven by civilian personnel.

The supplying of information to the newspapers in respect of crime appears to have been frowned upon as the advice in Howard Vincent's 'A Police Code and Manual of the Criminal Law' published in 1882 indicates —

> 'Police must not on any account give any information whatever to gentlemen connected with the press, relative to matters within police knowledge, or relative to duties to be performed on orders received, or communicate in any manner, either directly or indirectly, with editors or reporters of newspapers on any matter connected with the public service, without express and special authority.
>
> The slightest deviation from this rule may completely frustrate the ends of justice, and defeat the endeavour of superior officers to advance the welfare of the public service.'

Vincent did not stick strictly to his rules and admitted that, ' the press is a power in the detection of crime which we must not omit to take into account '.   He quoted the case of a fraudsman who had evaded arrest for many months until his portrait, description and handwriting were published in a newspaper, along with the offer of a reward, resulting in his arrest within forty eight hours.

The use of the press for the circulation of information concerning wanted persons is illustrated by the case of Percy Lefoy Mapleton whose portrait appeared in the Daily Telegraph in 1881 and resulted in his arrest for the murder of Isaac Frederick Gould on the London, Brighton and South Coast Railway in East Sussex.   Had it not been for the newspaper it was claimed that millions of reward notices would have required distribution throughout the world to achieve the same result.

It is not clear how often the Metropolitan Police took advantage of this method in its pursuit of criminals, although in 1910 the press were publishing details of the suspect (Crippen) wanted for the London Cellar murder.   A special department for disseminating news to the press had been created at New Scotland Yard by 1920 and in March, 1929 Press Bureau was extended and operated between 10 a.m. and 1 a.m. on weekdays and on Sundays between 6 p.m. and 1 a.m. (Monday).   Officers were instructed to give the greatest possible assistance to members of the Bureau staff and any enquiries from the press were referred to them.

Many of the public order problems which face the police in the 1980s were with them in the last century.   A riot, bombing or major disaster in London today will call for the setting up of a Special Operations Room from where manpower can be deployed and directed by means of advanced telecommunications systems.

Even though the transport of the 19th century was almost completely horse drawn (motor omnibuses for instance not being greatly developed until 1904) there were great difficulties in efficiently policing events without adequate communication.   In many cases the Commissioner would be present at the scene of a riot to direct operations. It is easy to draw parallels today to the public order events of the last century and consider the problems facing the police on the ground working without proper communication.

The year 1831 was to be the scene of riots over the Reform Bill which were particularly serious during October when, on one occasion, the mob smashed almost every window in Apsley House much to the annoyance of the Duke of Wellington. On the 7th November there was another scare when a mass meeting of extreme members of the Reform movement was advertised to take place. Preparations were made to swear in Special Constables by sending letters to the clerks of the various vestries. Police Orders of 6th November refer to the employment of two constables from each division as messengers during the night to convey any information of disturbances to stations where men were retained on reserve. Information obtained over night in respect of disorder was to be delivered to Scotland Yard by messenger at 7 a.m.

On 13th May, 1833 a meeting was held at Cold Bath Fields in Calthorpe Street off the Grays Inn Road. Organised by a group of agitators, who were known as the National Union of the Working Classes, the purpose was to ' adopt preparatory measures for holding a National Convention, the only means of obtaining and securing Rights for the People '. Police were prepared for the meeting which had been declared illegal by the Home Office. Colonel Rowan, the Commissioner, was to be present in a private house near the fields. Clearly the organisers' intention was confrontation with the police and this resulted in the death of one constable, Robert Culley, who had suffered stab wounds. Police faced the demonstrators who used stones, weighted cudgels and knives against them resulting also in the serious injury of two other officers. The murderer of PC Culley was never brought to justice and the biased jury recorded a verdict of 'justifiable homicide' which was later overturned.

The Chartist troubles of the 1830s and 40s provide examples of the difficulties in policing a continuing problem of unexpected violent meetings being held all over London and the rest of the country. Many of the speakers at London meetings were from other parts of England and would encourage their audiences to 'take up arms and claim their rights'. Co-ordination of police forces (and the army in those days) was an almost impossible task, although the electric telegraph did play a part (as described later in this Chapter).

The importance of gathering intelligence about the Chartists cannot be overstated and during the meetings of 1839 the Commissioner, Richard Mayne, employed private persons for a fee to enter the crowds and take notes of speeches. These observers prepared reports for the police supplying information of where future meetings were to take place and any likely disorder. Plain clothes constables were also used to observe and report on meetings. There was no telephone or Force telegraph, however, to disseminate this knowledge to those who may have required it with some urgency.

To go looking for evidence of Chartists drilling and training with firearms without some method of calling for assistance seems remarkable in these days of sophisticated radio systems. One reported occasion in 1839 is an interesting illustration of such an event where two constables, 'one disguised as a bird catcher and equipped with bird traps and cages and the other in the dress of a journeyman' set out and scoured the whole district of Brockley Wood, Sydenham Common, Forest Hill, Penge and every secluded place along the embankment of the railway nearly to Croydon looking for such evidence.

The Force in 1848, faced with widespread demonstrations by the Chartists, often without any prior notice, was still dogged by having no effective means of communicating information. The Trafalgar Square Riots of the 6th, 7th and 8th March were policed by large contingents of officers from all divisions of the Force, totalling 1,189, 2,842 and 2,460 respectively. Such was the concern that gunsmiths were warned that locks should be removed from their guns in case they should be stolen. In order to communicate any sightings of demonstrators to Captain Hay, the Superintendent in charge at Trafalgar Square, and to the officers on the beats around Buckingham Palace, a patrol of constables were on look out duty in St James' Park.

These days of unrest were not restricted to the Square and a meeting taking place at Clerkenwell Green on 'G' Division made it necessary for the night duty beat officers on 'A' to 'M' Divisions (except 'K') on 6th March to remain in their respective stations on reserve. In the event of any likely disturbance or movement of demonstrators the Superintendent of 'G' Division was to communicate the information to the Commissioner's Office and to adjoining divisions. Divisional messengers were on duty in the Clerk's Room at Scotland Yard ready to convey any instructions from the Commissioner. The 13th March saw 2,111 police on duty for the Kennington Common Meeting with a further 1,141 on the approaches to the meeting and 629 on reserve. This was followed by the April meeting, described later, during which, it is claimed, 150,000 Special Constables, were enrolled and the eighty year old Duke of Wellington took command of the police and military.

Passing instructions from Scotland Yard to divisions is highlighted by another Clerkenwell Green meeting of 29th May. At 9 p.m. on that evening copies of orders were sent by cabs from the Commissioner's Office to the Superintendents of 'A' to 'M' Divisions directing them to move all men to their stations as the Chartists had moved in procession to Finsbury Square. At 10.30 p.m. a further order went out by cabs for each Superintendent to keep up patrols and report to the Commissioner any Chartist movements. A total of 1,942 officers were mustered to deal with this unexpected meeting and the 'V' Division contingent of a Superintendent, two Inspectors and 104 constables (including six mounted) were still on their way on foot to central London when they were turned back at 1 a.m. by a messenger sent from Scotland Yard. It is amazing how, at comparatively short notice, large numbers of men could be assembled to deal with disorder notwithstanding the handicaps under which they were operating.

The policy of having men accommodated together when they were off duty in the Station Houses or in nearby apartment houses rented as Section Houses no doubt made it relatively easy to muster a contingent. At Albany Street Police Station in 1865 for example one married Inspector and fifty constables were accommodated.

The passing of information from one division to another rapidly was important as the Chartist leaders endeavoured to conceal the location of their meetings and movements. Police had to be continually vigilant and, during a meeting on 'G' Division on 30th May, a plain clothes constable was posted there from 'M' Division in order that he could be despatched for assistance in the event of trouble. The City of London Force had to be kept informed about any gatherings likely to enter their area.

On occasions the Commissioner would despatch a note instructing Superintendents as to their course of action during demonstrations. At a meeting on 1st June Superintendent Lewis of 'G' Division was to receive such a note instructing him that any person creating a disturbance was to be taken into custody.

Hyde Park was to be the scene of violent demonstrations during the 1850s, including the one resulting from the opposition to the Sunday Observance Bill of 1855 which resulted in the arrest of seventy people and injury to forty nine police officers. After the Reform League Disturbances of 1866/7, policing Hyde Park became the responsibility of the Force. Royal events, including the Coronations of William IV in September, 1831 and Queen Victoria in June 1838, all requred the services of the Metropolitan Police. State visits and funerals of Dukes probably created problems of crowds as large as they are today with all the attendant security responsibilities.

The need of an electric telegraph facility to improve policing efficiency could hardly have been disputed whether for passing information about crime or public order or even day to day routine communication; this was to be many years away.

As early as 1839 the Commission, Appointed to Enquire into the Setting up of a Constabulary Force in England and Wales, was recommending the use of the telegraph for police work. This Commission, which included Edwin Chadwick among its members, reported, when referring to the railways as a means of escape for criminals, ' One effectual means to countervail the increased facilities for escape by the new modes of communication would be the establishment of telegraphs along chief lines, a measure by no means costly, but one in which the company has for such purposes no interest. '

Many years before the Force made extensive use of the electric telegraph there were examples of involvement by the Metropolitan Police with this invention. In the 1830s two Englishmen, Charles Wheatstone and William Fothergill Cooke, who had formed a partnership after working independently for many years, succeeded in establishing the

Wheatstone and Cooke's Five
needle telegraph machine c.1837

Double needle telegraph
machine c.1842

1845 advertising for the Paddington to Slough telegraph using the
capture of Tawell.

[SCOTLAND-YARD, THE HEAD-QUARTERS OF THE METROPOLITAN POLICE.]

' Scotland Yard from 1829'

'New Scotland Yard
1890 to 1967'

first working 'electric telegraph' outside a laboratory. The earliest use of the facility in the country was by the railway companies. In 1837 the five needle telegraph system was installed on a stretch of the London and Birmingham Railway under construction between Camden Town and Euston Stations. Messages were successfully sent between the two stations.

The Great Western Railway telegraph line between Paddington and West Drayton, operating in July, 1839 using equipment designed by Wheatstone and Cooke, was extended to Slough in 1843. The original section used insulated wires through an underground hollow iron pipe, but the extension to Slough consisted of wires suspended from posts. Cooke came to an agreement with the railway whereby he took over ownership of the telegraph line but the railway continued to use it free of charge. The five needle telegraph machine operated at each end of the original section and at Hanwell. The extension of the service led to two needle machines being introduced as they were cheaper requiring only two wires instead of five. Although this reduced the cost, a specialist operator was necessary to handle the elaborate codes which were far more difficult than the relatively simple five needle system.

The Slough to Paddington telegraph became the first public telegraph system and shortly after its inception the potential for police use is illustrated by the extracts attributed to the Paddington Station Telegraph Book of 1844 which appear in the Quarterly Review of June, 1854. The Review states that this was 'the first intimation thieves got of the electric constable being on duty'.

The following extracts give a picture of the policing with the aid of the new telegraph machine in the early days of the Force. These messages would have been sent and received letter by letter and written down by the recipient. We can visualize the plain clothes police officers at Paddington mingling with the crowds spotting well known thieves and then hastening to the telgraph clerk's office to have the descriptions sent by him to Slough Station where other officers would be awaiting their arrival.

'Paddington, 10.20 AM — "Mail train just started. It contains three thieves, named Sparrow, Burrell, and Spurgeon, in the first compartment the fourth first-class carriage".

Slough, 10.48 AM — "Mail train arrived. The officers have watched the three thieves".

Paddington, 10.50 AM — "Special train just left. It contained two thieves: one named Oliver Martin, who is dressed in black, crape on his hat; the other named Fiddler Dick, in black trousers and light blouse. Both in the third compartment of the first second-class carriage.

Slough, 11.16 AM — "Special train arrived. Officers have taken the two thieves into custody, a lady having lost her bag, containing a

34

purse with two sovereigns and some silver in it; one of the sovereigns was sworn to by the lady as having been her property. It was found in Fiddler Dick's watch-fob".

It appears that, on the arrival of the train, a policeman opened the door of the 'third compartment of the first second-class carriage', and asked the passengers if they had missed anything? A search in pockets and bags accordingly ensued, until one lady pointed out that her purse was gone. 'Fiddler Dick, you are wanted' was the immediate demand of the police-officer, beckoning to the culprit, who came out of the carriage thunderstruck at the discovery, and gave himself up, together with the booty, with the air of a completely beaten man. The effect of the capture so cleverly brought about is thus spoken of in the telegraph book:—

Slough, 11.51 AM — "Several of the suspected persons who came by the various down-trains are lurking about Slough, uttering bitter invectives against the telegraph. Not one of those cautioned has ventured to proceed to the Montem".

Ever after this the lightfingered gentry avoided the railway and the too intelligent companion that ran beside it, and betook themselves again to the road — a retrograde step, to which on all great public occasions they continue to adhere'.

The first licensee to operate the Paddington to Slough system was Thomas Home who paid a rental of £170 per year and in a letter dated 2nd July, 1887 he describes the arrest of John Tawell, many years earlier.

On 1st January, 1845 the murder of Sarah Hart occurred at Salt Hill, Slough. After the suspected poisoning of Hart a man was seen leaving the house by neighbours, and depart hurriedly towards Slough railway station. The brother of the doctor who attended the scene went to the station where he saw a man, fitting the description given by the neighbours, board a train for Paddington, eighteen miles away.

Once the train had departed for its destination the doctor's brother went to the telegraph clerk's office from where Mr Howell, the station superintendent, sent a message via the telegraph to the Paddington Office over the two needle equipment.

The message was received letter by letter on a machine as follows —

"Murder has just been committed at Salt Hill. The suspected man was seen to take a first class ticket for London by the train which left Slough at 7.42 p.m. He is in the garb of a quaker with a brown greatcoat which reaches nearly to his feet. He is in the last compartment of the second first class carriage".

Some letters were absent from the apparatus including 'q' which resulted in quaker being spelt 'Kwaker'.

Sergeant Williams of the railway company police was found and given the message. When the train arrived at Paddington the suspect, John Tawell, was followed and later arrested in the City of London.

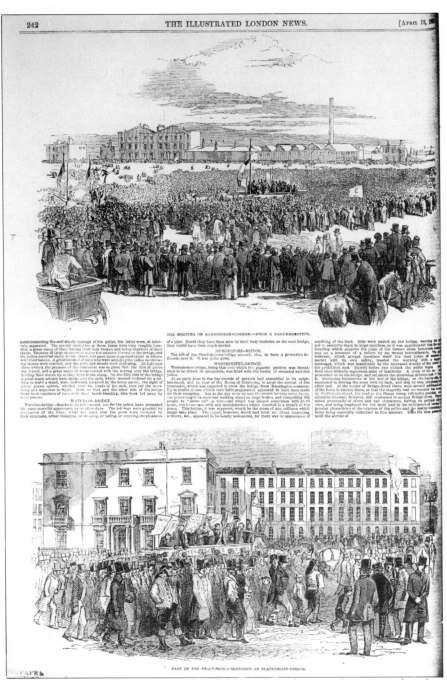

The Chartist Meeting of April, 1848 at Kennington Common (top).

Tawell, subsequently convicted at Aylesbury Assizes of the murder of Sarah Hart, eventually hanged for the crime.

It seems that subsequent years were to witness some use of the public telegraph in the pursuit of criminals. To quote the Quarterly Review of June, 1854, 'Does a murderer escape, the same wire makes the fact known to Scotland Yard, and from thence word is sent to the distant policeman to intercept him in flight. '

By 1848 the Electric Telegraph Company, under the Chairmanship of John Lewis Ricardo, had an extensive network of lines and telegraph stations throughout the whole country. The Central Telegraph Station was at Lothbury in the City of London (behind the Bank of England) ideally located for the business world. The four London branch stations were at 14 Seymour Street, Euston Square, the Eastern Counties Terminus at Shoreditch, the South Western Terminus at Nine Elms and the Great Western Terminus at Paddington. The Order Book of the Company for March, 1848 gives instructions as to the action to be taken by staff in the event of an attack on their offices. The Chartist troubles throughout the country in that year were causing a great deal of concern for the government. On 9th March the Chairman of the Telegraph Company offered to establish a line between the central station at Lothbury and the Home Office at £1000 per year which included the cost of communication, maintenance and clerks; this was not taken up.

On 10th April, the day of the planned Kennington Common meeting the likelihood of an uprising throughout the country was feared. The government were concerned that coded messages would be sent by Chartists over the wires encouraging members in other parts of the country to 'take arms and rise up.' Information, for example, was received from the magistrates at Nottingham that they had been informed that a cyphered message would be sent from London by the Chartists to Nottingham.

An act of parliament of 1846 had been passed to give the government power, in an emergency, to take control of the telegraph system operated by the Electric Telegraph Company. On 9th April a warrant had been issued by the Home Secretary, Sir George Grey, requiring the chairman of the company to take possession of all apparatus at the various stations for and on behalf of Her Majesty's Government for a period of one week. Ricardo complied immediately, requiring all stations to be closed to the public, and only messages addressed to the constituted authorities were to be received. Letters of authority were sent from the Home Secretary to the mayors of areas where Chartist activity was likely for production in the event of those authorities wishing to transmit a telegraph message.

At 11.40 a.m. on 10th April, a message was transmitted from the Mayor of Liverpool, Tomlis Horsfull, to the Home Secretary which said, 'Chartists at Manchester are organised armed with pikes and muskets. Mode of attack Special Constables to be first overpowered'. The message went on to describe how the Chartists obtained their information.

A message from the Mayor of Leeds said, ' Tranquility prevails here and the peace is not threatened '. At 2.15 p.m. the following transmission was received at the Admiralty, ' From Daniel Cameron, Superintendent of Police, Glasgow to Colonel Rowan, Commissioner. The Chief Superintendent of Glasgow requests that Colonel Rowan will let him know as early as possible per telegraph the result of the Chartist Meeting in London this day with any further information Colonel Rowan may consider useful '. Various other messages were received from mayors throughout the country giving information about the state of order in their towns.

Concern about support by sympathisers in Ireland resulted in telegraph messages received being passed on by packet boat to Ireland. Additional telegraph facilities were installed in order that information regarding troop requirements could be passed to and from Winchester. Equipment was installed at Kingston, Clapham, Harrow, Watford, Wolverhampton and Hampton for use during the anticipated disturbances on 10th April.

The cost to the government of taking over the telegraph for one week was £500. Whereas the Electric Telegraph Company had originally offered to instal equipment in the Home Office for £1000 per annum, on 3rd May 1848 a subsequent proposal to connect the Home Office and Horse Guards to the system was estimated at £6000 per annum.

Fears that Chartists intended to release prisoners caused the authorities at the Westminster House of Correction to maintain rockets ready for sending a warning to police, Special Constables and troops in the event of attack. A letter from the Chairman of the Committee of Visiting Justices says, 'I shall cause a rocket to be fired at intervals as a signal of our want of assistance and shall then hope to have the aid of the military'.

Prior to the Trafalgar Square Riots of 1848 Superintendent Ferguson was instructed to make contact with the railway authorities at Euston Square Station so as to ensure that police were informed about any attempt to disrupt the railway or telegraph.

The routine work of the Force could also benefit from the telegraph. In July, 1850 the Secretary of State sanctioned the conveyance of prisoners, committed to Maidstone Prison, by rail instead of police van; they were conveyed via the North Kent Line from the stations nearest to the courts, namely Dartford, Erith, Woolwich and Lewisham, to London; then via the South Eastern Railway train to Maidstone. On arrival of the train at Paddock Wood the sergeant in charge of the prisoners requested the station master to telegraph Maidstone to arrange for the van to be ready at the station to convey the prisoners to the gaol. By 1864, one sergeant and two constables were specially employed on the conveyance of prisoners by rail to Maidstone.

The Great Exhibition of Industry held in Hyde Park in May, 1851 presented the Force with a major policing problem. On 19th February, Richard Mayne had written to the Home Secretary requesting electric telegraph between the Commissioners' Office and the exhibition building which he emphasised was for use ' especially in cases of disturbance or tumult requiring reinforcement of Police. It would be most important to have means of instantaneous communication to prevent alarm on account of accidents that may occur on the unfounded rumours of such at the Exhibition '. The request was approved by the Home Office.

The large numbers expected to attend caused concern that the exhibition building would not accommodate them. From the beginning of March for six months officers from provincial and foreign police forces were engaged on duty. The officers from abroad were there to look for, and report sightings of, foreign criminals. Once the event started police officers controlled the movement of visitors and clear routes of passage were agreed. Constables were supplied with steps on which they could stand to obtain a good view of the crowds; on no account did they leave their position. Superintendent Pearce in charge of the operation regularly ascertained the numbers of visitors admitted at each entrance.

Prior to the opening of the exhibition a temporary wooden station had been built in Hyde Park at the west end of the Horse Guards Barracks near Princes' Gate. An officer was constantly on duty in the Reserve Room on the ground floor throughout the exhibition to deal with any public complaints or enquiries. Police were able to parade and have occasional meals at the station, and there was sufficient room in the basement to lock up ten to twelve prisoners. The electric telegraph machine was located in the station and Richard Mayne's report on the policing of the exhibition stated that communication "between the office of the Commissioner of Police and this station was constantly kept up".

From the east and west entrances of the exhibition building communication could be made by electric telegraph to the south entrance giving information about the numbers admitted at each. Once the total number reached 50,000 then the doors were to be closed. Notices were then to be posted on the various routes leading to the exhibition advising the public of the position.

Once the doors closed the instructions were that this information was to be immediately communicated by telegraph to the Commissioner's Office and from there to railway stations. In the event of an alarm of fire being received by an officer at the entrance telegraphic communication was to be sent to Scotland Yard. The machines used were probably one or two needle instruments requiring skilled operators, although no reference has been found respecting this. The single needle machine operated in 1846 by the Electric Telegraph Company had letter codes adapted from the two needle codes with the added advantage of a single wire. Morse code was used on the equipment in later years.

King Street, Vine Street and Rochester Row Police Stations received information concerning the exhibition from Scotland Yard although it is not clear whether by telegraph or messenger. Mounted patrols or cabs were used to convey the information to the police stations at The Triumphal Arch, Marble Arch, Marylebone Lane and Walton Street. Similarly the various army barracks were kept informed.

Letters, which are written in 1852, confirm that there was still telegraphic communication between Whitehall Place, the office of the Commissioner, Sir Richard Mayne, and his home.

A letter from John Wray, Receiver of the Metropolitan Police, dated 5th March 1852 refers to the Commissioner's telegraph and the possibility of extending the use to police stations. The letter reads:-

"The decision of the Sec of State should be got. I suppose he wd (would) require an opinion of the Commr (Commissioner) for the continuance of this alone wd (would) be of no value. I requested the Secretary of the Telegraph Company lately to let me have a statement for making communications from this office to most of the Police Stations, this he promised to send, & (and) I shd (should) like to see it before bringing the question before the Sec of State. When will the year expire.

(Signed) J Wray Receiver"

This letter indicates that the Commissioner's telegraph line was the only one in existence in the Metropolitan Police and had been connected for less than a year. The agreement entered into by the Receiver with the Electric Telegraph Company at Lothbury, was to pay £500 for one year or £86 each year to ten years. It appears that this was the system installed for the exhibition as the accounts of the Force for the year ended 31st December 1852 detail an expenditure of £500 for the use of Electric Telegraph during the Great Exhibition.

The Electric Telegraph Company
single needle c.1846.

Other letters from the Electric Telegraph Company to the Receiver, dated 8th March and 12th March, refer to the enclosure of the company's account to 31st December 1851 and the latter acknowledges receipt of a letter requesting an 'estimate of the probable cost attending the laying down of a communication between Whitehall and the Principal Police Stations of the Metropolis by means of the Electric Telegraph'.

On 8th September a letter from The Electric Telegraph Company (which, incidentally, was formed in 1846 when Wheatstone and Cooke's shares in the various patents were bought out) to Sir Richard Mayne accompanied a "statement of this company's claim against the Commissioner of Police to June 30th, 1852 amounting to £93.14s". The statement shows £53.14s to 31st December, 1851 and one half year's rent of £40 to 30th June.

Sir Richard seems to have been unimpressed by the value of the telegraph for everyday policing and wrote a letter to the Receiver from Hastings on 17th September, 1852 in which he refers to the account of the company and appears to have effectively squashed for many years any ideas there may have been to use this form of communication for improving police efficiency.

The letter reads:-

"The letter from the Electric Telegraph Company of the 8th Inst is referred to the Receiver that the claim may be settled according to the agreement entered into by him.

I have no intention of recommending to the Secretary of State the proposal of the Company for a general communication to the Police Stations by the Telegraph and this single line of communication is of no use. I think therefore it should be closed.

(Signed) R. Mayne".

In accordance with the Commissioner's wishes the Receiver requested the telegraph company to remove his line which was met with a reply dated 23rd September claiming £500 from the Metropolitan Police.

Even The Times of 3rd August, 1852 announced 'shortly various police stations in the metropolis and its outskirts will be connected with one and another and the railways by electric telegraph'. This does not appear to have materialised for many years although Punch Vol.XXIII of that year was also commenting upon 'the arrangements now in the course of being made to connect all Police Offices, with the Electric Telegraph'. The magazine referred to 'a terrible new foe' which criminals would have to contend with; 'The Law had now added the Lightning. They were to be nabbed through Electricity; they were to be collared by the agency of magnetism'.

Only a few references to the use of the electric telegraph by police can be found after the installation for the 1851 exhibition. During the lying in state of the Duke of Wellington in November, 1852 information about the closing times of the hall at Chelsea Hospital, where the body rested, were passed by telegraph to railway stations on the route to the

41

Taking the prisoners away by Police Van.

Constables on parade ready for their beats c.1860.

hospital.   Two women had been killed in the crowds during the event making it essential to pass information ensuring that crushes of people did not occur after the hall had closed.

Commissioner's Orders of 12th August, 1852 stated that, 'Superintendents may make use of the Electric Telegraph from (Railway) stations for sending information of a fire to the Fire Brigade Stations, they will arrange with the Telegraph Company that the information shall be forwarded without delay to the nearest Fire Brigade station'. The expenses of the telegraph on each occasion were to be approved by the Commissioner and forwarded to the Superintendent of the Fire Brigade for payment.   Discretion was to be used by constables thus avoiding calling the brigade unnecessarily to small fires or to fires five or six miles from London in small buildings, which were unlikely to spread through a town or village; not very reassuring for the residents.

Communication with foreign police forces today is through the extensive Interpol network, however, Police Orders of 26th January, 1853 instructed Superintendents and Detective Inspectors not to communicate with the 'Police of France'.   If such communication was felt to be necessary a report requesting authority was to be submitted to the Commissioner who, if approved, would arrange for it to be passed to the officer of the electric telegraph for transmission.

Although there were no verified references found respecting internal Force telegraph links between 1852 and 1867 it is difficult to accept that some did not exist; after all by 1854 there were a number of branch telegraph stations throughout the capital located often at railway stations. Many London clubs had the telegraph installed as did the Opera House on which Members of Parliament could receive information regarding debates taking place in the House of Commons. Although it has not been possible to find records there is reference in the Quarterly Review of June, 1854 to a branch telegraph line which ran from Scotland Yard to Charing Cross Station and then on to the Central Telegraph Office.   The central office of the Electric Telegraph Company was located at Lothbury and after 8.30 p.m. the wires were put through to Charing Cross where the night work was carried out.

Consideration was being given to establishing communication between some police stations and the Commissioner's Office in 1859. Superintendents were asked to consider a list of stations and other places detailed in a memorandum distributed to them in December of that year as to whether they were sufficient and suitable for installation of the telegraph.   The observations of the Superintendents are unavailable and it can only be assumed that no installations took place at this time.

The Admiralty were in touch with Plymouth and Portsmouth via the railway telegraph by 1854 and there was a proposal that all dockyards should be linked.   The outcome of this proposal is not known.

The Force on occasions required access to private telegraph messages and a resolution forwarded to the Secretary of State by the Electric Telegraph Company in 1855 states:-

43

The Great Exhibition of Industry, (South entrance) 1851.

The Submarine Telegraph Company, Cornhill — First London-Paris circuit, 1852.

"That Superintendents and Clerks in charge of Stations be authorised on receiving a written application signed by a Magistrate to give, in Criminal cases only, such information to the Police respecting Telegraph Messages as may be required for evidence in furtherance of the ends of justice.

That this resolution be communicated to the Secretary of State for the Home Department accompanied by a request that it may be communicated to the Bench of Magistrates".

The 'Irish problem' was beginning to raise its head during the mid 1860s and considerable communication in respect of suspects took place between Sir Richard Mayne, Liverpool and Ireland. In November, 1865, Timothy Hegarty was arrested on a warrant granted in Cork for Fenian practices namely pike making. A telegram was sent immediately to the police in Cork in order that an officer could be sent over to identify him and, if necessary, escort the prisoner back to Ireland.

The following year detectives from the Metropolitan Force were directed to Liverpool to assist officers from that Force and the Irish Police with investigations into a Fenian conspiracy. The telegraph service was used on a number of occasions to pass information from one force to another. The Mayor of Liverpool sent a telegram to Sir Richard providing the description of a suspect, Brooks, who was believed to have sailed into London.

Letters passed between Major Greig, the Chief Constable of Liverpool, and the Commissioner concerning stolen arms of the Volunteer Rifles discovered in Liverpool and the payment of an informant for evidence leading to the arrest of the conspirators. The Acting Commissioner, Labalmodiere, and Major Greig, communicated with each other by telegram concerning the case and Detective Sergeant Mulvany and three non-commissioned officers of the volunteer regiments were sent to Liverpool to give evidence. Again Labalmodiere invited the Chief Constable to 'telegraph or write if I can in any way further aid you'.

In November, 1866 the Commissioner received a telegram from Dublin concerning the seizure of rifles at Cork which he passed on to the Chief Constable of Liverpool. This rapid means of communication was proving its worth for police work and in the following year Major Greig and the Commissioner were again in touch by telegram on a number of occasions concerning Fenian activity. Telegrams also passed between Paris and London concerning Irish suspects travelling to England from France.

A telegram in cipher was sent by Labalmodiere from the Home Office to Major General Sir Thomas Larcom at Dublin Castle enquiring about a warrant for a Fenian named Burke whose house was being kept under observation in London. Unfortunately the cipher did not appear to have been understood by the recipient and had to be followed by a letter requesting that a telegraph message be sent if the observation on premises should cease.

45

In September, 1867 a police van was broken into in Manchester and a police sergeant murdered by two Fenian leaders, Kelly and Burke, who escaped. Telegrams were received from Manchester concerning Fenian escapees, Kelly and Deasy, on 18th September. Costs incurred in respect of these messages were normally recovered from the Irish Government. The Chief Constable of Liverpool was requested to arrange for observation to be kept on passengers travelling by boat to Ireland or America in an attempt to identify the two escapees. In November, Superintendents were instructed to select intelligent constables for observations to find the Fenians Thomas Kelly and Patrick Lennon.

Fenian activity reached a climax in December, 1867 when a cask of gunpowder was placed against the wall of the Clerkenwell Prison in an attempt to release two prisoners, Casey and Burke. The prison wall was demolished and houses nearby damaged resulting in the deaths of four people and injury to forty others. Three persons were arrested for the crime and a fourth, Michael Barrett, was captured later in Glasgow. Barrett was executed on 26th May, 1868 and was the last person to be publicly hanged in Britain.

The photographing of prisoners at police stations, in certain circumstances, was arranged from 1868, undoubtedly due to the problems with the Irish; all Fenians of note had to be photographed. This was clearly the best method of communicating a description and, in fact, Kelly's photographs had in 1867 been hung in each station to assist in identifying the escaped Fenian.

The City of London Force were ahead of the Metropolitan having finally established telegraphic communication between their stations in September, 1860. The London District Telegraph Company was registered on 4th January 1859 and the Universal Private Telegraph Company on 20th September 1860; these two companies were to provide the telegraph service for central London until formally taken over by the Postal Telegraphs Department (Post Office) on 4th February 1870. Due to the high cost and difficulties of laying telegraph cables underground in busy city streets there had been much pressure prior to the formation of the companies for over-house telegraph. In 1855 Sydney Waterlow, a member of the Common Council of the City of London, suggested to the Police Committee that the efficiency of the City Police would be enhanced if the headquarters at Old Jewry were to be connected to the Commissioner's home at Finsbury Circus by way of over-house wires.

The over-head wires included one which linked Waterlow's offices in the City to a branch in Parliament Street. This spanned the Thames to a warehouse on the Surrey side, than along the south side until a wire a quarter of a mile long brought it back to Westminster. This tortuous route was necessary as mud banks formed the Victoria Embankment at that time and wayleaves over the bridges were refused.

Again the City of London Commissioner was approached and a suggestion that telegraph wires for City Police communication should be suspended between church steeples to avoid unauthorised interference was agreed by the Police Committee. The Commissioner's subsequent link to his headquarters and five other City Police Stations at the cost of about £300 led in 1861 to Sydney Waterlow receiving a vote of thanks from the City Corporation for introducing police telegraphs.

With the formation of the two telegraph companies they rapidly set about erecting over-house wires between masts fixed to roof tops which, of course, required the permission of the landlords or occupants. In some cases the companies were forced to lay cables under the streets. Whereas the Universal's business was gained by connecting direct private telegraph facilities to business or private premises the District concentrated on providing a service to the public through a series of telegraph offices. The latter required more staff in the form of telegraph clerks and delivery boys and its slowness and inefficiency was often the subject of criticism.

The Universal's method of operation, which had the rights of Wheatstone's ABC instrument, was more successful than that of the competitor although the District did complete a private network linking London fire brigade stations under Captain Shaw. The District Company operated eventually from about eighty telegraph stations throughout the centre of the capital with an establishment in the region of 150 telegraphists. Morse code was normally used on the apparatus at these stations and some were in a small room with one machine, a telegraphist and messenger boy. The overhead wires were subject to break during storms and gradually underground cables became more extensively used particularly after the Post Office took control.

By the mid 1860s Sir Richard Mayne had little option but to reconsider his abandonment, many years earlier, of the concept of a Force telegraph network. The telegraph was in widespread public use throughout the country by 1865 with a total of 16,066 miles of telegraph line and 2,040 telegraph offices operated by various private companies. The Force had been slow to accept the values of modern technology a symptom which continued into the twentieth century.

CHAPTER II

WEAVING THE WEB OF WIRES –
THE METROPOLITAN POLICE TELEGRAPH SERVICE

Police Orders of 7th June, 1866 instructed divisional Superintendents to report the name and description of any telegraph company having wires near their respective stations for communication within the Metropolitan Police District. There is little doubt that unrest over the Reform Bill and the subsequent riots of July were to have some influence on the need to pursue, as a priority, more efficient communications. Fenian troubles were also looming on the horizon.

The potential of the telegraph was at last realised in this year when companies were requested by the Commissioner to tender 'for the performance of the telegraphic service of the Police of the Metropolis'. The latest date fixed for receipt of the tenders was 8th October, 1866, a printed specification detailing the requirements of the Force was approved by the Commissioner.

A schedule to the document indicated the 21 divisional stations (including Thames) along with three private residences which were, the following year, to be connected to Scotland Yard.

A	or	Whitehall	King Street, Westminster
B		Westminster	Rochester Row, Westminster
C		St James'	Vine Street, Piccadilly
D		Marylebone	Marylebone Lane
E		Holborn	Clark's Buildings, Bloomsbury
F		Covent Garden	Bow Street
G		Finsbury	King's Cross Road
H		Whitechapel	Leman Street, Whitechapel
K		Stepney	Arbour Square, Stepney
L		Lambeth	Kennington Lane
M		Southwark	Stones End, Boro'
N		Islington	Kingsland Road
P		Camberwell	Carter Street, Walworth
R		Greenwich	Blackheath Road, Greenwich
S		Hampstead	Albany Street, Regent's Park
T		Kensington	Brook Green, Hammersmith
V		Wandsworth	Wandsworth
W		Brixton	High Road, Brixton
X		Paddington	Harrow Road, Paddington
Y		Highgate	Kentish Town Road
Thames		Wapping	

Sir Richard Mayne, KCB, Commissioner of Police, 1829 to 1868.

Residences
Sir Richard Mayne, 80 Chester Square
Captain W.C. Harris, 17 Porchester Square (Assistant Commissioner)
Captain D.W. Labalmondiere, 13 South Audley Street, Grosvenor
Square, (Assistant Commissioner).

Three new divisions of W, X and Y had been created in 1865, (the temporary 'X' Division formed for the 1862 International Exhibition, being made permanent). Additionally two years or so after the introduction of the telegraph 'F' Division was incorporated into 'E' Holborn Division, mainly due to the reduction of work resulting from slum clearance.

The statement of requirement for the Metropolitan Police telegraph service clearly defined the needs of the Force and stated that ' all wires are to be carried into the said principle office underground, from distances not less than one quarter of a mile from the same office respectively, but except for such distances from the same office all wires may be carried either over house-top or underground, or partly over-house top and partly underground'. The statement indicated that 'as many of Wheatstone's patent instruments as were required to carry telegraphic messages along every wire should be furnished by the Contractor'. The service, planned to be ready for use by 1st March, 1867, included a contract for a period of seven years from that date during which time the Contractor would be required to keep the wires, instruments and apparatus in working order.

Tenders for the service were received from The Universal Private Telegraph Company and the London District Telegraph Company. The former quoted a price of £786 per annum for the provision of the whole service. The cost of purchasing the wires, instruments and apparatus at any time during the currency of the contract was £3,200. The tender of the London District Telegraph Company arrived at a rent of £900 per annum with a purchase price of £4,000. They quoted the cost per mile for any additional wires at £50, £20 more than that of the competitor.

The contract, granted to the lowest tender offered by the Universal Private Telegraph Company, was finalised on 30th September, 1867 with a letter from their office at 4 Adelaide Street, West Strand, London, WC to Sir Richard Mayne which reads:

"Sir,

I have the honour to inform you that the various lines of Telegraph undertaken to be supplied by this company under contract with the Receiver of the Metropolitan Police are now completed and in perfect working order.

I am Sir,
Your obedient servant
Wm Breltargh
Secretary".

The completion was about six months later than the statement of requirement had originally indicated as the final date.

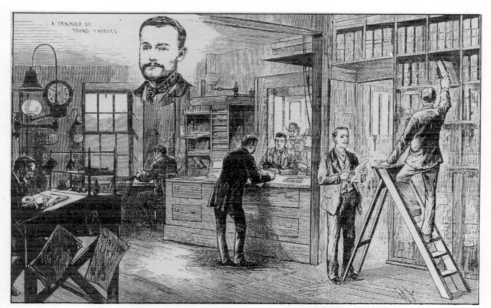

Convict Supervision Office, Scotland Yard, 1883.

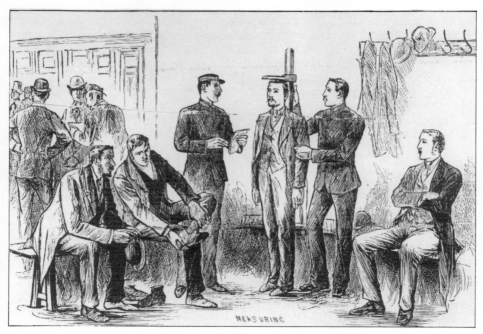

Measuring recruits for the Force, 1883.

(i) Vaccinating recruits (top left) (ii) Howard Vincent with his detectives (top right) (iii) Telegraph Office at Scotland Yard, 1883 – instructing the County Constabulary. ABC instruments and a wall telephone (below).

The tender from the Universal Private Telegraph Company offered the provision at each station of one complete set of Wheatstone's Alphabetical Telegraph Instrument (ABC Machine) consisting of communicator, indicator and bell. At the Telegraph Office at Scotland Yard four indicators and twenty four bells with four switches or turnplates, to enable each instrument to communicate with any one of six stations, and any or all such stations to call attention at the chief office were to be supplied. The cost of renting any additional instruments per annum was £6 for a complete set or £5 without bells.

The ABC machine had been patented in June, 1858 thus overcoming the difficulties of the single and double needle machines which required great skill by an operator. The ABC equipment was simple to operate leading to more use of private telegraphs by public bodies and offices. The machine consisted of an upper and lower dial, the top was the receiver and the bottom the transmitter. The key, located opposite to a letter on the lower dial, was pressed and a handle turned to generate the power when sending this letter. The pointer on the receiving dial moved to the same letter and was written down by the person receiving the message. Skilled operators could reach speeds of twenty to thirty words a minute.

Wheatstone's ABC telegraph
machine patented 1858.

From 5th November, 1866 an Inspector or Station Sergeant from the principle stations of the first six divisions attended Scotland Yard daily for instruction in working electric telegraph instruments.

Police Orders of the 30th September 1867 announced the arrival of the Force telegraph linking the divisional stations with Scotland Yard along with the homes of the Commissioner and Assistant Commissioners. The Force telegraph, albeit in a more advanced form, continued until the introduction of a computerised Message Switching System on 20th July, 1984. In those far off years there were no alternative forms of rapid communication in the nature of telephone or wireless, consequently this revolutionary development had a tremendous impact on the Force.

The original Police Order directed that one sergeant and one constable would always be on duty at the Commissioner's Office commencing at 10 a.m. 1st October and the duties would be in eight hour shifts. For this purpose three sergeants and three PCs were augmented (P.O. 20.8.1867 — on 'A' Division establishment); a report was required by the Commissioner at the end of three months as to the sufficiency or otherwise of the number employed along with the efficiency of the office arrangements.

Measures for the arrival of the system were carefully prepared and telegraph offices were immediately made the subject of regulations which included that no persons were permitted to touch instruments, other than those authorised to send messages, and message books had to be maintained both in division and at Commissioner's Office for recording all incoming transmissions. The metal work of the instruments had to be carefully cleaned with leather and the alarm bells were to be wound up every morning. Each line required testing at 8 a.m. daily, the results being sent to the Engineer of the telegraph company. In January, 1868 each station with a telegraph instrument was issued with a polished mahogany case for holding telegraph forms.

The service was gradually extended and in December 1867 authority was given for communication between the Commissioner's Office and the Home Office at a rental of £32 per year (removed in April 1880) and in the following January from C.O. to the Houses of Parliament at £36 per annum. A Police Order of 31st May, 1869 directed that during the session of parliament a police constable was to be appointed to attend to the telegraph instrument from 2 p.m. until 10 p.m. daily in that building. Outside those hours he was to be nearby to hear the bell ring. Less than six months after introduction the Metropolitan Fire Brigade Headquarters Station in the City, Horse Guards and the City Police were connected to the Metropolitan Police Office.

Sir Richard Mayne replied to a question concerning riots to the Committee Appointed to Enquire into the System of Police in 1868, ' each superintendent is first of all responsible for the preservation of peace and the prevention of any disturbance within his own Division as far as his means go, and directions are that he is immediately to communicate by telegraph to me and the Assistant Commissioners and to the superintendents of the adjoining Divisions'. During the night the Commissioner said that a message would be telegraphed to his home and the homes of the Assistant Commissioners. Quoting Paddington Police Station as an example it was assessed that within half an hour at night four hundred constables could be assembled.

There were now a total of 138 police stations in the Metropolitan Police District 117 without telegraphic communication and in February divisional Superintendents were instructed to report details of their most important stations with a view to connecting them to the divisional station. The Receiver, Maurice Drummond, followed by requesting Home Office approval to extend the telegraph to the greater proportion of police stations in the outer districts. On 18th April the approval for an extension, without tender, by the Universal Private Telegraph Company was granted. Unfortunately Sir Richard Mayne, who died in December, was not to witness any further development of his system.

An estimate was subsequently received for the extension quoting an annual rent of £1936. It appears that this work was never undertaken by the company as , resulting from the Telegraph Act 1868, the General Post Office were to take control of the telegraph service. In May 1871 the Post Office agreed to carry out the extension for an annual rental of £1,525 which was authorised by the Home Office.

The recommendations of the Committee set up after the Clerkenwell explosion led the Metropolitan Force, in 1869, to divide its area into four Districts each under a District Superintendent. A memorandum of the 3rd March in that year instructed divisional Superintendents to telegraph at 8 a.m. each day to the District Superintendent's Office the number of defaulters to be dealt with by him and any occurrence of a serious nature requiring his presence. These messages gave the District Superintendent an opportunity to assess in which order he should make his visits after which he would telegraph back his programme to the divisional stations.

The communication was between the following District stations and their divisions:-

No. 1 District	— (G)	Kings Cross	(G, H, K, N and Thames)
No. 2 District	— (S)	Albany Street	(D, E, S, X, Y)
No. 3 District	— (B)	Rochester Row	(A, B, C, T, V)
No. 4 District	— (W)	Brixton	(L, M, P, R, W)

Messages were taken by messenger to the residence of the District Superintendent when he was not at the office.

The years between 1871 and 1873 saw the programme of considerable improvement to the system as a number of stations on divisions were linked to their chief stations. During this period stations were connected as detailed below and Police Orders of 19 December, 1871 indicated the signal code to be used for each location. Divisional stations were identified by the divisional letter followed by 'D' as they are today. Other locations had no divisional identifier making it difficult on occasions to identify the stations from the code.

1/8/1871	A.	(King Street	(AD)
		(Hyde Park	(HP)
1/12/1871	B.	(Rochester Row	(BD)
		(Cottage Road	(CR)
		(Walton Street	(WS)
	C.	(Vine Street	(CD)
		(Marlborough Mews	(MM)
	D.	(Marylebone Lane	(DD)
		(Molyneux Street	(MS)
	E.	(Bow Street	(ED)
		(George Street	(GS)
		(Hunter Street	(HS)
	G.	(King's Cross Road	(GD)
		(Old Street	(OS)
	H.	(Leman Street	(HD)
		(Church Street	(CS)
9/1/1872	K.	(Arbour Square	(KD)
		(Poplar	(PR)
		(Shadwell	(SL)
		(Bethnal Green	(BG)
		(Bow	(BO)
		(West Ham	(WH)
		(Ilford	(IF)
	L.	(Kennington Lane	(LD)
		(Tower Street	(TS)
	M.	(Southwark	(MD)
		(Bermondsey	(BY)
12/4/1872	N.	(Kingsland	(ND)
		(Islington	(IN)
		(Hoxton	(HX)
		(Hackney	(HK)
		(Walthamstow	(WA)
10/5/1872	P.	(Walworth	(PD)
		(Peckham	(PK)
		(Norwood	(NW)
		(Bromley	(BM)
		(Sydenham	(SY)
4/6/1872	R.	(Greenwich	(RD)
		(Woolwich	(WL)
		(Lee Road	(LR)
		(Shooter's Hill	(SH)

		(Rotherhithe	(RI)
		(Deptford	(DF)
8/4/1873	S.	(Albany Street	(SD)
		(Portland Town	(PT)
		(Hampstead	(HA)
		(Barnet	(BA)
		(Edgware	(EG)
4/12/1872	T.	(Hammersmith	(TD)
		(Kensington	(KE)
		(Chelsea	(CH)
		(Brentford	(BR)
		(Bedfont	(BE)
		(Chiswick	(CK)
5/10/1872	V.	(Wandsworth	(VD)
		(Kingston	(KI)
		(Richmond	(RM)
		(Battersea	(BS)
4/12/1872	W.	(Brixton	(WD)
		(Clapham	(CM)
		(Croydon	(CN)
		(Streatham	(SM)
		(Sutton	(SU)
11/2/1873	X.	(Paddington	(XD)
		(Notting Hill	(NH)
		(Harrow Road	(HR)
		(Hanwell	(HW)
		(Hillingdon	(HI)
5/3/1873	Y.	(Kentish Town	(YD)
		(Somers Town	(ST)
		(Highgate	(HG)
		(Caledonian Road	(CL)
		(Enfield	(EF)
		(Holloway	(HY)
		(Tottenham	(TM)

Some further extensions continued over the following few years between chief stations and their stations on the division. For example, in 1874 Walthamstow was connected to Woodford, in 1875 Poplar to Plaistow and in 1882 expenditure of £146 per annum was authorised to extend the system to Bexley, Erith, Penge and Chislehurst. Waltham Abbey was connected to Enfield Lock in June, 1883. The Royal Small Arms Factory located at Enfield Lock, was policed by an establishment of two sergeants and fourteen constables in 1868.

Maintenance and servicing of an expanding system was a major undertaking and in 1874 approval was given for the Metropolitan Police to enter into an agreement with the Postmaster General for keeping in repair the telegraph lines between the Metropolitan Police Office and the principal divisional stations, the residencies of the Commissioner and Assistant Commissioners, the Home Office and Houses of Parliament at an annual cost of £798 to terminate on 31st March 1880. Together with the extended service to other stations the total annual rental in 1874 amounted to £2435 (for the financial year 1873/74 it was £3,147.11s.9d). It is interesting, however, that the expenditure on lanterns and their upkeep for the same financial year reached £5,389.10s.9d, far in excess of that spent on the telegraph.

During the 1868 enquiry Mayne admitted that there was no organised method of passing information to and from other constabularies although there had been communication between Liverpool Police and the Force in respect of Fenian movements. Mayne agreed that better liaison was necessary and the use of the telegraph was suggested as a means of achieving this.

The Force did make some use of the public telegraph. On 12th April 1870 a foreigner named Christian Lieb enticed a young German woman from home in Hamburg, Germany. On arrival in London they stayed one night at a coffee house at 118 Leman Street, Whitechapel, leaving luggage belonging to the female at Kings Cross Railway Station. The next day he collected the luggage and decamped. After a telegram had been sent to Southampton he was traced and apprehended. All property recovered he was brought back to London, convicted and sentenced to 12 months hard labour.

The internal network was soon an essential feature in policing the Metropolis and in August, 1871 Post Office engineers were engaged in surveying fixed point boxes on divisions with a view to establishing telegraphic communication with police stations. It does not appear that this work was ever carried out. Although regulations stated that the system was only to be used for police business, during the illness of the Prince of Wales in 1872 the public in outer areas who did not have access to the late editions of the daily newspapers, were informed of his condition by means of the Force telegraph. A breakdown between Scotland Yard and divisions in March 1876 made it necessary to send messages through the Postal Telegraph Office the cost being recovered later.

Informations of special significance, where an arrest was likely, were circulated by telegraph and inserted in the next issue of the publication. At 2.50 p.m. on 18th December 1871 information was received by wire in 'L' Division from 'B' Division that a horse and cart containing a quantity of meat had been stolen. This message resulted in a constable stopping a man in possession of the property at 4.20 p.m. on the same day thereby highlighting the value of a system which had undoubtedly led to the rapid arrest of a felon and the recovery of a stolen vehicle and its contents.

Burglary, the entry to an occupied dwelling house between 9 p.m.

and 6 a.m., required the attendance of a 'superior officer' to obtain details of property stolen and any suspects seen nearby. He was instructed in appropriate cases to telegraph these details to the Telegraph Office at Commissioner's Office for circulation to divisions.

Connections continued to outside establishments and included Woolwich (R) to the Royal Arsenal, Woolwich Dockyard in 1874, Vine Street (C) to the Geological Museum, Jermyn Street by alarm bell in 1878 and the Royal Mint to Leman Street (H) in 1881. Over the years the Force provided officers on permanent special employment to many public offices, museums and other premises at a charge paid to the Receiver. The establishment at the Royal Arsenal in 1864 was four Inspectors, ten sergeants and 64 constables; the Royal Mint was policed by one sergeant and six constables and the Geological Museum by three PCs. Prior to the installation of the internal Force telegraph at the Royal Mint instructions were that, in the case of fire, a constable was to proceed by cab to the police station for further assistance and telegraph to the fire brigade station.

Although by 1872 approval had been given for a telegraphic line between Buckingham Palace and King Street it had still not been installed by 1874.

The Criminal Investigation Department was formed in March, 1878 and on 20th May a letter from the Home Department to the Receiver authorised that 'Mr. Howard Vincent, Director of Criminal Investigations in the Metropolitan Police should have telegraphic communication laid on between Scotland Yard and his private house and the same facilities as the Assistant Commissioner with a Telegraph Opertant at the same rates of pay £45 a year'. These telegraph operators were employed in the residences for many years. The cost of their services are shown in the accounts of the Force up to 1882/83.

The London Fire Engine Establishment, maintained by commercial and private funds, had provided a fire service for the inner areas of the capital under the command of James Braidwood (until he died in 1861) and in 1862 a Select Committee recommended that a brigade should be instituted under the control of the Commissioner of Police. This did not occur but in 1866, under the new Metropolitan Board of Works, the Metropolitan Fire Brigade, commanded by Captain Eyre Massey Shaw, who had succeeded Braidwood, was formed. In addition to the Fire Engine Establishment the new brigade took over, a year later, the escapes of the Royal Society for the Protection of Life from Fire and by 1877 was operating from forty eight fire engine stations, one hundred and seven fire escape stations and four floating stations; coupled with this there were fifty six telegraph lines.

Whereas Braidwood had resisted the use of the telegraph Shaw could appreciate its value right from the start and immediately began to install connections between fire stations. A further Select Committee during Edmund Henderson's term as Commissioner again recommended, much to his disagreement, that police should take over the brigade. Although this never happened, the Force co-operated with the fire authorities by allowing an extensive telephone and telegraph network between police and brigade stations to assist with the rapid reporting of fires.

Shaw split his brigade into four districts roughly divided 'A' North West (extending to Hammersmith and Highgate), 'B' North (extending to Holloway), 'C' East (taking in the docks and extending to Hackney) and 'D' (covering South of the River as far as Sydenham). The Head-quarters were initially at Watling Street in the City but later moved to Southwalk Bridge Road to the south of the Thames.

As early as 23rd December, 1872 the Metroplitan Fire Brigade at Woolwich were connected to Shooters Hill Police Station. In November, 1882 the Commissioner sanctioned the establishment of telegraphic communication between various fire brigade stations and police stations on P, R, V and W Divisions.

Officers on duty at stations were instructed to afford engineers engaged on installation work every assistance. The communication agreed —

From Fire Brigade Station		To Police Stations
P.	Lewisham	Lewisham
	Camberwell	Camberwell Green
	Sydenham	Upper Norwood
	”	Sydenham
	”	Lower Norwood
R.	Woolwich	Woolwich
	Greenwich	East Greenwich
	Blackheath	Lee Road
	”	Eltham
V.	Wandsworth	Putney
	Battersea	Battersea Bridge Road
W.	Brixton	Dulwich Road
	Tooting	Streatham
	”	Lower Tooting
	Clapham	Smedley Street, Clapham
	”	Battersea Park Road

It is unlikely that all these links were ever established as by 1888 the majority of locations were connected by direct telephone wires as described in the following Chapter. An article in the Journal of the Telegraph and Electrical Engineers in 1888 (Vol.17) entitled 'The Present State of Fire Telegraphy' indicates that the maximum number of telegraph lines between the brigade and police in London was four and by 1886 there were only three.

Superintendent Kittle, in charge of the Executive Branch, was responsible for telegraph staff at the Commissioner's Office. The introduction of the telegraph resulted in numerous Police Orders and Instructions being issued over the years which included specific guidance on how officers on telegraph duty were to contact other stations through the system. The method to be used was published separately for each station by way of Police Order and regulations for working the machines were hung in a convenient place over the instrument for easy reference.

By the end of 1871 the number of messages had increased to 49,109 compared with 14,719 in 1868 and the pressure on the Telegraph Office at the Commissioner's Office in 1874 was so great that a Police Order of May in that year directed that unnecessary telegraph messages were not to be sent. Completed Telegraph Message Books were retained for a period of seven years before being destroyed.

Details of the increases in telegraph message traffic (such as are still available) are interesting to consider.

Year	Messages Handled
Division 'N'	Station Kingsland Road, Islington
1875	5,922 (transmitted)
1876	12,409
1877	13,595
1878	17,656
1879	21,679
Division 'E'	Bow Street
1876	8,731
Division 'V'	Wandsworth
1877	4,056
Division 'B'	Rochester Row
1880	8,066
Division 'G'	Kings Cross Road
1887	12,496
Division 'W'	Brixton
1887	12,405 (received)
Division 'X'	Paddington
1887	11,345 (received)

Concern was beginning to be expressed about the time Inspectors at divisional stations were required to spend on sending and receiving telegraph messages to the detriment of their other duties. Superintendent Hayes of 'B' Division said, in 1879, 'Telegraphy in fact is becoming of so much importance that I think Constables should be appointed for the purpose of attending the instruments'. Superintendent Harris of 'S' Division suggested that a Telegraph Clerk should be employed on a permanent basis throughout the day. His view was that the post would be good opening for youths leaving the Metropolitan and City Police Orphanage at the age of 15 years, and referred to them as a cadet corps.

He even suggested a salary of ten shillings each week and recommended that on reaching manhood they be considered for employment as constables. An Order of 1885 directed that 'intelligent Constables' in each division be instructed in the use of telegraph instruments to assist the Inspector. By 1887 the use of constables for telegraph work was approved, and the Reserve Constable assumed a responsibility which was welcomed by divisional Superintendents who could then abandon the use of Inspectors for this time consuming work.

Proficiency in telegraphy was viewed with great importance for those officers seeking advancement in their career. A Police Order of 2nd October 1872 reads — ' Sergeants and Constables undergoing instruction in drill at the Preparatory Class, prior to promotion, are also to attend Commissioner's Office for instruction in working the telegraph. The Superintendent for the Executive Branch is to certify on the printed Recommendations Form that the Officer is competent to work the telegraph, previous to the form being submitted to the Commissioner for directions as to forwarding recommendation for promotion to the Home Office '. To quote Charles Clarkson from his book 'Police!' published in 1889, ' The A.B.C. instrument is practically the marshal's baton of the police force. Facility to read messages has frequently been the means of bringing a constable under the notice of his superiors, which is the first step to promotion '.

A free telegram service for police courts using the public network, was announced on 30th September, 1878. From July, 1881 reports of serious crimes including murder, manslaughter and serious burglary were sent by wire to the Director of the Criminal Investigation Department as soon as the offence became known. Regulations even directed that Police Notices were not to be affixed to Post Office telegraph poles and in 1881 Superintendents were instructed to submit returns of postal wires fixed, whether or not by pole, to their stations.

In 1882 the Secretary of State approved the sum of £30 being paid to Superintendent Williamson of the Criminal Investigation Department in recognition of his service in the compilation of the new telegraph code for use by police. Revised message forms were distributed to divisions in 1883 onto which messages were copied from the Message Book for distribution by messenger to the addressees.

An official ambulance service did not operate in London until 1915 when a number of stations were opened under the control of the Chief Officer of the Fire Brigade, although the Metropolitan Asylums Board did provide a service for fever sufferers. The London Ambulance Service was not formed until 1965; consequently in the last century police had a role to play in this field.

Horse Ambulance Wagons were based at Carter Street and Stoke Newington Police Stations and were available for use, except in 'seedy cases', at a charge. The scale of charges ranged from five shillings for up to two miles to ten shillings for six to ten miles. There was a charge of two shillings extra between 8 p.m. and 9 a.m. In August, 1883 Police

Orders directed that the telegraph could be used on application by medical men or other responsible persons to direct the ambulances to where their services were required.

Praises for the Force telegraph were coming from all quarters as the full benefits became appreciated by management and many Superintendents were urging extensions. On more than one occasion in the early 1870s Superintendent Gernon of 'P' Division voiced his approval by reporting that 'the telegraph is the most useful introduction the service had had.' In 1874 he indicated that the extension of the system to subdivisional stations was of 'great and important' service to his division and recommended extension to all stations. The Superintendent for No 2 District, Robert Walker, in 1875 was highlighting in the Commissioner's Annual Report the efficiency of the telegraph over the old means of circulating information.

"I have the honour to submit my annual report of the state of the Police Force in the Second or N.W. District of the Metropolis for the year 1875. It comprises the Divisions D, E, S, X, and Y, the first two being Town Divisions, and the other Country Divisions, from their extending to the limits of the Police radius in the quarter above indicated, but yet embracing a considerable proportion of the Town. The advantage of this combination of town and country, or, what is now nearer the fact, town and suburb, is that the communication along the great lines of road may be carried on as far as possible by a Division of Police, having its principal Station and Superintendent's Office within the five-mile circle from Charing Cross, and thus available for speedy intercourse with the Chief Police Office close to the latter locality. Until within the last few years the means of circulating information was by the Police on foot, or, in emergencies by the mounted men, whose field of duty is necessarily along the highroads and the lanes for the protection of travellers, as in former days. But a great step has been gained latterly by uniting by telegraph the principal Station of a Division with the Inspector's Station, and it would be of still greater advantage for the public service in my opinion, were every Station along the main roads from Town thus connected for immediate aid or action. I may cite an instance here:-

A line of houses, or street it may be called, extends from Shoreditch onwards to Kingsland, Stoke Newington, Stamford Hill, Tottenham, Edmonton, Enfield Highway, Waltham, and Cheshunt. The last-named parish reaches the limit of the radius, where the Bucks Constabulary take up the "patrol". The few breaks in this almost continuous street are becoming fewer year by year as roadside fields and hedges disappear and houses and gardens take they place. The Police telegraph "points" along this 15-mile "street" are at the Inspectors' Stations in Shoreditch, Kingsland, and Tottenham, the two first, however, being in a different Division from the last, but beyond this telegraphic communication does not go although new stations, in charge of Sergeants, are at Edmonton, Enfield Highway, and Cheshunt. I would respectfully urge that it is as important to householders in the outskirts for the Police to have means at their command for the speedy circulation of information in respect of crime, fire, or the like, as to those in the more favoured inner districts where telegraphic connexion is close. It may also be urged that the claim is greater to have the means of swift intelligence where the Police are fewer in number, have longer beats, and the Stations further apart, seeing that it would not add a single Policeman of any grade to the strength but would rather help to keep those on duty on the alert for the summoning bell to receive a message. The telegraph instrument cannot be too fully appreciated for the purposes of Police, and its value is really not known until it is at hand. That it inspires a wholesome dread in the minds of the depredatary class is certain, and it may be appropriately termed in this "line" the modern "hue and cry". Were its use made general at all Stations on the principal roads the Sergeants and acting Sergeants or Constables would become skilful in what may now be termed a branch of Police duty, seeing that every rank above that of Constable has to pass a test of proficiency, after a course of instruction in telegraphy at the Chief Office of the Force, although the officers may be afterwards sent to do duty where the knowledge is not called into requisition.

I trust that while thus urging on the Commissioner an extension of the telegraph system over portions of the Police District I am not overstepping my proper limits in this report."

Superintendent Digby of 'V' Division was so impressed with the system that in 1879 he suggested that not only should all Metropolitan stations be connected but also the chief stations of each County and Borough Constabulary throughout the United Kingdom. Robert Walker (then No. 1 District Superintendent), again praising the system in 1881 for the quick dissemination of information, said that it 'helped to expose, track and stop the criminal classes'.

Superintendent Thomas Butt of 'P' Division reported that several cases of theft of carts and harnesses from outhouses had occurred during the Spring and Summer of 1881 indicating in his report that telegraphic communication would have made the likelihood of apprehending the criminals more probable. He quoted a case at Penge where a dairyman gave the description of three men who had stolen some new harnesses during the night and made good their escape. These men, from Deptford, were arrested by mounted patrols at Brockley some days later and the proceeds of several crimes found in their premises.

Howard Vincent, the Director of Criminal Investigation, from March, 1878 to June, 1884 provides some advice regarding the use of the telegraph in his instruction book 'A Police Code and Manual of the Criminal Law' published in 1882.

'The telgraph, if properly utilised, is of the utmost value in the detection of crime. If the arrest of any person is sought, of whom there is a good and recognisable description, a multiple telegram should be sent to every adjacent force on the route he may possibly have taken, so as to block his escape as far as possible.

When serious burglaries occur in provincial districts, the fact should be notified by telegram to all the neighbouring towns. It is sometimes assumed that the thieves have betaken themselves to London, whereas the probability is quite as great of their seeking refuge in nearer and more unsuspected places'.

The Illustrated London News of 20th March, 1886 under an article headed 'Sketches by Telegraph', suggested that a portrait of a burglar could be sent over the electric telegraph by adopting the alphabetical messages for the purpose. The periodical claims, 'It was shown to Sir Edmund Henderson at Scotland Yard; but we do not know whether the Detective Department has resolved to adopt the process'. There is no evidence to suggest that the Force used anything like this.

Many years later in 1921, Detective Superintendent Collins published his booklet 'A Telegraphic Code for Fingerprint Formulae' which proposed a method of passing details of fingerprints across the world using the telegraph. The method was used subsequently to send such information to Australia and New Zealand in 1924 and the reply received from those countries confirmed that the subjects of the information possessed criminal records.

The Riots of 1886 and the outcome

After the extension of the telegraph service from 1871 to 1873 there appears to have been very little alteration or improvement for some years except to provide a method of intercommunication between divisions by means of switches placed at the Commissioner's Office. This system commenced on 24th February, 1883 and reduced the need for Telegraph Office to record messages for onward transmission from one division to another.

On 8th January, 1886 the inefficiency of the Metropolitan Police communications was highlighted during the riots which occurred as mobs of demonstrators left Trafalgar Square after a meeting of the London United Workmen's Committee which had been disrupted by the Social Democratic Federation. Serious damage had been caused to property in streets over a wide area of central London. Police had failed to prepare adequately for the meeting although warnings of disorder had been given prior to the event and the number of officers on duty were in excess of those normally employed at such an event.

The meeting was very large with many of the 'rougher element' of unemployed present and groups frequently had to be broken up by police charges. It was difficult to keep the roads around the Square open even with the 563 officers on duty in the area. At about 4 p.m. a portion of the crowd, which the police had assumed would return to the east and south from where they had come, moved west from the Square.

Colonel Sir Edmund Henderson, KCB, RE, Commissioner of Police, 1869 to 1886.

They caused damage to premises in Pall Mall and in particular the Carlton Club; a messenger went to Scotland Yard giving information about this incident and the mood of the crowd. A reserve of 100 officers had been moved prior to this from St George's Barracks to a position outside Buckingham Palace and could not be found to deal with the trouble when a messenger went at 4.20 p.m. to the barracks to alert them. The Commissioner, who was on duty at the Square, stated that he had sent a verbal order at 4 p.m. to Superintendent Hume at the barracks to take his men to Pall Mall and it was alleged that the constable messenger had incorrectly directed them to go to The Mall.

There were a number of 'fixed points' where police officers were always on duty in the vicinity of Pall Mall but there was no communication between the points and police stations. A constable posted to the War Office was unaware of the existence of a telegraph link from there to Horseguards and a telephone link from Horseguards to Scotland Yard. It would have been possible for this officer to have passed immediate information to Scotland Yard about the rioters.

From the club the crowd continued westward along Pall Mall and the leaders ran up St James Street and into Piccadilly breaking windows as they went. They were seen by Inspector Knight and twenty officers to pass Arlington Street, where the officers were protecting Lord Salisbury's house, and eventually entered Hyde Park. From the Park they went to South Audley Street at 4.40 p.m. where very serious damage was caused to property.

Their riotous course continued into Oxford Street destroying windows and stealing from shops as they went. The group was about 1000 strong when they were confronted with a group of sixteen police officers led by Inspector Cuthbert in Marylebone Lane and, as a result of the energetic effort of these officers, were dispersed.

At 4.55 p.m. Inspector Cuthbert had telegraphed to Scotland Yard for assistance after receiving information about the approaching mob. This was the first communication received at the Yard since 4 p.m. although the rioters had been on the rampage since that time.

A Committee was appointed under the Chairmanship of the Honourable Hugh C.E. Childers, M.P., to enquire into the origin and character of the disturbance. The Committee's findings and recommendations were that the administration and organisation of the Metropolitan Police Force required to be thoroughly investigated. The Commissioner, Sir Edmund Henderson, was the subject of much criticism and subsequently resigned from the Force in March. Although many of the findings were not in relation to police communications much of the criticism was levelled at the inadequacy and improper or lack of use of the existing telegraph.

The Committee found that it was a mistake not to warn by telegraph from Scotland Yard all stations to the west of Trafalgar Square as soon as it was known that mobs were approaching causing damage. Their report says, 'We have also to call attention to the very inadequate arrangements made for telegraphic communication between the police in the streets and the Commissioner's headquarters at Scotland Yard. We find that no Constable was aware that from the War Office it was possible to have sent a telegraphic message to Scotland Yard at any time.

Had the police constable, who is always on duty in front of the War office, been aware that he could send such a message, he could easily, when the mob had assembled in front of the Calrton Club, have informed Scotland Yard of the fact, where arrangements could have been made for heading the mob'.

The Committee also said that police should have the power to enter a postal telegraph office and order the telegraphist on duty to clear the line at once to Scotland Yard in order that an emergency message could be sent. Attention was drawn to the fact that at Scotland Yard, and at police stations generally, there seemed to be no telegraphic signal by which the urgency of any particular message could be specially indicated.

They found that the practice of sending important messages by word of mouth was liable to misinterpretation and felt that such messages should be in writing. In the case of verbal messages the precaution of sending two or more messengers at five or ten minute intervals should be taken to ensure that at least one reached the destination. The messengers should ensure that they return and report delivery of the message, and that they had seen the order attended to.

The following extract from the evidence given to the Committee during the questioning of Lieutenant Colonel R. Pearson, an Assistant Commissioner, gives a picture of the Metropolitan Police communications as they were in 1886.

"You have no system for communicating from the various parts of London to the central office in Scotland Yard except at your police stations, by telegraph? — By Telegraph.

But you have no other system of communicating? — None.

Except that a constable can go into any telegraph office and tele-graph to you at Scotland Yard? — There was one telegram which came on Monday to Scotland Yard, a postal telegram, which arrived an hour after the whole thing was over.

From a Constable? — No, from a private person; I merely mention that as showing that the delay would be so very great if that course were adopted.

Not if you cleared the line? — We have no power to do that, and I do not suppose they would do it for us.

But have you ever asked about it? — Never.

There is no system like the American one of constables communic-ating by telegraph; that has never been thought of in this country? — No, but we have now a system of telegraphing, which has only been established quite lately, with all our stations. Formerly it was only telegraphing with the principal stations of the division, but now it

is all the stations, and we ought to get quicker telegraph communication through our own means than we should through the Post
Office.

Take, for instance, this last affair we are talking of. Now there is in
every public office that I know of in London a telephone for communicating with the other public offices and with Scotland Yard.
Within 150 yards of the stone throwing at the Carlton Club, there
was a telephone in the War Office with a constable on duty in front
of that office; he might simply have gone in and telephoned to you
in Scotland Yard, and told you that there was a disorderly crowd
breaking windows? — I think the telephone there might have been
utilised to very good purpose.

And he might have told you further that the police were not there?
— Yes.

And the same thing with reference to the end of St James's Street,
at the corner of Cleveland Row; there is a regular postal telegraph
there, from which, if it had been arranged with the postal authorities
that the superintendent or constable on duty should have the power
of clearing the line you would have known, in two or three minutes,
what was going on. That has never been contemplated at all? —
Never.

You know very well what the American system is? — Yes, I think
the Chicago system is a still better one. The mayor of Chicago gave
me a description of it. It is a sort of box where a constable is always
stationed, worked by electricity. By touching a certain button
inside that box he can telegraph to the nearest police station,
"Assault," "Drunken women," "Riot," or as the case might be; and
the inspector on duty would send down the number of men thought
necessary. You simply touch a button and either two men come to
fetch away a drunken woman, or 20 men to quell a riot. They
gallop down in open vans just like the fire brigade system.

(Sir Henry T. Holland) Are those boxes put up in the street? — In the
street, and, I believe, not subject to injury.

(Viscount Wolseley) Am I then to understand that the police constables on duty by day and night in London have no instructions at
all to make use of the telegraphic offices that exist in London for
the purpose of giving you information? — No, none whatever.

(Chairman) Nor of the telephone in the Government offices? — No.
My impression is, though I do not know, that the Post Office would
probably make a great deal of difficulty about it; we rent all our
telegraphs from the Post Office.

(Viscount Wolseley) The constables on duty by day and night have
the power to telegraph to the fire stations to give warning of fires in
their different localities? — They get anybody that they possibly can

to jump into a cab or go to the nearest police station as quickly as they can, remaining themselves to render any assistance for getting the turncock, and so forth. I mean that is in addition to the alarm-posts. Of course you may break the glass at an alarm-post; we have all that in operation.

The constables know that they may use that? — Yes.

And the same sort of system in an extended way could be applied to riots also? — Yes no doubt, I did not quite understand the question at first."

As a result of the findings of the Committee the then Secretary of State authorised a special expenditure of a sum not exceeding £2000 per annum to carry out certain improvements to the telegraph service.

By the next meeting of the Social Democratic Federation on 21st February, 1886 in Hyde Park the Force seems to have learned by the earlier mistakes. There were 2,450 officers on duty and very specific instructions for communicating messages were given. Each Superintendent had the ground to which he was to be assigned pointed out to him and Inspectors were instructed to inform him promptly of any crowd movements. In addition each Superintendent, Inspector and sergeant on duty was supplied with slips of paper on which all information sent or orders given were to be written to avoid any mistakes.

A telegraph message was sent every fifteen minutes, or more often if necessary, from Hyde Park to Scotland Yard giving a situation report. Similarly each divisional station was required to telegraph a report every half an hour.

A return (obviously as a result of the riots) dated February, 1886 prepared by Chief Inspector Cutbush, of the Executive Branch, details the police stations connected by the telegraph to Scotland Yard, via divisional and sub divisional stations. Mr. Cutbush's document shows that the residences of the Commissioner and Assistant Commissioners were still connected as were the Houses of Parliament, the Royal Mint, Woolwich Arsenal, the National Gallery, the City Police and the office of the Telegraph Engineer. Some outside bodies were already connected to the telephone (as described in the following Chapter). A total of about 122 police stations are shown to have a telegraphic link and even though the service appeared to lack efficiency a large communications network had been set up throughout the Metropolitan Police District. Certainly the riots had shown the importance of good communications.

A letter from the Metropolitan Police to the Home Office dated 17th March, about a month after the riots, indicates that all but a few stations in the country districts were on the system. The letter drew attention to the faults in the network and the problems which were encountered in the West End during the riots. It was emphasised that for one divisional station to operate to another it was necessary to pass through the system of switching at Scotland Yard. The letter goes on to give specific examples of inadequate communication —

"Vine Street can only speak to CO and Marlborough Mews and if attention cannot be gained at CO and the signal wait is given nothing further can be done. Hyde Park can only speak to King Street and this message would have to be taken down and repeated to CO. Hyde Park cannot speak to Molyneux Street or any other in the neighbourhood of the Park in the direction of which a disorderly crowd might be moving and if necessary send such a message. It would have to be telegraphed to King Street, there taken down. King Street would then telegraph to CO and ask to be switched to Marylebone Lane. This done the message would be sent there, taken down and repeated to Molyneux Street".

The letter indicates that arrangements had been made to link Wellington Arch to King Street and Hyde Park to C.O. The Force admitted that the recent events had shown that an extension to the system was desirable. Centralisation of trunk wires at Scotland Yard caused the system in an emergency to be used in excess of its capability often delaying important messages. Any wire which was out of order caused great inconvenience as there was no alternative. The suggestion that there should be cross wires from one division to another would be useful in the event of riots or other emergency.

On 23rd September, authority was given to take the necessary steps for the extension of police telegraph so as to establish a complete inner circle of communication between the principle station of each division. This inner circle of wires was subsequently completed in December at a cost of £595.15s; considerable improvement was reported.

The following Table details the connections referred to:-

Inner Circle of Wires

Connection.

Division	From	To	Thence to
A and D	Marble Arch	Marylebone Lane	C.O.
B and T	Walton Street	Hammersmith	"
C and D	Vine Street	Marylebone Lane	"
C and E	Vine Street	Bow Street	"
D and F	Marylebone Lane	Paddington	"
E and G	Bow Street	King's Cross Road	"
F and X	Paddington	Harrow Road	"
G and S	King's Cross Road	Albany Street	"
H and K	Leman Street	Bow	"
H and TA	Leman Street	Wapping	"
J and K	Bethnal Green	Bow	"
J and N	Bethnal Green	Stoke Newington	"
L and V	Kennington Lane	Wandsworth	"
L and W	Kennington Lane	Brixton	"
M and R	Southwark	Blackheath Road	"

M and TA	Southwark	Wapping	"
N and Y	Stoke Newington	Kentish Town	"
P and R	Peckham	Blackheath Road	"
P and W	Peckham	Brixton	"
S and Y	Albany Street	Kentish Town	"
T and V	Hammersmith	Wandsworth	"
T and X	Hammersmith	Harrow Road	"

The next proposal for an outer circle of wires was questioned by the Receiver on the grounds of expenditure. Sir Charles Warren, the Commissioner, in a letter dated 11th April, 1887 objected to the Receiver's criticism of the requirement and authority was granted by the Home Office for an outer circle on 9th May. This was completed in September at a cost of £755.15s with the following connections:-

Outer Circle of Wires

Connection

Division	From	To	Thence to
G and N	King's Cross	Islington	Stoke Newington
J and K	Barkingside	Ilford	West Ham and Barking
J	Woodford	Barkinside	Ilford
J and N	Woodford	Edmonton	Tottenham & Enfield Lock
K	Barking	Plaistow	Canning Town and North Woolwich
N and Y	Edmonton	Enfield	Enfield Highway and Wood Green
P and R	Bromley	Chislehurst	Lee Road and St Mary's Cray
P and W	Penge	South Norwood	Croydon and Thornton Heath
R	Bexley	Sidcup	Eltham
S and Y	Barnet	East Barnet	Southgate and Potter's Bar
S	Edgware	Barnet	Whetstone and East Barnet
S and X	Edgware	Harrow	Willesden and Hanwell
T and V	Hampton	Kingston	Ditton and Epsom
T and X	Brentford	Hanwell	Ealing and Uxbridge
T and X	Staines	Uxbridge	Hayes and Hanwell
V and W	Sutton	Epsom	Kingston
X	Hanwell	Harrow	Willesden and Edgware

An electric apparatus, separate from the telegraph instrument, was installed at each divisional station to enable staff to alert Telegraph Office at Scotland Yard, by bell and drop indicator, when it was required to send a message. In the event of an urgent transmission being necessary division would operate the bell continuously until C.O. had answered. When a breakdown of wires between a division and Scotland Yard occurred an alternative route, using the outer or inner wires through another division, could be used. Normally one division wishing to communicate with another would send to **C.O.** the code of the station to which the message was to be sent over their **ABC** machine and await the connection.

Resulting also from the riots the Commissioner's Office was connected to the General Post Office Central Telegraph system on 18th March, 1886 which afforded police an additional means of communication in an emergency. This connection was a supplement to the Force network and was not to be used when other means were available. Each message had to be marked 'On Police Service'.

Section Houses at Ambrosden Avenue, SW1, Charing Cross Road and Mile End were connected to the chief station of the divisions in which they were located thereby making it relatively easy to muster a contingent of men in the event of public disorder arising. Other connections provided valuable facilities in the event of demonstrations, for example those between Hyde Park and Wellington Arch and Marble Arch. Wapping was linked to the Thames Division ship 'Royalist', used as a station.

In October, 1886 the District Superintendents became known as Chief Constables. From the outset the Commissioner and Assistant Commissioner's homes were either connected by the telegraph to Scotland Yard or a police station. However, at the time of the riots only the District Superintendent No.2 District, A.C. Howard (AH), had telegraphic communication from his residence to Marylebone Lane Police Station on 'D' Division. The need to have immediate contact with senior officers in the event of an emergency became essential and by 1888 the following additional lines had been installed in residences (code signals shown in brackets) —

(AW) A.F. Williamson, Chief Constable CID to Scotland Yard (10.3.1887)

(EX) Superintendent Cutbush, Executive Branch to Scotland Yard

(RE) Lt Col W.A. Roberts, Chief Constable, No.3 District to Kensington (F) (1.4.1887)

(ML) Lt Col B. Monsell, Chief Constable No.1 District to King's Cross Road (G) (4.4.1887)

(GT) Major W.E. Gilbert, Chief Constable No.4. District to Brixton (W) (14.10.1887)

The three Assistant Commissioners were connected as follows:-

(AB) A.C. Bruce to Kensington (F)

(JM) J. Monro to Gipsy Hill (P)

(RP) Lt Col R.L.O. Pearson to Scotland Yard

Chief Constables' residences continued to be connected to the system into the early years of this century as did those of the Commissioners and Assistant Commissioners. When an officer moved from his address for his own convenience he was required to pay for the transfer of the telegraph line.

The year 1887 witnessed more disorder in the capital. November 13 at Trafalgar Square was the scene of the most serious of the rioting involving unemployed socialist groups leading Charles Warren, the Commissioner, to call on the aid of the Life Guards. This day became known as 'Bloody Sunday' but fortunately, although many of the crowd and about seventy police were injured, the army were not required to fire a shot. As with Henderson, Warren was the subject of undeserved criticism from the Home Secretary for his handling of the trouble. These events placed a great strain on the telegraph system and a proposal for the duplication of the lines between the Commissioner's Office and the principal stations of the divisions was implemented.

During the years 1887 and 1888 a number of extensions to the system were carried out, many due to the formation of the new 'F' and 'J' Divisions, and the consequent alteration in boundaries. Several wires were also provided resulting from the opening of new stations or owing to the development of some special need for the facility.

By June, 1888 the only stations not connected to the telegraph system were:-

Chigwell (J)
Chadwell Heath (K)
Forest Gate (K)
Purfleet Magazine (K)
Royal Gunpowder Factory (N)
(Waltham Abbey)
Farnborough (P)
Elstree (S)
Shenley (S)
South Mimms (S)
Harlington (T)
Heston (T)
Banstead (W)
Harefield (X)
Ruislip (X)

Maintaining and Extending

In 1887 the Post Office wished to change their contract with the Metropolitan Police relating to the maintenance of the system. The maintenance clause had been prepared prior to the Post Office taking control of the telegraph from the private telegraph company. The police wished to retain the right to decide which lines should be repaired first in the event of failure as they felt that the Post Office would repair those bringing the most revenue first. The original agreements with the Post Office in 1871 and 1873 allowed the police to arrange repair if the Post Office did not do so within three days and they would in due course be required to repay the Receiver. The Post Office objected to this clause which had been taken over from the Universal Private Telegraph Company.

In December, 1886 half of the police wires had been destroyed by snow storms and the Post Office took many weeks replacing them. This event emphasised the need to retain control over the priority of repair work which would not be possible if the maintenance clause in the contract was altered to suit the Post Office. On 'T' Division the total communications were destroyed prompting Superintendent Fisher of that division to say, 'The feeling of isolation this caused, as well as the difficulty in obtaining information has led me to thoroughly appreciate the immense advantages which are gained by this system of communication'. Mr. Fisher was again praising the accuracy and efficiency of the system in the Commissioner's Annual Report the following year.

A compromise agreement reached in January, 1888, stated that all practical steps to restore communication were to be taken by the Post Office. If a telegraph facility remained interrupted for seven days or the Receiver did not consider due diligence was being used he would be at liberty, after giving the Postmaster General 72 hours notice of his intentions, to employ persons to execute such works as necessary to repair. The Postmaster General would be required to repay the cost.

During 1887 and 1888 Boards were convened under Lt Colonel Monsell and the Superintendent of the Executive Branch to consider alterations and additions to the system. Various divisional Superintendents made recommendations.

In June 1888 the police were renting 205 ABC sets from the Post Office along with 214 switches. A total of 650 miles of wire existed (some running side by side) and by 1889 the system had been completely revolutionised with the establishment of the Inner and Outer circle of wires (already mentioned), and the introduction of the Type Printing system in that year (described later). The additional lines between Scotland Yard and divisional stations together with Type Printers cost £795.10s per year rental. James Monro by then Commissioner, had his residence connected to Scotland Yard by telegraph on 30th May by which time there were only 12 stations without the telegraph; recommendations for further extensions were continually being made.

It is interesting to examine the increase in annual rental costs of the telegraph over the years —

1868	—	£786 (rental from the Universal Telegraph Company)
1869/70	—	£1,124.17s.6d. (inc £45 per annum for Commissioners' and Ass. Comms' Operators at their homes)
1873	—	£1637 (1st agreement with the Post Office)
1874	—	£2435
1880	—	£2543.10s
1881	—	£3097.15s
1883/4	—	£3524.16s.3d.
1884/5	—	£3502.19s.4d.
1885/6	—	£4794.13s.8d
1887	—	£5960.15s.

1888 — £5783.4s
1889 — £6090.13s.

The end of 1889 was to see the cost rise to over £7000 a year and the Receiver raised the question of these heavy annual charges, which had increased rapidly over the previous few years, and asked whether it was necessary to retain all the existing wires. A report dated 18th November from Superintendent Cutbush of the Executive Branch made it quite clear that to reduce the service would affect efficiency and, in fact, he recommended that further improvements were necessary. He indicated that a considerable improvement could be made by reducing the length of some of the circuits. His report stated, "In many instances, communications have to pass through four or five stations before reaching their destination, the constant switching, connecting, disconnecting etc. involved by this process, gives trouble and tends to greatly complicate the working of the system, and it is moreover liable at times to render the electric current weak and consequently not reliable".

A further report answering the query of the cost says, "The service is one of supreme importance to the Police both as regards the pursuit and apprehension of prisoners and speedy communication of emergencies such as disturbance, or a fire, while as a general labour saving appliance its benefits are incalculable. It is possible, however, to pay too dearly for anything however important and, although the question was thoroughly gone into in 1887, there are points in which some modification may be possible."

The residence at 58 Ecclestone Square of a new Commissioner Colonel Sir Edward Bradford, was connected by telegraph to Scotland Yard in August, 1890; Monro's link was removed. In December of that year the Commissioner's Office which had been gradually overflowing into the buildings adjoining Whitehall Place and Scotland Yard, was relocated in the purpose built offices, designed by Norman Shaw, on the Embankment. This building, known as New Scotland Yard, saw the Telegraph Office along with the offices of other senior officers and the Executive Branch located on the third floor. In April, 1891 the Metropolitan Police took up the high telegraph rental charges with the Post Office resulting in a reduction from £7307.2s. to £6052.7s.

A request for a line from Uxbridge to Harefield and similar lines to country stations had been questioned on the grounds of cost and the small population in those areas. A suggestion that messages should be directed to the Post Office in the village via the postal telegraph created objections on grounds of the confidentiality required for police messages which often gave information about local residents. On 27th June, 1890 Uxbridge and Harefield were linked.

Hanwell Police were connected to the Central London District School in March, 1891 and by the following year there was telegraph communication between Hounslow and Hounslow Barracks, North Woolwich and Beckton Gas Works, and New Scotland Yard and Marlborough

House. There were continual extensions and improvements to the system over the last twenty years of the century which included many telegraphic links between stations and section houses.

In February, 1891 the Superintendent of 'V' Division requested a telegraph connection between Battersea on 'V' Division and Battersea Park Road on 'W' Division on the grounds that 'the inhabitants of Battersea were of a turbulent class and many of the principle Social Democrats and agitators resided there. During demonstrations very large numbers of the disorderly class assemble on 'V' Division and pass through 'W' Division on the way to town'. This link was established in January 1892.

Instructions of 24th June, 1892 directed that sub-divisions and sectional stations were not to be switched through to C.O. but messages were to be taken down at the chief divisional station and re-transmitted.

On 1st January, 1895 the rental agreement between the Receiver and the Post Office was renewed for a further seven years at a total cost of £6,254.10s. annually. There were by then a total 239 ABC sets and 244 switches installed throughout the Force.

At New Scotland Yard there were 22 ABC sets providing direct connections, in addition to all divisional stations, to Waterloo Pier, the House of Commons, the National Gallery, Great Scotland Yard, Marlborough House, the two Central Telegraph Offices and the residence of the Commissioner and a Superintendent Davis. The outer divisions had a large number of ABC sets located throughout the divisions including the residences of senior officers.

In addition to the ABC machines there was a Column Printing Syndicate transmitter (referred to as Q.Y. System) at New Scotland Yard and 22 receivers located one at each divisional station (development of this system is described later). The call system from twenty four stations to Scotland Yard was still operating. The pneumatic pump presumably ran the internal pneumatic tube telegraph which obviated unnecessary journeys between connected Branches; associated with this system were two bells and two buttons. A greatly improved tube system operated between Registry, C.1. Branch, Special Branch, C.R.O., Back Hall, Press Bureau and Information Room in 1937 for the rapid transit of messages between departments. A memorandum in that year emphasised the necessity for staff to use the system in preference to the telephone thereby avoiding errors. A written message was placed in a carton and an indicator on the carton turned to show its intended destination.

On 24th December,1902 Home Office authority was given for the payment of £17 per annum in respect of a new private telegraphic circuit from Paddington Police Station to the residence of Mr. Edward Henry, Assistant Commissioner, at Campden House Court. This ceased in 1904 after a telephone had been installed. The two years that followed saw telegraph communication established between C.O. and the residences of Mr. F.S. Bullock, the Chief Constable of the Criminal Investigation Department which included a bell and extension bell, and Major Parsons, the Chief Constable of the Western District. Six years later Mr. Bullock

Lamson Pneumatic Tube Telegraph at New Scotland Yard, c.1940s/50s.

was requesting the removal of the ABC machine; he was by then on the telephone, and the machine never received any use.

Direct communication with surrounding constabularies was generally slow to be implemented although the City of London Force was connected to Scotland Yard from the early days of the system. A telegraph link existed in 1886 between Woodford Police Station, then on 'N' Division (in that year the divisional boundary changed to bring it within 'J' Division), and Epping Town in the Essex Constabulary. Superintendent Sherlock in charge of 'N' reported this link to be 'an advantage with no difficulty or inconvenience experienced'.

On 13th November 1890 Colonel Henry Daniell, the Chief Constable of Hertfordshire, wrote to the Assistant Commissioner, Mr. A.C. Howard

"My Dear Howard

I am desirous of putting my Police Force in direct telegraphic communication with the Metropolitcan Force.

The local Police Authority for Hertfordshire has agreed to my suggestion and the county will bear all the cost.

My suggestion is that there should be telegraphic communication between the Ware Police Station and Cheshunt. Herts Constabulary Headquarters at Hatfield with Potters Bar. Watford Police Station with Bushey. From three points there, bordering on the Metropolitan District, I shall be in immediate communication with the whole of the Metropolitan Police District. It would of course be an immense advantage to Hertfordshire, while I cannot help thinking that any addition to the radius in which the Metropolitan Police can receive immediate information of crime in adjoining jurisdiction would be of considerable advantage to them.

Would you kindly submit the matter to the Commissioner

and Believe me

Yours very sincerely

Henry Daniell".

On 22nd November the Assistant Commissioner replied to Col. Daniell supporting the suggestion providing no expense was placed upon the Metropolitan Police Fund. The Superintendent of the divisions concerned within the Metropolitan were asked to report their views. Superintendent Beard of 'S' Division, where Bushey was situated, felt that there was a need to ensure a proper understanding between the Forces on what type of messages should be passed. An extract from his report reads, ' unless some definite instructions are promulgated I am of the opinion that officers on duty would be sending all AS (All Station) telegrams and we might be getting some very frivolous ones '.

The connections to Potters Bar on 'Y' Division and Chehunt on 'N' were supported by the divisional Superintendents. Both reiterated Mr. Beard's concern that proper regulations for the guidance of both Forces should exist.   Acting Superintendent McFadden of 'Y' Division said that in all AS messages the original sender should state if the Hertfordshire Constabulary was to be included.   In the case of a message from Hertfordshire the originator should state ' AS North of Thames ' or ' AS in N, S and Y ' as required.

A Memorandum from the Executive Branch of the Commissioners Office dated 9th December, endeavours to set a procedure for communications and reads—

"Telegraphs

The question of dealing with messages received from the Herts Police appears to be a very simple one.   No *fixed* rules could be adopted with advantage since the nature of each message must be considered before deciding what action is to be taken upon it, but, generally all telegrams containing description of thieves, stolen property, stolen horses or cattle, persons wanted for offences committed, person missing, and etc., should be repeated to the Commissioner's office by the Division receiving the information for transmission to all stations in the MP District, while other less important matters such as descriptions of children found, animals found or strayed, and etc. should be repeated to the Divisions and Stations bordering on the Constabulary district only.

There is but little probability of any difficulty arising if the Station Officers of the Herts Constabulary are instructed that only such information as would be likely to be of service in the detection of crime, recovery of stolen property or other matters of importance is to be wired to the Metropolitan Police, and that telegrams containing information which obviously does not affect this force are not to be sent.

Signed Superintendent of

Executive Branch"

Details of this memorandum were sent to the Hertfordshire Force in order that they could prepare instructions.   It appears that before the telegraphic links were installed Hertfordshire were requesting telephonic communication and it is not certain that the telegraph was ever connected between the Forces.

A telegraph link was announced between Old Jewry in the City Force and Leman Street on 5th August, 1889 but this was abolished in 1903 and replaced by telephone communication.

More Modern Machines and Methods

For over twenty years the Wheatstone ABC machine appears to have had the privilege of exclusive use by the Force requiring the operator to write each message down letter by letter as it appeared on the machine. This was a slow process, and with almost 100 separate locations on the system by the 1880s, it is not difficult to imagine that the lines often became cluttered with telegraphic traffic. The last decade of the century saw considerable activity by the Commissioner in his pursuit of a more efficient labour saving machine.

As early as 1858 the Electric Telegraph Company had tried the American Hughes Printing Telegraph without approving general use although it did operate extensively on the Continent. The Company continued to experiment with other type printing instruments including Wheatstone's automatic machines. For many years the Press Association, taking advantage of the Post Office's favourable cheap rates provided to them, used the telegraph considerably for passing reports to provincial newspapers. In 1872 the Exchange Telegraph Company, formed to notify Stock Exchange news, was using the familiar piano-type keyboard and glass domed receiver which remained operational for many years. A paging function was available on some telegraphic machines by the late 1890s.

The Force waited until 3rd April 1889 for a Type Printing System to be introduced at Scotland Yard with receiving machines at the chief divisional stations on A, B, C, D, E, G, H, J, L, M, S and Y. All AS (all stations) messages were sent over this line with division retaining the printed tape after entering the contents in manuscript in the Telegraph Message Book in red ink thereby distinguishing them from other messages.

This new system ran separately from the ABC equipment which still handled the bulk of the traffic. In the event of the Type Printing system becoming defective AS messages would be sent via the ABC equipment and forwarded from one divisional station to another. Scotland Yard would send to 'A' Division, 'A' would then repeat to 'B' Division and so on until all divisional stations had received the message.

In 1892 a major advance in the telegraph system was being discussed known as Simultaneous Column Printing. A memorandum for the Receiver, Sir Richard Pennefather, from Colonel Sir Edward Bradford, the Commissioner, dated 17th October, indicates the Commissioner's enthusiasm for installing the new system —

Telegraphs

'The Commissioner has to acquaint the Receiver that his attention has been called to the system of simultaneous column printing telegraphy which is in use by the Exchange Company which appears to be the most effective means of telegraphic communication now in existence. It is much in advance of the tape system which is in use in this office.

There is a considerable amount of mechanism in connection with the apparatus in use at CO terminal 'relays'. With the new instrument 'relays' are unnecessary, and worked by electricity supplied direct from the accumulators this obviating the necessity for the employment of complicated machinery and risk of error.

Moreover all the tape messages require to be *written* in the Telegraph Books, but, if the column printer were used, messages could be cut from the strip and pasted in the Telegraph Book. It is estimated that had this system been in use by Police since 1st January 1891, it would have obviated the necessity for the written entry in the Telegraph Book of CO and Divisions of 280,000 messages.

Some enquiry has been made at the General Post Office and it is stated that there would be no difficulty in arranging for the alterations if it were decided upon, but there might be a small increase to the annual cost of rental. Mr. Barker (of the GPO) suggests the advisability of making an experiment with one of the Column Printing Recorders as at present the officials of the Post Office have had no experience with these instruments. Such trial would not be made the subject of any charge.

Having regard to the circumstances stated the Commr will be glad if the Receiver will kindly arrange for an experiment as suggested. There is a spare wire to King Street Station and the recorder could therefore be very conveniently fixed there for the purpose.

Signed E R Bradford".

Exchange Telegraph Company
Receiver, latter 19th century.

By November 1892 a column printer from the Column Printing Telegraph Syndicate Limited, which had been under observation by the police, was recommended for adoption. In December, however, the Post Office Telegraphs commenced a competitive test of two column printing apparatus; one provided by the above company and the other by the Exchange Telegraph Company. The Post Office sought permission to have each Company's sending instrument at New Scotland Yard and receiving instruments at King Street or another suitable police station.

The acceptance by the police of the Column Printing Syndicate printer in November 1893 led the Exchange Telegraph Company to complain that the trials were unfair seeking an extension of the evaluation. The Company alleged that the Post Office Inspector responsible for the test gave a biased assessment as he was related to an engineer employed by their competitor. In fact the engineer complained of had been withdrawn prior to the trials.

Obviously a contract with the Metropolitan Police was of considerable prestigious value to the E.T.C. who tried every tactic to sway the decision. This included a complaint that their machine, being installed five months earlier than the Syndicate's, gave the competitor an unfair advantage as operators' experience had been gained on the E.T.C. apparatus before the other had been installed. The clear proof that the Syndicate's equipment gave a superior performance did not dissuade the Post Office from suggesting a further trial in February the following year.

On 4 July 1894, following a recommendation, the Central News Column Printing Machine was placed on trial over long and short circuits on 'T', 'V' and 'X' Divisions. Soon a transmitter at New Scotland Yard and twenty two receivers at divisional stations, supplied by the Column Printing Syndicate, were being rented from the Post Office at £798 per annum. A duplicate transmitter, installed in 1903 at a rental of £20, provided an essential back up.

The equipment available during the last decade had considerable sophistication. The Murray Automatic Printing Telegraph machine, introduced in 1896, for example, provided the Post Office with an apparatus for extensive use on their public circuits after 1901. With the keyboard, not unlike a typewriter, for sending and a printer at the receiving end converting the five unit code back into characters, it produced a paper tape in plain language. This equipment was combined with the Baudot Multiplex system between 1907 and 1912 to produce the Murray Type Printing Multiplex. It is not apparent that this system ever operated on private police internal wires but it does illustrate the advances which had been made in telegraphy by the beginning of this century.

On 12th November 1897 the Printing Telegraph Recorder Company Limited, 5 Newbridge Street, EC wrote to the Commissioner, Sir Edward Bradford —

Pattern No. B**189**

TYPEWRITING TELEGRAPH SET.

(Steljes' Patent).

Comprises Complete Transmitter, and Receiver; the mechanism being actuated by clockwork, and the magneto sending the current being driven by hand.

Pattern No. B189—This is an apparatus by which any person is enabled to telegraph messages, on either a telegraph, or telephone line, which messages appear on the instruments at each end of the line, similarly printed in Roman type on a paper ribbon.

Anyone can learn in a few minutes to use the apparatus.

No one need be at hand to receive the message as it is printed automatically at the receiving end, so that if the addressee is absent, or engaged the message remains awaiting his return. Privacy can be secured by keeping the apparatus under lock, and key.

ACCURACY—No operator being necessary at the receiving end, only one person handles the message, thus decreasing the chance of errors. Moreover, as the message appears word for word on the tape in front of the sender as he transmits it, he is able to discover, and rectify any error he may make.

If required the transmitter can be fitted with an electric motor, or a treadle (in place of a handle as above illustrated) for driving the magneto, the mechanism in any case being actuated by either springs, or weights.

A portable type for field telegraph, &c., purposes, can be supplied.

The instruments can be purchased outright, or the Company will supply them on hire, and maintain them for an annual charge.

Particulars, and prices on application.

Steljes patent tape machine.

"Dear Sir

We have a most ingenious instrument which we have adapted to the present ABC telegraph instrument and which gives a printed record of each message sent. It can be worked between two stations or the man transmitting can send to a whole series of stations.

It works in the Tape System similar to the enclosed, and its great advantage is that in sending messages there can be no questions whatever as to the actual words sent. I believe it would be of the greatest value to the Metropolitan Police System.

The machines have been submitted to the Engineers of the General Post Office, and have been subjected to tests therewith, I understand, every success.

I shall be happy to send machines for your approval if you desire it — or possibly the General Post Office might supply you with machines and at the same time give you their views as to their utility.

Yours faithfully
John Lanyou
Secretary"

The Commissioner expressed interest in these ABC Recorder machines (which appear to have been supplied by the Column Printing Syndicate) and early in 1898 a trial was commenced between New Scotland Yard and King Street Police Station. On 5th March that year the trials were reported as very satisfactory and, with a view to testing the capabilities through switches, the Commissioner asked the Receiver to arrange for equipment to be fixed for a short time to Hammersmith and Wandsworth Police Stations. These trials were carried out and both the police and Post Office reported once again their satisfaction. The Post Office agreed to provide and maintain the new apparatus in place of existing ABC machinery at a cost of £8 per year per instrument.

The Commissioner indicated that the future requirement would be for a total of 254 of the new instruments throughout the Force and that initially about 40 should be fitted at C.O. and the chief stations of divisions. The remainder were to be fitted as soon after as practicable. Home Office approval for the 40 instruments, given in August 1898, indicated the locations as follows:—

Divisional Stations	—	22
Commissioner's Office	—	11
Hyde Park Station	—	1
Residences of Commissioner	—	1
Assistant Commissioners and	—	3
Supt. of Executive Branch	—	1
Kensington Police Station		
(to Mr. Bruce's residence)	—	1

The Post Office reduced the final price to £7 per annum for each recorder with additional cost for the bells and circuits, totalling £300.2s.6d per annum. A reduction of £156 was made for the recovery of 39 ABC machines, rented at only £4 per annum. In July, the Commissioner and Assistant Commissioner, Sir Charles Howard, indicated to the Receiver that they did not consider that a recorder would be of any service in their private residence.

An overall reduction in the telegraph charges in March from £6,311.5s. to £4,706.8s. per annum meant that the introduction of new equipment did not in effect increase costs. It had been necessary to retain one ABC instrument at all stations in order that those without the new instruments were able to maintain communication with their divisional stations.

In September, the following year, the Acting Commissioner Alexander Bruce, informed the Receiver that the removal of one of the ABC instruments at stations where the Tape Recorder had been fixed had caused inconvenience. The only contact stations on a division had with their divisional station was normally through the ABC machines. If the one remaining ABC machine at the divisional station broke down, which was more likely due to the additional strain, then there was no communication with other stations. After correspondence with the Home Office it was finally agreed to return the ABC machine at eleven stations as a temporary measure until the tape machines had been installed throughout the Force. They were reinstalled at Bethnal Green, Limehouse, Stoke Newington, Peckham, Blackheath Road, Albany Street, Hammersmith, Wandsworth, Brixton, Harrow Road and Kentish Town.

The recording of messages appearing on the old system required considerable attention by operators whether employed at Scotland Yard or the police stations. Prior to 1905 messages received via the ABC telegraph would normally be recorded by the reserve officer or the station officer standing in front of the machine writing each letter, as it appeared, onto a slate. The message would then be transcribed into a Telegraph Message Book and the slate would be cleaned.

An illustration of this method of recording a message can be found in the Strand Magazine of 1891 when a reporter visited Wapping Police Station, Thames Division, and described the scene in the communications room.

'Just in a crevice by the window are the telegraph instruments. A clicking noise is heard, and the Inspector hurriedly takes down on a *slate* a strange but suggestive message:- "Information received of a prize fight for £2 a side, supposed to take place between Highgate or Hampstead." — What has Highgate or Hampstead to do with the neighbourhood of Wapping, or how does a prize fight affect the members of the Thames Police, who are anything but pugilistically inclined? In our innocence we learnt that it is customary to telegraph such information to all the principal stations throughout London. The steady routine of the Force is to be admired.'

This interesting illustration is also used in Peter Evans' book 'The

Telegraph Office, New Scotland Yard – before the Creed machines.

Police Revolution'.

The inefficiency of the system was brought home on 5th August, 1904 when, at the Metropolitan Cattle Market, Caledonian Road, a Mr. Henry Wallestein was given into the custody of police by a private person who identified him as a man named Bamberger. Bamberger was wanted on a warrant held at Kensington Police Station for larceny. Subsequent enquiries revealed that Wallestein was not, in fact, the wanted man but before the truth had been established he had been detained at Caledonian Road Police Station from 1.30 p.m. until 10.40 a.m. the following day. He complained of his unlawful detention which resulted in an enquiry being carried out by the Assistant Commissioner 'A' Department.

Station Sergeant Collins and Sergeant Wilson of 'Y' Division were interviewed in respect of their delay in establishing Wallestein's innocence. This had occurred because the original telegraph message sent from Caledonian Road to Kensington at 2 p.m. had allegedly never been received consequently, neither the officer holding the warrant, nor the prosecutor attended Caledonian Road. Not until 5.30 p.m. was the message repeated resulting in the attendance of the officer. The prosecutor, however, the only person able to identify the prisoner, had left his home and was not available until the following day. When he did finally attend he failed to identify the prisoner who was then released.

The AC 'A' reprimanded the sergeants for their negligence but indicated that "there was a laxity in the methods of the telegraph operators, also that the wires, or instruments were apparently not in satisfactory working order".

The evidence of the enquiry shows that a message from Caledonian Road to Kensington had to be routed through a number of stations depending on which lines were clear. An earlier message, sent prior to Wallestein's arrest to confirm the existence of a warrant at Kensington, had been routed through Kentish Town (YD), Albany Street (SD), Marylebone (DD), Paddington (FD), and Notting Hill before reaching Kensington. This highlights the problems in sending such messages as each station had to be 'rung' in turn to obtain the connection. The route depended on the availability of links.

The message at 2 p.m. sent to YD from Caledonian Road contained a request to forward it to Kensington. The officer at YD, unable to send the message through Albany Street, requested C.O. to open the line to XD (Harrow Road) through which route he said the message had been sent. Staff at Kensington denied receiving this message.

This case emphasised the inefficiencies in the recording of telegraph and telephone messages where the original record was wiped from the slate after transcription into a book. The consequent recommendation was that 'Rough Books' should be introduced along with indelible pencils for the original recording of messages and these would be retained for a period of six months. In September, 1904 they were placed on trial at Cannon Row, Vine Street, Bow Street, Bow, Peckham and Blackheath Road with a view to adopting them throughout the Force.

The Superintendents of five of the divisions concerned found the system to work satisfactorily and four recommended its permanent adoption. The Superintendent of 'A' Division saw the advantages of the permanent record but found the book to be cumbersome. He suggested that smaller books or message pads with numbered perforated sheets would be more suitable.

In addition a decision was made that each station should be supplied with books of message forms, with counterfoils numbered consecutively, onto which messages for transmission would be written. This form, handed to the officer responsible for sending the message, would, once transmitted, be marked with details of the sender and the person receiving it and pasted onto the counterfoil. This method would obviate the need to copy a message into the Telegraph Book. Messages received via the telephone or telegraph were to be recorded initially in the 'Rough Book' and then copied onto the message form and filed in the message book.

Reports were called for from divisional Superintendents who raised many objections to the proposals. Their fears were that more work would be placed upon station officers and communications would be slowed down due to the time taken to deal with each message, particularly if a succession of stations on a line were required to give details of the person receiving the message.

The view was that delays were being caused by sub divisional and sectional stations being switched through different divisions rather than their own divisional station recording the message and re-transmitting it. The proposals were considered to be too elaborate and not likely to lessen mistakes.

The views of the Superintendents were considered at a board convened on 16th December, 1904 presided over by Colonel Bolton Monsell, Chief Constable Northern District. The board concluded that the use of slates would be entirely discontinued and substituted by the Rough Books and indelible pencils. Messages to be sent would be recorded on a message form (form 133) and handed to the officer sending it. After sending, it would be entered in the Telegraph Message Book and the original forms filed every 24 hours and kept for six months. Messages received by telephone or telegraph from other stations would be recorded in the Rough Book and numbered. These would also be retained for six months. Also recommended was that connections established between stations for the purpose of communication should be cleared as soon as possible.

Every message book was to be carefully examined by every station officer taking over charge of a station to ensure that all messages had been properly dealt with. Although instructions were given that Rough Books were to be used, slates were still being used on 'F' and 'Y' Divisions for recording telegraph messages in 1908. Many other divisions had not adopted the new system fully.

Another recommendation of the board was that constables employed on telegraph duties, at the discretion of the Superintendent, would be retained on that duty for a period not exceeding six months. Telegraphy was again considered as a necessary qualification for promotion, and a certificate as to efficiency or otherwise in this respect was to be attached to recommendations for promotion. Constables were to be permitted to qualify in telegraphy by attending occasionally, in their own time, at stations arranged by the Superintendent.

The Executive Department of the Commissioner's Office, housed on the second floor in 1903, included the telegraphs in Room 210 and the Telephone Room (209) next door. The telegraphs were staffed by six sergeants and two constables in three reliefs. The years 1906/7 witnessed a considerable number of defects on the ABC machines throughout the Force although the Post Office claimed that this was due to operator mishandling or even suggested that no fault existed when their engineer arrived. The staff employed on telegraph duties at New Scotland Yard's Telegraph Office in 1909 amounted to three sergeants and eight constables. After the decline and replacement of the manual ABC machines little development occurred in the Force telegraph system for many years. The onset of the Great War required the introduction of procedures involving the extensive use of the telegraph and telephone.

During the First World War instructions were given regarding the methods to be used in the warning of an impending attack on London. The warning was to be transmitted from C.O. to all stations where, on receipt of the message, the officer on duty would immediately form a reserve of police, including cyclists, to act as messengers. In the event of an actual attack telegraph operators at Scotland Yard were required to transmit any messages received to the Admiralty and War Office in addition to the Commissioner, Assistant Commissioners, Special Constabulary Headquarters and other senior officers. Police Orders of 26th December, 1914 refer to 'Measures to be taken by Police in the Event of Bomb Throwing from aircraft or otherwise, or in case of Incendiarism'. In the event of an unexploded bomb being found in the street the Air Department and Admiralty in Whitehall were to be informed by telegram or telephone.

The first officer at the scene of a bomb explosion was required to raise the alarm and call the fire brigade. Unless they were guarding vulnerable points, Special Constables, whether on or off duty, had to proceed to the scene of any attack by hostile aircraft or to the police station, whichever was the nearer and report to the senior officer. Those at vulnerable points were instructed to be particularly alert to prevent 'destructive action'. The officer in charge of the police station was required to acquaint the chief station and all surrounding stations for the purpose of obtaining assistance. Local hospitals and doctors were to be notified and all available police and ambulances sent to the scene.

Observation Posts were manned by Special Constables watching and listening for enemy aircraft in outer parts of the Metropolitan area. These posts, often on the roofs of buildings, included one at the Kings Oak Hotel, High Beech, Loughton where the Specials maintained a look

METROPOLITAN POLICE.

Air Raid by Day

Instruction to Station Officer.

I. The first message will probably be "Take Air Raid Action." On this, proceed as detailed in the printed instructions, but **ON NO ACCOUNT** fire sound signals (rockets) or send out "Take Cover" Notices.

II. When the attack is believed imminent, the message will be "Commissioner's Warning, Take Cover," on which act as follows :—

> All Stations will send out "Take Cover" Notices.
>
> Stations authorised to fire sound signals will fire two rockets.

III. When the attack is known to be over, the message "All Clear" will be received. On receipt of this, Stations will send out "All Clear" Notices, and Police, regular and special, Air Raid Relief and Ambulance parties, Doctors, and others called out, may be dismissed unless their services are required in connection with casualties or damage.

New Scotland Yard, S.W.
28th July, 1917.

E. R. HENRY,
Commissioner of Police of the Metropolis.

out.   In some cases the posts were in communication by telephone.

Police officers were in some areas required to cycle around the town blowing on whistles and wearing sandwich boards bearing a written warning of an attack.   Maroons were also fired and a bugle often announced an 'All Clear'.   In addition to the regular constables and Specials who performed the task at some stations, boy buglers were employed to sound the 'All Clear' after a raid.   Much of the inner area was covered by the buglers operating from Scotland House and included scouts, schoolboys and cadets.

On receipt of a message notifying an explosion the officer in charge of the police station was required to issue pistols to all qualified men and mounted men were to saddle up and remain with their horses in readiness. Single men not required for duty were to remain at the Section House.

Any information received locally had to be transmitted to New Scotland Yard for circulation.   Fortunately, unlike the Second World War, the instructions did not require implementation to such a great extent with zeppelins imposing the main threat.

Although a short local newspaper article suggests that prior to 1909 carrier pigeons had been used by Chingford police for carrying 'swift, private messages to other forces' no positive evidence of the employment of this form of communication by the 'Met' has been found in the numerous records examined.   However, during the First World War many directions were made under the Defence of the Realm Regulations in respect of homing and carrier pigeons used by the armed services for the purpose of passing messages.   No person was allowed to keep these birds without a permit issued by police which included a description of the pigeon.   The Admiralty and War Office made use of homing pigeons as a means of communication and police were instructed to do all in their power to prevent interference with them whilst in passage.   In the event of a bird being found by private persons the police were to telegraph their message and ring number to the Admiralty or War Office as soon as possible.

The War Office Pigeon Service normally required the birds to be conveyed by rail to their destination and liberated by the Station Master. Police were not involved in the liberation of pigeons.

The twenty second division of the Force 'Z' Division was formed in 1921 and covered the County Borough of Croydon.   This required the re-arrangement of other divisional boundaries.

As already indicated the period up to the early 1930s saw Column Printers, supplied by the G.P.O., used in all head divisional stations, Marlborough Street and Kennington Road connected to equipment at Scotland Yard.   In 1929 only transmission of messages from Telegraph Office to divisions via the Column Printers was possible as receiving machines were the only apparatus of this type installed there.   There were two transmitting machines and two receiving machines at Telegraph Office the receivers being used for test and record purposes.   A device at the station was used to notify Scotland Yard that a message had been received. Each message had to be neatly cut off and pasted into a message book. Some years earlier Police Orders of 7th February, 1916 had instructed that, in the event of a breakdown of the Column Printers, messages will be transmitted by means of telephone or ABC system from C.O. and then passed on in accordance with a table'.

At Telegraph Office six Steljes Recording Instruments were installed for the receipt of messages transmitted from similar machines installed at 21 land divisions. Although the machines could be used for transmitting to divisions from New Scotland Yard they were almost exclusively used for incoming traffic. All Station (AS) messages were sent by Column Printer to the chief stations and from there by telephone to sub-divisional and sectional stations.

The Steljes Recorders, apparatus which replaced the ABC indicators and printed messages in Roman characters on paper tape, were used on many private wires in this country. A light wheel in the equipment inked a type wheel. W.S. Steljes also invented the Rebesi typewriting telegraph, battery operated, incorporating a standard typewriter keyboard. The receivers on this equipment were either tape or column printing.

Creed, a name famous in British telegraph history, became prominent in printer technology during the first half of the twentieth century, although the Force do not appear to have used the early machines. In 1902 the Company's new pneumatic printer decoded the perforations in the automatic Wheatstone tape and printed the message in ordinary Roman characters on gummed tape for adhesion to a telegraph form. Perforated tape, reproduced at the receiving machine, could be subsequently used for re transmission of the message. The pneumatic printer with its small air compressor was capable of operation up to 125 words per minute.

In 1921 Messrs Creed and Co produced their first teleprinter, a concept which had been first developed in 1915 in the United States by Kleinschmidt and Markum. The Creed teleprinter, a revolution in message handling, provided an important part of the Post Office's system by the end of the 1920s.

In February, 1929 Creed and Co.Ltd wrote to Superintendent Abbott of A.3. Branch offering to demonstrate their 'typewriting by telegraph' system to police. A suggestion that the machines would be suitable for communications between station and police box, did not materialise.

The Creed Start-Stop Telegraph System was already in use at the offices of the Central News Agency and the Evening News. Representatives of the Force, including the Assistant Commissioner 'A' Department, Sir Charles Royds, examined the system there. Trials between Croydon Police Station and New Scotland Yard were agreed and the 23rd to 25th April 1929 saw the Creed Transmitter and Receiver successfully used at the locations. The Commissioner, Viscount Byng of Vimu, the Receiver, John Moylan, and Sir Charles Royds, all inspected the equipment during evaluation.

The system was found to be a great improvement over the existing Column Printers with transmission much quicker and the type clearer. The wider paper used by the Creed required less returns of the carriage for new lines. A good operator at the trials attained a speed of 40 words per minute compared with 15 words per minute on the existing machines. The keyboard of the Creed was identical to that of a typewriter.

As a result of the satisfactory trial Superintendent Abbott recommended that these machines be installed for communication between Telegraph Office and all divisional, sub-divisional and some additional important stations. The proposal was that once the printers had been installed the Column Printers and Recording Instruments could be dispensed with.

Considerable correspondence took place with the Post Office regarding the adoption of the Creed Start-Stop apparatus. It was anticipated that the police would hire the machines from the Post Office and maintenance would be under contract as with the Column Printers. The GPO were not entirely happy with the reliability of this Creed model and recommended that the Force adopt the Creed tape machine which they (the Post Office) were using at the time. However, the demand for this tape machine was such that some delay in supply occurred. A completely new page printer, developed by Creed and tested satisfactorily by the Post Office, was not to be available for 18 months. A decision was made to defer implementation of the page system until the new Creed machines were available.

On 16th/17th December, 1930, New Scotland Yard was connected to Vine Street (C) and Limehouse (K) by the Creed tape machines. An experimental Creed Switchboard was installed in January, 1931 at Scotland Yard and connections were made to tape instruments at four other recommended sites — Kings Cross Road (G), Blackheath Road (R), Brixton (W) and Paddington (F). These machines were capable of sending and receiving messages. A Police Constable Coote had been recommended to attend the Post Office Central Station for instruction on the equipment. The tape machines were also installed at Lewisham (P) and Balham (W) in January, 1932 but, due to a switching problem, were not in use until the following month.

The new Creed page teleprinters were ready by April, 1931 and the G.P.O. wrote to the Commissioner requesting trials between the Yard and Croydon Police Station at the company's expense. In July it was proposed that the printers should replace the existing Column Printing machines at Scotland Yard and at the chief stations of divisions along with Marlborough Street and Kennington Road Stations. The apparatus incorporated transmitting and receiving capability combined in one machine. Six machines were suggested for Telegraph Office with a switching system allowing a great deal of flexibility in transmitting messages to various divisions. Installation would allow for the removal of all existing Column Printers and Steljes Recorders.

Certainly a modernised system was long overdue as equipment had changed little in twenty years suffering regular breakdowns and poor maintenance by the G.P.O. Even the experimental Creed tape system was not being maintained adequately; one machine at Paddington was out of service for nineteen days. The Force expressed considerable concern about the Post Office's ability to provide a good service on a new system.

The Post Office offered free special instruction at their Central Telegraph Office to a member of the Force who would be required to instruct other personnel prior to implementation. The training of constables to operate the new Creed teleprinters commenced in June, 1932 and consisted of two hours instruction in Telegraph Office at the Yard. A previous knowledge of typing was normally expected from the trainees.

The Lancashire Police were already using the new Creed 7A machines in 1932 connecting their headquarters at Preston with divisions. A keyboard perforator was used there to prepare punched tape for automatic transmission. The police in Ceylon, Amsterdam and Berlin were also using Creed machines.

In November, 1932 the programme for the installation of the new 7A teleprinters was carried out at 23 divisional stations and Rochester Row (A), Marlborough Street (C) and Kennington Road (M) sub-divisions. Operating successfully by the end of the month, within a few weeks the old equipment was all removed including the Creed 3A machines still being used at Vine Street, Kings Cross, Blackheath and Brixton Stations. With the removal of the old equipment from Telegraph Office the new Creed switchboard was moved to its permanent position. A modern facility, available to broadcast messages to all divisional stations simultaneously or to a selected number, provided two way communication at all locations. An indication when a station broke out of a broadcast was also incorporated into the system. During August, 1933 a total of 1001 messages were received in Telegraph Office 756 of which related to stolen motor vehicles.

An earlier recommendation to extend a system of Creed receiving instruments to sub-divisions (62 locations) was discussed further in July, 1933 with a reorganisation of divisional boundaries. As wireless communications between stations were to be explored, an extension of the network was not implemented. The rental costs were likely to have been in the region of £3,100 per year. In fact, in 1938, Chief Inspector Fallon of the Communications Branch (D4) recommended that the equipment be transferred from Rochester Row, Marlborough Street and Kennington Road sub-divisions to the District Headquarters at Great Scotland Yard, Paddington and Peckham which at the time had no access to the Creed system. This became a particular priority for the passing of Air Raid messages during the War. Not until 18th June, 1948 was the teleprinter service extended to sub-divisions and District Traffic Garages.

Two week courses of instruction were introduced when operators proved to be very slow in sending messages. By 1937, it had become clear that police officers at divisional stations lacked efficiency in the

Telegraph Office, New Scotland Yard – the Creed Teleprinters and switch board.

operation of the equipment and a decision was made to have eight constables from each division trained by the G.P.O. at Scotland Yard.

The equipment in use in the 1930s, varying little from the teleprinters operated until recent years, established a modern system of message handling serving the Force well for many years. The view of the Commissioner, Sir Philip Game, in 1937 was that once wireless had been installed in divisional police stations the Creed printers could be scrapped. This, of course, never happened as wireless would not have been able to cope with the excessive amount of traffic which built up over the succeeding years. Consequently a teleprinter network remained until the introduction of a computerised Message Switch System in July, 1984.

By 1931 clear instructions were necessary to reduce the amount of traffic sent by telephone and teleprinter to all stations. Types of incidents where AS messages were inappropriate were published in Police Orders and included such matters as persons found, articles of a trifling nature coming into the hands of police and animals found such as donkeys and goats.

By the 1930s the instances of motor cars being stolen were increasing and methods of speeding up circulation of information respecting vehicles were considered. Particulars of stolen vehicles, passed to all stations via the teleprinter, resulted in some divisions, on receipt of the message, having a constable on a cycle visit the officers on traffic duty and give them the details. Often the Inspector would collect the information from the station officer and pass it to the men on the beat while patrolling in his car. When a vehicle suspected of being stolen was found a message was sent to A.2. Branch and once the owner had been located an appropriate message cancelled the report.

Police Orders of 11th March, 1936 announced a major revision of station code signals. Unlike the old codes, the first letter always represented the division and the second symbol was, wherever possible the first letter of the station name. Divisional headquarter stations continued to use the letter 'D' after the divisional letter. The new system made it far easier to identify a station from the code and indicated immediately to the operator its division. A disadvantage occurred when divisional boundaries changed, moving a station into another division thereby making a change of code necessary.

On 14th December, 1932 the Telex (Teleprinter Exchange) service was installed at Scotland Yard thereby establishing links with other police forces throughout the country. This gave the advantage of a printed copy of a message for the receiver and sender. Preparation of a message could be made on punched tape and then sent at high speed to the receiving station.

In 1935 the Force were examining the new Siemens 'Hell Schreiber' direct writing telegraph machine which incorporated the use of a wireless receiver. Although the machine was not actually used by the Force the Commissioner considered that its development should be monitored acknowledging the potential for police communications.

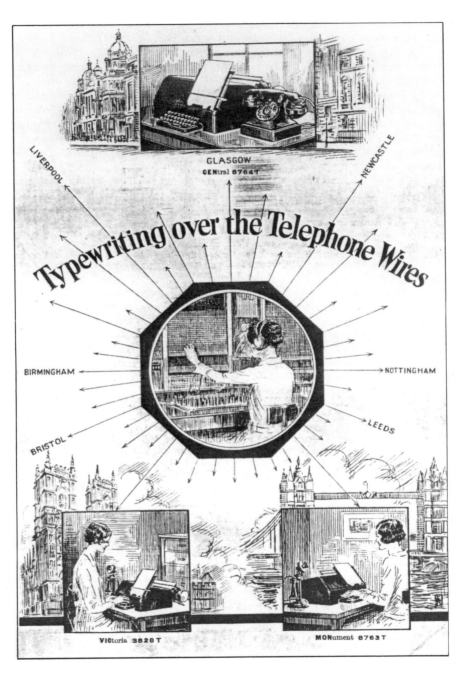

Messrs. Creed and Co.Ltd. Publicity, 1930s.

98

The Telegraph Office, albeit relocated during the War and again with the move of New Scotland Yard to the Broadway in 1967, remained an important communications centre until the introduction of the Message Switching System. It is rather sad that the name Telegraph Office, which remained with the Force for over one hundred and fifteen years, a constant reminder of the rather primative electric telegraph, has now been replaced by Message Switch Office. Today's computerised systems with Visual Display Units (VDUs) and fast copy printers are a far cry from the needle and ABC machines which gave service for so many years.

CHAPTER III

SPEECH OVER WIRES – THE TELEPHONE

Superintendent Foinett of 'B' Division observed in 1880 that he did not consider the telephone suitable for the police 'as the voice cannot be heard if there is any noise and it would necessitate the knowledge of shorthand to ensure accuracy at anytime'.   This opposition continued into the twentieth century when a remark, claimed to have been made by a disgruntled Sergeant in 1901, really expressed the fears of the Force, "I don't know what we're coming to.   Why if this sort of thing goes on, we'll have the public ringing us direct".

In 1878 the Telephone Company Limited was formed to market Bell's patent telephone and the following year the first telephone exchange, with a subscriber capacity of 150, was set up at 36 Coleman Street, London E.C.   The Postmaster General was forced to take legal action against this Company and the Edison Company in 1879 on the grounds that the Post Office's exclusive privilege to operate the 'telegraph' was being breached.   Although the companies argued that the telephone, an entirely new invention, was not subject to the Telegraph Acts, the judgement favoured the Post Office.   This meant that operators required a licence issued by the G.P.O.   In May, 1880 the two companies amalgamated to form the United Telephone Company which could operate within a radius of five miles from the centre of the Metropolis.

Many years passed before the Metropolitan Police took full advantage of the telephone system as a means of rapid and efficient communication although, as early as 1886, the U.T.C. applied to have their system of telephones connected with the police for the benefit of their subscribers; this was refused.

The earliest use of telephone by the police in London was by means of direct wire links between the Metropolitan Police Office in Whitehall Place and various government buildings.   In the early 1880s approval was given for direct telephone communication between Scotland Yard and the Home Office, Wellington Barracks and Horse Guards.

On 26th April, 1881 a direct telephone line between the residence of Mr. Howard Vincent, the director of Criminal Investigations at 8 Ebury Street and Scotland Yard was approved at a cost of £21.5s per annum. It appears that this telephone was handed over by the General Post Office for use in July.   In February, 1883 the Home Office authorised another arrangement with the United Telephone Company to establish communication between Mr. Vincent's home and Scotland Yard at the cost of £31.

In 1888 a private bill was placed before parliament (United Telephone Company Limited Act, 1888) 'to afford the company additional facilities for telephone communication and other purposes'.   One of the clauses related to the fixing of poles to premises.   The solicitor for the Metropolitan Police petitioned against the bill as police buildings would

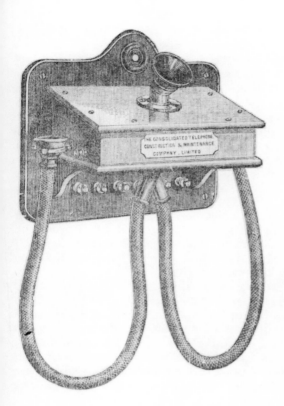

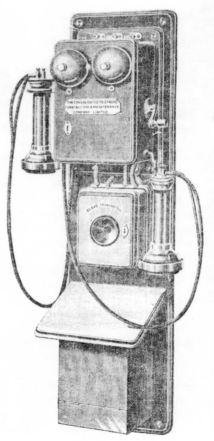

Bell-Blake wall apparatus
(below)

Gower-Bell Post Office
telephone (above)

Telephones of the 1880s.

101

not be protected from poles being fixed to them. Many disputes occurred between the two London telephone companies (the U.T.C. and the National Telephone Company) over the locating of their wires until in 1889 they merged adopting the N.T.C's name.

Certainly the use of the telephone was very limited, communication being mainly through the telegraph, as no telephone lines had been installed between police stations and Scotland Yard. In addition to those with the Home Office (the offices of Mr. Murdoch, Principal Clerk, and Mr. Ruggles Brise, Private Secretary), Horse Guards, and Wellington Barracks, by 1886 private telephone wires existed between the Executive Branch of the Commissioner's Office and the Metropolitan Fire Brigade, the British Museum, the Receiver, Richard Pennefather's Office, and the offices of Sir Charles Warren, the Commissioner, and James Monro, Assistant Commissioner. By June, 1888 connections between Walton Street (B) and the South Kensington Museum, Gerald Road (B) and the Army Clothing Factory, the Gunpowder Factory, Waltham Abbey (N) and the Grand Magazine had been established. In 1893 Hanwell Police Station was connected to Hanwell Lunatic Asylum.

The Gunpowder Factory at Waltham Abbey had been policed by the Metropolitan Force from 1st April, 1860 and by 1871 the fully fledged police station and barracks operated on the site at Powdermill Lane. Policing involved the maintenance of security and the prevention of persons entering with smoking materials; in 1868 an establishment of two sergeants and 22 constables carried out this work. Major accidents occurred on the site over the years and included one in 1870 where five people died as a result of an explosion. The rather interesting telephone connection between the police station and the Grand Magazine about a mile away seems to have been installed to aid communication between constables employed on security duty. The produce from the factory was stored in the Magazine before being transported by barge to Woolwich Arsenal.

The Army Clothing Store had an additional responsibility for the examination of police uniforms and boots after delivery by the contractor. The telephone may have been used for communication in respect of this function as well as general duties. An establishment of two sergeants and 12 constables were specially employed at the Store from 1864. The South Kensington Museum, policed by a large strength of officers, consisted that year of two sergeants and thirty four PCs; additionally one Inspector and four constables were policing the British Museum. These private wires clearly gave staff protecting valuable call system (described in the following Chapter), which increased to £349.0s.1d the following year.

The link between the police station and the asylum at Hanwell was undoubtedly useful for reporting immediately details of escapees.

The financial year 1889/90 saw £89.2s. 6d expended on the public call system, described in the following chapter, which increased to £349.0s.1d the following year.

A police station switchboard.

The police hand ambulance normally used to convey drunken persons.

Whereas constabularies surrounding the capital were keen to establish links with the Metropolitan Police the Commissioner did not show a great deal of enthusiasm for the idea; any proposals were instigated by the other Force.

On 29th June, 1891 Lieut Colonel Henry Daniell, the Chief Constable of Hertfordshire, wrote to the Commissioner, Colonel Sir Edward Bradford, informing him that the police authority of the county had sanctioned the establishment of telephonic communication between all the larger police stations in his Force for police purposes only. He requested permission to extend the system to the Metropolitan police stations at Bushey or Potters Bar, or both, thereby bringing the forces into direct telegraphic and telephonic communication. The Chief Constable indicated that 'all expenses connected with the erection, fitting, maintenance and repairs of the poles, wires and instruments connecting the forces would be borne by the County'.

On 26th August, 1892 the National Telephone Company (Watford Branch) installed and connected a telephone in the Inspector's office at Bushey Police Station thereby linking the station with Watford Police Station in the constabulary. The 'Watford Observer' of the following day announced the connection stating that, 'This will be a great service to the Herts Constabulary as direct communication can now be made through Bushey police with Scotland Yard'.

Telephonic communication was established in March, 1894 between Chelmsford Station in the Essex County Constabulary and Chadwell Heath Police Station on 'K' Division. Prior to this a link existed between Epping in Essex and Loughton on 'J' Division. The line to Chelmsford, taken out in 1916/7 temporarily, was finally removed in 1919.

The Surrey Standing Joint Committee at County Hall, Kingston-Upon-Thames wrote to the Commissioner on 28th June, 1898 informing him of the intention to establish telephonic communication between police stations in the county. A suggestion that the Surrey Constabulary Police Station at Egham should be connected to the Metropolitan Police at Staines was not met with a great deal of enthusiasm. The Commissioner's views were sought on the proposal and the possible sharing of the cost.

The Superintendent of 'T' Division, requested to report on the matter, expressed the view that the communication was of greater value to the Surrey Police. He said in his report, 'We very seldom have any occasion to communicate with County Police beyond informing them of previous convictions against prisoners for minor offences but on the other hand Egham Police communicate with Staines on all petty offences in the Surrey District, for instance, a coat and vest stolen from Ottershaw 6 miles out of MP District, they sent particulars to us. It would be far greater advantage to the Surrey Police who now have to walk or cycle to give us information of their cases'. He recommended that the cost, or at least the greater part of any cost, should be borne by Surrey. The Commissioner agreed and consequently the connection did not go ahead.

On 19th January, 1903 the Surrey Standing Committee again wrote to the Commissioner indicating that the principle stations in the county had been connected by telephone. The Committee stated that the telephone had proved to be of very great assistance to the Surrey Police and again suggested a link with the adjoining district in the Metropolitan area.

The early 1900s saw the telephone links with other forces gradually being implemented. In 1900 the police office of the Dock Company was connected with Canning Town Police Station and in January, 1902 Belvedere Police Station on 'R' Division with Dartford Police Station, Kent County Constabulary. Police Orders of 15th October, 1903 announced a link between Leman Street, 'H' Division and Old Jewry in the City of London; the existing telegraph was abolished. By 1907 Uxbridge on 'X' Division was connected to Slough in the Buckinghamshire Constabulary, Hillingdon Workhouse and Uxbridge Post Office.

Captain Shaw did not share the police reluctance to use the telephone and as early as 1879 he was pronouncing its value for his fire brigade's purposes when he reported, '. . . there seems no room for doubt that within a very short time we shall be able to use the telephone for our purpose; but we must make sure of getting a clear sound'. Within five years he was obtaining estimates to replace the brigade's existing telegraph although lack of finance prevented this happening immediately. Certainly the fire brigade chief tended towards telephone for the connections with police stations in preference to telegraphs.

An article entitled 'The Present State of Fire Telegraphy' in the Journal of the Telegraph and Electrical Engineers (Vol 17, 1888) states that in 1883 there were thirteen telephone connections between the Metropolitan Fire Brigade and London police stations which had increased to eighteen two years later (these figures have not been confirmed by police records). Fire brigade stations were connected to the local police stations as follows by 1888:-

Div.	From			To			
K	North Woolwich Police Station			Poplar Fire Brigade Station (Abolished 1894)			
”	Isle of Dogs	”	”	Millwall ” ” ”			
P	Gipsy-hill	”	”	Sydenham ” ” ”			
”	Penge	”	”	” ” ” ” (Abolished 1902)			
”	Lewisham	”	”	Catford ” ” ”			
”	Sydenham	”	”	Sydenham ” ” ”			
”	Knight-hill	”	”	Lower Norwood ” ”			
”	East Dulwich	”	”	Peckham Road ” ”			
”	Camberwell	”	”	” ” ” ”			
”	Brockley	”	”	Catford ” ” ” (Abolished 1903)			
R	Park Row	”	”	Blackheath-hill ” ” (Abolished 1903)			

"	Woolwich	"	"	Sun Street "	"	"
"	Eltham	"	"	Shooter's-hill	"	"
				(Abolished 1905)		
V	Putney	"	"	Wandsworth	"	"
"	Battersea	"	"	Battersea Park Road	"	
				(Abolished 1900)		
"	Kingston	"	"	Kingston "	"	"
W	Battersea Park Road "		"	Clapham Common	"	
				(Abolished 1895)		
"	Clapham	"	"	Clapham Common	"	
				(Abolished 1900)		
"	Streatham	"	"	Tooting "	"	"
"	Tooting	"	"	Tooting "	"	"
				(Abolished 1900)		
"	Sutton	"	"	Sutton "	"	"

Operating alongside the Metropolitan Fire Brigade, and outside the area under the jurisdiction of the Metropolitan Board of Works were the volunteer brigades and those administered by the local parish boards. There were numerous 'volunteers'; for example in 1877 an attempt at amalgamation was made between those at Barnet, Alexander Palace, Hendon, Tottenham, Wood Green, Hornsey, Willesden, Kilburn, Highgate and Tufnell Park. Many of the 'volunteers' were short lived often due to lack of finance. In many instances these brigades sought communication of one form or another with local police stations.

In 1889 the privately run volunteer 'Finchley Fire Brigade' was formed receiving a grant of £150 each year from the parish board. A letter, circulated to the ratepayers of Finchley, requested contributions to assist in building a fire station. Any subscriptions in excess of the amount required were to be used to purchase horse-carts to be stationed in different parts of the district.

The brigade proposed to fix alarms at three locations in the district including one outside Finchley Police Station. Telegraphic communication to the firemen's houses and the livery stables was to be installed. A request for a private telephone link between the new police station at Ballards Lane and the fire station was initially refused, although at that time a constable had to sprint a mile to the fire station to alert the brigade in the event of a fire being reported in the vicinity of the police station. It appears that the fire brigade preferred to have a telephone in the police station rather than the originally proposed alarm outside.

Finally Superintendent Beard of 'S' Division persuaded the Commissioner, James Monro, to agree to the request for a telephone line on the grounds of public safety. In the case of a fire occurring in the Whetstone area the police there would in future be able to contact Finchley by telegraph who could in turn telephone the brigade. On 10th December, 1890 the telephone link was established between the police and the fire station at Hendon Lane. The equipment was tested at 7 p.m. each day until in about 1897 the wire, broken during a gale, remained out of use until replaced some years later.

In 1905 barracks were built in Mill Hill resulting in a large number of messages being received by telegraph at Finchley Police Station for the military. This required the reserve officer at the station to walk two miles either way to deliver the messages. On occasions the military authorities required police attendance to take persons into custody for making false attestations on enlistment. This meant sending a message to the police station from the barracks by hand.

The barracks were already connected to the fire station by telephone and it was agreed with all concerned that the disused line from the police station to the fire station should be repaired. This would allow a connection through the fire station.

Although the Receiver disapproved of this method of communication the line to the fire station was reconnected in March, 1908. Later that year Finchley's connection to the public exchange made communication between the two organisations more efficient. The direct line to Finchley fire station was removed in 1935.

In March, 1889, in view of the burglaries occurring in the Muswell Hill and Crouch End areas, the Hornsey Local Board adopted a recommendation of their Fire Brigade Committee that Hornsey and Highgate Police Stations should be connected to the Board's telephone facilities. The telephone system included connections to the pumping station, mortuary, hospital, the Local Board offices and the fire station in Highgate and a fire box in Stroud Green.

As the Board's wires passed the stations at Highgate and Hornsey they could be connected at very little cost. If approved it would enable constables to communicate with their stations from the Board's telephones. Messages could also be sent from the 24 fire alarm posts in the area by way of coded signals. Such a connection would also allow telephonic communication between the two stations through a switch at the Board's offices or fire stations.

The Superintendent of 'Y' Division, in favour of the connection, recommended that police should take up the offer. The Board agreed to pay the cost of the wires but the annual charge of £2 for each telephone instrument was to be met by the Police Fund. The public would clearly benefit from the ability to speak with police from any of the telephones located in the Board's premises. Although approved it is not clear from records whether implementation ever took place.

At Devonport Dockyard there were special electric and telephone arrangements to give an alarm of fire in 1889. The police fire brigade often gave additional help in the town.

It is interesting to consider some of the other early telephone links between the police and local fire brigades prior to 1900 —

17.7.1889	—	T Teddington	— Teddington Fire Brigade Station
7.11.1889	—	X Ealing	— Ealing Fire Brigade Station
19.11.1889	—	X Kilburn	— Willesden Local Board (Electric Bell)

25.6.1891	—	X Willesden	—	Willesden Local Board Fire Station, High Street, Harlesden (telegraph abolished)
17.10.1891	—	V Kingston	—	Residence of Chief Fire Officer and Kingston Local Fire Brigade (also to the Fire Station)
17.3.1892	—	T Hounslow	—	Superintendent of Local Fire Brigade
19.3.1892	—	T Chiswick	—	Local Board Fire Brigade Station
5.8.1893	—	P East Dulwich	—	Peckham Road Fire Brigade Station
20.2.1894	—	R Lee Road	—	Blackheath Fire Brigade Station
7.7.1894	—	R Erith	—	Erith Local Fire Brigade Station
9.3.1895	—	N Walthamstow	—	Walthamstow Fire Brigade Station
1.9.1898	—	P Gipsy Hill	—	Westow-Hill Fire Brigade Station Upper Norwood
Installation date unknown	—	K West Ham	—	West Ham Fire Brigade Station
,,	—	K Plaistow	—	Canning Town Fire Brigade Station
,,	—	K Canning Town	—	Canning Town Fire Brigade Station

The discussions and correspondence concerning the various arrangements to improve the efficiency of the brigades through police co-operation were extensive. On 22nd February, 1895 a letter from Brentford Urban District Council written to Inspector Mumford at Brentford Police Station requested authority to fix telephones and electric alarms at the police station for the purpose of ringing up the firemen in the case of fires. Arranged as an interim measure prior to the erection of a new fire station the apparatus would be transferred after completion of the station. At that time firemen in the area were called by runners.

The intention was that the police station should be connected with the residences of the Superintendent of the Fire Brigade, his Deputy, and the Assistant Deputy, the turncock and the existing fire station. There were also to be electric alarms to the residences of 18 firemen in various parts of the town and the horse keeper's residence in order that the station officer could call them as and when their services were required.

The Inspector indicated that space existed for the equipment in the Inspector's office but the Superintendent's opinion was that to fit such alarms in the station would entail considerable work for the police in calling every member of the brigade. The Inspector opposed this view feeling that the work of police would in fact diminish by avoiding the procedure prevailing at the time where, when a fire was reported at the police station, one officer had to be sent to call the brigade runner and another the turncock. The engine then had to be collected by firemen from the fire station located in a shed at the extreme end of the town.

Fire, and Police Alarms—continued.

FIRE ALARM GENERATOR.

Pattern No. B127 (10)

Comprises Hand Combination Transmitter, and Receiver, Cord, Automatic Switch-hook, Induction Coil, Lightning Arrester, Magneto Generator, Switch, and Galvanometer for testing the Lines.

Pattern No. B127—The object of this apparatus is to transmit a fire signal received at the station, to the fire brigade men, and officers, in whose houses, and offices, bells are fitted.

These bells are connected in groups on the lines, and both ends of the circuit through each group are connected with the terminals of the generator used for that purpose.

When signalling the handle is turned rapidly, and the switch in the middle of the apparatus is brought from one contact to another, whereby the current is led out to the different groups of bells.

The apparatus is provided with a galvanometer, and keys for ascertaining whether the lines are in proper working order; it is, moreover, fitted with a Hand Combination Transmitter, and Receiver for speaking to those officers who are provided with telephones.

Price **£12 0 0**

Police stations often had alarm lines to the brigade — c.1903 equipment.

In June, 1895 the District Council arranged for a board with bells and a battery cupboard to be fitted at Brentford Police Station along with the telephone. The Receiver expressed concern about the permanent character of the work having the view that, with their alarms installed in the police station, a new fire station would not be built. In June, 1898 the alarms were removed from the station, but the fire brigade's telephone remained at an agreed rental of 5 shillings per annum.

In 1895 telephonic communication existed between Erith Police Station and the fire brigade which had been fitted without the approval of the Receiver much to his disgust. Six keys had been supplied to allow use of the telephone in fire alarm posts for police purposes when, in 1905, permission was given to connect them to the police station at Erith. A similar system operated at Bushey.

The Surveyor of the Southgate Urban District Council requested a telephone link between their chief fire station, the residences of three firemen and New Southgate Police Station in November, 1897. At that time when a fire occurred Wood Green Police Station received a message and then, by hand, took it to the fire station three quarters of a mile away.

A letter from the Cheshunt Urban District Council in June, 1899 notified the Superintendent of 'N' Division that the council were to keep their own horses for the purpose of the fire brigade and general work. They requested the services of the police at Cheshunt to fire signal rockets in the event of a fire to warn the drivers of the engine. There were objections by the Superintendent and it does not appear that the police ever undertook this responsibility.

Another letter to the Commissioner from the Clerk to the Enfield Urban District Council in November 1899 suggested that the police stations at Enfield and Enfield Highway should be in connection by telephone with each other and the local fire brigade. Considered desirable for use in the event of fire the idea, supported by the divisional Superintendent, could be seen as being of value for the communication of normal police messages between the two stations as an addition to the telegraph. Connection at least to Enfield went ahead; Enfield Highway was in due course connected to Ponders End Fire Station.

In 1907 the Carshalton Urban District Council asked that fire calls be received at the local police station for passing to the call boy of the fire brigade who lived opposite. The houses of five members of the local volunteer fire brigade were connected in April, 1908 by call bell from Belvedere Police Station. A similar system operated at Bexley and Loughton; Ditton was another station connected to the local fire alarms. In return for the police testing the fire alarm daily at Creekmouth, Barking they were permitted to use it for 'telephonic communication'. A number of agreements were reached over the years that followed between the police and local authorities in connection with local fire alarm systems; the Force generally co-operated with the local brigades.

On 25th July, 1898 the Clerk of the London County Council (res-

110

ponsible for the Metropolitan Fire Brigade from 1889) wrote to the Commissioner informing him that the Chief Office of the brigade had suggested that telephonic communication should be established between the Superintendent's station of each division and the Superintendent's station of a fire brigade district. The proposals were as follows:-

Divisional Letter	Police Stations	Fire Station
A	King-Street, Westminster	Clerkenwell (Installation not confirmed)
B	Chelsea	Manchester-Square
C	Vine-Street	" "
D	Marylebone-Lane	" "
E	Bow-Street	Clerkenwell
F	Paddington	Manchester-Square
G	Old-Street, St. Luke's (Kings Cross Road)	Clerkenwell
H	Leman-Street, E.	Whitechapel
J	Bethnal-Green	"
K	Bow (Limehouse)	"
L	Kennington-Lane	Kennington (Installation not agreed)
M	High-Street, Borough	Head Quarters
N	Islington (Stoke Newington)	Clerkenwell
P	Peckham Clock-House, SE.	New-Cross (Installation already connected)
R	Blackheath-Road, SE.	"
S	Rosslyn-Hill, Hampstead	Manchester-Square
T	Hammersmith, W.	" "
V	Wandsworth, SW.	Kennington
W	Brixton	" (Abolished 1903 and substituted by Clapham Common)
X	Harrow-Road	Manchester-Square
Y	Kentish-Town, NW.	Clerkenwell
Thames	Wapping (near the river)	Whitechapel

In some cases alternative police stations appear to have been selected for the connection and the original proposal abandoned. These stations are shown in brackets. ( ).

The Commissioner had no objection to the majority of the above proposals, providing the Council met the cost, apart from Peckham which was already connected, and Kennington located very close to the police station. Once these links were completed existing lines between Battersea, Camberwell, Tooting and Clapham Police Stations and their local fire stations were to be discontinued. By 1900 telephonic connection had been completed as suggested with some exceptions including Bow, positioned next door to a fire station.

Connection to the chief fire station of the area was not always efficient as, in many cases, those stations were many miles from the police station. Often it was easier for police to attend the nearest fire station for assistance. The brigade, two years later, introduced a single wire system and found it necessary, due to interference, to use shorter lines and connect fire stations to the nearest police stations. Extensive communication existed between the two organisations on the formation of the London Fire Brigade in 1904.

An improved form of telephone apparatus in fire stations in 1907 made it possible to link a number of police stations with their local fire station. Some lines to the Fire Superintendent's stations were disconnected leaving only those to the nearest police station. An example of this more efficient method was Hammersmith, connected to Hammersmith Fire Station instead of Manchester Square some miles away as it had been previously. Sixty police stations were connected by telephone to fire stations.

On 2nd November, 1912 the Commissioner, Sir Edward Henry, requested the removal of all telephone connections to the London Fire Brigade Stations which was complied with soon afterwards. The only one remaining, between Putney Police Station and Wandsworth Fire Station, was not disconnected until 1914 when night fire-escape duty in Upper Richmond Road ceased.

By 1938, a number of local fire brigades still had direct telephone links with police stations:-

Police Station	Fire Brigade
Chiswick	Chiswick
Brentford	Brentford
East Molesey	Esher and East Molesey
Richmond	Richmond
Uxbridge	Uxbridge
Shenley	Radlett
Edmonton	Edmonton
Tottenham	Tottenham
Leyton	Leyton
Waltham Abbey	Waltham Holy Cross
Barking	Barking Town
East Ham	East Ham
Forest Gate	East Ham
North Woolwich	East Ham
West Ham	West Ham
Canning Town	West Ham

Plaistow	West Ham
Chislehurst	Chislehurst and Sidcup
Kenley	Coulsdon and Purley
Croydon	Croydon

The line to Edmonton was considered most useful as the police could contact all schools in the area through the brigade. The system at Waltham Abbey, connected to each fireman's private residence in 1912, included bells fitted and operated by a hand generator in the communications room at the police station. Another hand generator operated the fire alarm system on the roof of the Town Hall. Additionally there were lines from two street call points. In August, 1929 the Receiver approved the operation, during the daytime, from the police station of a siren fixed over the fire station to alert the firemen in the event of fire. The magneto generator was mounted on the wall next to the Inspector's office.

During the First World War the motor ambulances of the Metropolitan Asylums Board could be summoned in the event of an attack by enemy aircraft by sending a message on the telephone, telegraph or by messenger during the daytime (9 a.m. to 11 p.m.) to the Head Office (Ambulance Department) Embankment, EC where they had thirteen exchange telephone lines. At night time messages were sent by telephone or messenger to one of the following stations:-

Eastern Ambulance Station,
Brooksby's Walk, Homerton.

North Western Ambulance Station,
Lawn Road, Fleet Road, Hampstead, NW

Western Ambulance Station,
Seagrave Road, Fulham, SW.

South Western Ambulance Station,
Landor Road, Stockwell, SW.

South Eastern Ambulance Station,
New Cross Road, SE.

Brook Ambulance Station,
Shooters Hill, Woolwich.

These stations all had lines on the City Exchange as did the headquarters. Additionally ambulances of the hospitals, Boards of Guardians and Local Authorities, some of which were horsed and others motorised, were called by police.

In 1915 the fire brigade took control of the ambulances, apart from those organised by the local Boards of Guardians. In some cases, where they existed, the direct lines could be used to summon the ambulances of the local authority.

The British Red Cross Society presented three ambulances (two Austins and one Harold-Johnson) to the Commissioner in 1918 which were allocated to divisions for use.

The internal Force telephone extensions were gradually increased at New Scotland Yard and indicated below are the connections in 1903. Some were rented from the National Telephone Company and others from the General Post Office.

Telephones at New Scotland Yard on the National Telephone Company System in 1903

FROM	TO
Telephone Rooms Nos. 209 & 210	Home Office (Mr. Troup). (Room 146). (Private Secretary).
	Wellington Barracks.
	Home District Office, Carlton House Terrace.
	Supt. Executive Office. (Room 221).
	Commr's Private Sec. (Room 162).
	Recr's Waiting Room. (Room 132).
	Commr's Chief Clerk's Room. (177).
	Asst. Commissioner's Room (93)
	City Police, Old Jewry.
	Asst. Commr. (Major Wodehouse) (Room 179).
	Commissioner's Room (174).
C.I.D. Room 102	Mr. Bullock's Room (89) (abolished 1908).
	Supt. Kirchner's Room (90).
	Mr. McNaughton's Room (93).
	Supt. Hare's Room (77).
Asst. Commr's Room No. 93	Commissioner's Room (174).
	Clerk's Office (125).
Commr's Chief Clerk's Room No.177	Telephone Room (210).
	Room 260.
	Commr's Registry (Room 152).
	Commr's Accountant's Room (196).
Receiver's Office Rooms 132 & 133	Receiver's Store (Room 259).
	Receiver's Accountant (Room 110). (abolished 1908).
Room 228 (Ch.Inspr. Ex. Branch)	Printers. (Room 182).
	Supt. Executive. (Room 221).
Basement	Receiver's Store.
Supt. Ext. Branch Rooms 221 & 212	Clerks Office (Room 220) *
	Chief Inspector's (Room 206) *

Record Office (Room 200) *

Printer's Room (182) *

* Later abolished

Asst. Commr's Room (161)

Back Hall. (Room 47).

Back Hall (Supt's. Office - Room 37).

Carpenter's Shop   Clerk's Office (Room 139).

Telephones on the G.P.O System in 1903

FROM	TO
Chief Office Room 209	Asst.Commr's Residence (Major Wodehouse).
	Fire Brigade Head Quarters.
	British Museum.
	House of Commons (Home Sec's Room).
	Asst. Commr's Residence (Mr. Macnaghten).
	Commissioner's Office.
	Commissioner's Residence.
	Battery Room.
	Treasury Switch.
Exchange 553 Victoria	Room 136. Surveyors.
552 "	Room 144. Receiver's.
554 "	Room 259. Storekeeper.
Leman Street	City Police, Old Jewry.

Major Arthur Griffiths in his book 'Mysteries of Police and Crime' describes the office of Robert Anderson, Assistant Commissioner from 1888 to 1901, 'The Chief of the Investigation Department has, of course, to be in close touch with his sub-ordinates; from his desk he can communicate with every branch of his department.   The speaking tubes hang just behind his chair.   A little farther off is the office telephone which brings him into converse with Sir Edward Bradford, the Chief Commissioner or with colleagues and sub-ordinates in more distant parts of the 'house'.'

The following connections with the Scotland Yard switchboard and other police premises show that by 1907 the telephone was in widespread use throughout the Force although resistance to the general connection to the public telephone exchanges was only just diminishing.

29/03/1897 — Cheshunt Police Station to the Police Cottages at Goff's Oak.

1898 — The cottage of a constable at Stanwell connected by telephone to Staines Police Station.

15/12/1899	—	Telephone between Kensington Police Station and Kensington Palace.
23/06/1902	—	Direct telephone link between Cannon Row Police Station and Buckingham Palace.
1/07/1902	—	Authority for the Registry, the Store and the Surveyor (Branches of the Receiver's Office) to be connected to the Post Office telephone system.
15/07/1902	—	Authority for a telephone link between New Scotland Yard and Buckingham Palace.
28/08/1902	—	Direct telephone communication between Cannon Row and Marlborough House.
17/12/1902	—	Direct telephone link between the Commissioner and Buckingham Palace and York House.
1903	—	Extension of the telephone from the NSY switchboard to the Room of the Commissioner's Private Secretary at a rent of 5/- per annum.
24/04/1903	—	Telephonic communication established between the residence of the Commissioner, Edward Henry, and New Scotland Yard at a rental of £23.2s.6d. per annum.
29/06/1905	—	Approval for telephonic communication between Buckingham Palace and Wellington Arch by means of a double wire circuit.
09/1905	—	Extension telephones in C.I.D. offices at Divisional Stations.
07/1906	—	Approval for an additional telephone at Hyde Park Police Station at a rental of £1.10s. per year.

From the very early days of the telephone premises with a security risk or with other needs for regular and immediate communication with the police stations were connected by direct lines to local stations and included (some already mentioned) —

'B'	Natural History Museum	to	Walton Street (01.04.1905) (telegraph abolished)
'B'	Victoria and Albert Museum	to	Walton Street
'B'	Royal Army Clothing Store	to	Gerald Road (prior to 06.1888)
'C'	National Gallery	to	Vine Street
'C'	Museum of Practical Geology	to	Vine Street (29.9.1904)
'G'	Messrs De La Rue, Bunhill Rd.	to	City Road
'J'	Bethnal Green Museum	to	Bethnal Green (9.7.1902)
'K'	Poplar Casual Ward	to	Bow
'K'	Victoria Dock and Royal Albert Docks	to	Canning Town
'K'	Naval Store Depot	to	Poplar (27.9.1899)
'N'	Gunpowder Factory, Waltham Abbey	to	Grand Magazine (prior to 06.1888)
'R'	Royal Hospital School, Greenwich	to	Park Row (14.3.1903)

'R'	Royal Arsenal (Main Gate)	to	Woolwich	(20.10.1902)
'T'	Hounslow Barracks	to	Hounslow	
'T'	Hampton Court Palace	to	Hampton	
'T'	Brentford Union Offices	to	Brentford	
'X'	Hanwell Lunatic Asylum	to	Hanwell	(10.7.1893)
'X'	H.M. Prison, Wormwood Scrubs	to	Notting Dale	
'X'	Hillingdon Workhouse	to	Uxbridge	
'X'	Central London District School	to	Hanwell	
'Y'	Enfield District Council Office	to	Enfield	
'Y'	District Council Office Palmers Green	to	Southgate	

The policy adopted by the Commissioner for approving direct telephone links is unclear although they were often refused as with the applications in October 1898 from the Association for the Care of Friendless Girls, the Discharged Prisoners Aid Society and the Willesden Hospital. Professor Herkomer of Bushey and Messrs Williamson of Farrington also tried unsuccessfully to arrange direct communication with the police.

On 18th June, 1903 the Receiver, Richard Pennefather, wrote to the Commissioner, Edward Henry, forwarding an estimate of the annual Post Office rental for establishing telephonic communication between certain police stations and New Scotland Yard. This most important advancement in internal Force communications, previously based solely on the telegraph network, would provide divisions with an effective and much needed facility.

The Commissioner, who only came to office a few months earlier, was convinced that the introduction of a telephone link with the more important divisions and stations 'would lead to more effective administration and control of the Metropolitan Police Service'. Prior to its introduction divisional Superintendents were often called to C.O. to discuss business which could easily have been dealt with over the telephone. This was a very time consuming exercise particularly when the officer had to travel from an outer division.

The telephone could also provide a 'back up' for the telegraph in the event of a break down. A station, situated on or near the routes of processions or demonstrations, would gain additional convenience for rapidly passing information concerning the events.

The Metropolitan Force were still considering this facility when all stations of the City of London were already connected by telephone. The Commissioner recommended that the divisional stations of sixteen of the twenty two divisions should be connected to his office by trunk lines. In addition branch lines from Whitechapel to Arbour Square on 'H' Division, Vine Street to Marlborough Street on 'C', Marylebone to Tottenham Court Road on 'D' and Bow Street to Grays Inn Road on 'E' were suggested mainly due to their position in areas where demonstrations often occurred. In September the following estimate from the

117

G.P.O. was received (extract from letter)—

GENERAL POST OFFICE, LONDON
17th September 1903.

Sir,

With reference to your letter of the 21st July last on the subject of the proposed telephone circuits between New Scotland Yard and the various Divisional Stations, I am directed by the Postmaster General to say that the rentals will be as shown below, under the usual agreement for 7 years.

From	To	Apparatus	Rental	Remarks
			£ s. d.	
A. New Scotland Yard	Divisional Stations C.D.E.G.H.J.K.L. M.N.P.R.S.V.X and Y.	20 Telephones 16 holes on Switch at New Scotland Yard	378 15. 0	
B. New Scotland Yard	Divisional Stations B.F.T and W.	4 Telephones 4 holes on Switch at New Scotland Yard	97 0. 0.	
C. Divisional Station H (1) do. do. G do. do. D do. do. E	Arbour Square. Gt.Marlborough St. Tottenham Court Rd. Grays Inn Road	8 Telephones	*56 10. 0.	*Including a charge of £15 for new pipe work to cease at end of lease.
C. Divisional Section H (2) do. do. C do. do. D do. do. E	Arbour Square Gt.Marlborough St. Tottenham Court Rd. Grays Inn Road.	4 Switches 4 Telephones	*34 10 0.	*Alternative to C(1) provided proposal A is accepted.

The rental for proposals A B & C(2) combined would be £508. 15. 0 per annum. This rental provides for 4 additional telephones and 20 additional holes in the switch at the Chief Office.

Home Office approval was given on 24th September, 1903 for the connection to all divisional stations with the exception of 'A' Division due to its close proximity to Scotland Yard. The memorandum from the Executive Branch directed that the telephone instruments were to be isolated so that the Commissioner could speak to his Superintendents confidentially. A suggestion that a sound proofed box be constructed in the Inspector's Office at the divisional station was considered but not implemented.

The four additional stations recommended were to be connected by means of switches at their divisional stations. The divisional stations were to be equipped with a telephone transmitter and receiver in the Inspector's Office with another in the Superintendent's Office at an additional annual rental of £34.10. A confidential conversation with the Superintendent in his office would require the telephone to be switched on there and the one in the Inspector's office turned off.

Work on installation was well under way by December, and thirteen divisional stations were in communication by telephone with New Scotland Yard in January. The outstanding divisions followed shortly afterwards. The annual rental finally amounted to about £556.

On 23rd January, 1905 the Commissioner reported the system of 'immense advantage to the Police Service'. He added that the valuable time of superior officers of the Force had been saved by discussing matters of the moment with Superintendents without bringing them to Scotland Yard. He observed that, although the telephone had been regarded at first with misgiving by many experienced officers, none of the anticipated difficulties had arisen. The fears that inaccurate transmission or reception of messages would occur had been unfounded. The Commissioner recommended an extension of the system to the principal stations of inner divisions.

In July 1904 a line from the new switchboard at the Commissioner's Office to the Convict Supervision Office was requested thus enabling officers employed there to communicate with divisions in respect of finger print identification and other crime related matters. Later that year the completion coincided with a connection to Public Carriage Office, the section of the Force responsible for the licensing of Hackney Carriages and associated matters.

Sir Edward Henry notified the Home Secretary that the representations he had received were for the extension of the telephone system throughout the Force. Although the Commissioner did not request such extension at this time he felt that the system should be extended to principal stations of river divisions which would allow speedy communication in the event of 'labour troubles or disturbances in the Metropolis, or other of the many exigencies of Police administration'.

The Commissioner quoted, as an example of the need for better communication, a report from the Superintendent of Thames Division at Wapping —

"I beg to report that the communications between Wapping Station and the Commissioner's Office are unsatisfactory and altogether inadequate to the requirements of the principal Station of a Division. The only means at present provided for the transmission of urgent or confidential messages to Commissioner's Office is an ABC telegraph, this is constantly blocked with messages passing to and from Waterloo Pier Station there being no other means of communication between Wapping and Waterloo Pier. All messages for the latter station have to pass over the ABC wire to CO, where they are switched through. This line is also the only medium of communication with the Chief Station of other Divisions. During the year 1903, 9756 messages were received or transmitted at Wapping Station while during the current year 10973 have been dealt with up to the present date (12 Decr.) With this amount of telegraph work, constant delay and inconvenience are inevitable where the means provided for dealing with it are so inadequate, and I submit that the time has arrived when it becomes necessary to afford increased facilities for dealing with urgent or confidential messages in a more expeditious and satisfactory manner.

As an instance of inconvenience which is so often experienced, it may be mentioned that many of the communications which have recently passed between the Divisions and the Treasury and the Commissioner's Office relating to the prosecution in the case of the torpedo des? Caroline have had to be put into writing and conveyed by hand from Wapping to Westminster thereby wasting valuable time and incurring expense which might have been avoided had it been possible to exchange a few minutes conversation by telephone".

On 17th April, 1905 approval to extend the telephone system to a number of additional police stations and locations was granted by the Home Office. This extension involved linking one station with another on a division by way of switches. Additionally the following lines were authorised —

'A' Cannon Row to Ambrosden Avenue Section House
'C' Vine Street to Charing Cross Road Section House
'H' Leman Street to the Royal Mint
'H' Leman Street to the Tower of London

The annual rental for the extended system amounted to £593. 5s, approved by the Home Office in May, 1906.

The following year authority for many more sub-divisional stations to be linked up by telephone was given and interconnections between certain divisions were also implemented. With the Executive Branch at C.O. already connected to each divisional headquarters station communication with a large proportion of the M.P.D. through a very extensive network of private wires had developed.

The Commissioner opposed a suggestion that telegraph connections should be dispensed with in certain locations where telephones had been installed. However in 1910 he did ask the Receiver to arrange for all the stations on 'X' Division to be connected to the internal telephone system in order that all telegraph communication could be discontinued as an experiment.

On 19th March, 1903 authority was given for the Post Office to connect New Scotland Yard to the offices of Ellis and Ellis, the Force solicitors, at 5 Delahey Street, Westminster. On 12th August, 1905 the Metropolitan Police solicitors, Wontner and Sons, of 40 Bedford Row WC were similarly connected which ensured much more efficient communication with divisions in connection with pending prosecutions.

The Prison Commissioners requested in 1906 that telephonic communications be established between the Metropolitan prisons and

120

the courts and police stations. If Brixton Prison were to be connected to Brixton Police Station this would give access to the private wire network and other prisons would be able to pass their messages for police through that prison. The problem existing without telephone communication was demonstrated by a case where a constable had been posted outside Brixton Prison for three weeks waiting to arrest a debtor on a criminal charge who may have been released without notice had his debt been paid. With a telephone the prison could have contacted the police station prior to his release. By 1907 the police connection to the telephone exchange made the private wire unnecessary.

Divisional Surgeon's homes were often connected to the police station which they served by a private wire installed at their own expense. Illustrations are Doctor Goddard's residence linked in 1896 to Caledonian Road and two years later Doctor Neville's connection to Gerald Road.

The Chief Surgeon of the Force indicated in November, 1904 that, as far as was practicable, a private wire should be insisted upon as a condition of service for doctors applying to become Divisional Surgeons. In 1905 the Chief Surgeon requested such a line himself between his house and Marylebone Lane or Vine Street in order that he could speak with New Scotland Yard; his house was subsequently connected to Marylebone. The requirement for direct lines was re-enforced in 1908 when a coroner's jury at Hornsey heard, during an inquest, that there had been a case involving serious delay in procuring medical assistance. They added a rider to the verdict that Divisional Surgeons should, as a matter of course, be connected to their local police station. Although by 1907 eight Divisional Surgeons were so connected it became less important as the Force proceeded towards the installation of exchange lines.

Mr. Kirk, a Veterinary Surgeon, frequently required by police to attend Bow Street Court, was connected in 1907 by a private telephone wire to Bow Street Police Station. Messrs Harrison, Barber and Co., the horse slaughterers, were in direct communication with the Executive Branch at C.O. in September, 1904.

Marylebone, Tower Bridge, North London and West London Courts were connected to their divisional stations in 1905. The following year the Brentford Guardians urged the need for a telephone link between their offices and Isleworth police in anticipation of possible disturbances by unemployed and other offences on their premises. Permission was granted to the authority.

Harefield Police Station, which was closed at night, had an extension bell fitted in 1911 to the police officers' quarters. Public Carriage Offices, which were often situated some distance from the police stations to which they were attached, were provided with a telephone extension from the station, thereby avoiding the delay of an officer having to call there with messages. This work, carried out by the Post Office on a number of divisions, cost an annual total rental of about £23.

Extension telephones were placed in C.I.D. offices at the twenty one divisional stations and Thames Division at an annual cost of £35.15s.

The offices of Mr. Bullock, the Assistant Commissioner, and Superintendent Hare were connected at annual rentals of £1. 7s. 6d and £1. 12s. 6d respectively.

Other direct lines from the Executive Branch at C.O. to outside offices in 1916 were —

The Treasury switchboard
Admiralty - Anti Aircraft Department
War Office
British Museum
National Gallery
Special Constabulary Headquarters
Central Criminal Court
Wellington Barracks
Home Secretary - House of Commons

In 1905, as a result of the proposals to use Rough Books for recording messages, a survey of four stations, made on behalf of the Superintendent of the Executive Branch, ascertained the facilities available for officers to write down messages from the telephone. No accommodation for writing existed at Walton Street or Bow Street and at Peckham the top of the Inspector's wash stand was being used. Many of the telephones were of the wrong type for efficient use or were wrongly sited.

Over the twenty five years prior to the Force being connected extensively to the exchanges a variety of telephone instruments were available. Specific details of the earliest types of telephone used by the Force have not been found but would have included the standard designs supplied by the United Telephone Company, the General Post Office or National Telephone Company. The central Telegraph Office at Scotland Yard (depicted in an illustration in the Illustrated London News) was fitted with a wall instrument in the early 1880s in addition to the ABC telegraph machines. Illustrations in this book of the earliest apparatus in general use provide an idea of the Victorian police network.

It is possible to identify a number of the designs fitted in 1905 at police stations. The Ericsson table telephone was in widespread use and one such instrument was definitely connected at Vine Street. Walton Street Police Station operated with three different types for specific purposes. A 'Deckert' magneto ringing instrument, with a switch for the Superintendent and Scotland Yard, comprised of two earphones, a transmitter and bells similar to those of the G.P.O. supplied equipment. The Deckert transmitter, consisting of a more efficient granular carbon microphone to that previously used, was introduced on many of the telephone designs in the latter years of the nineteenth century. The connection to the South Kensington Museum from this station was by way of a 'Deckert' battery ringing instrument similar in design to the single receiver G.P.O. apparatus. A magneto wall set with a single receiving earpiece was available for communication with the Natural History Museum. Many companies produced wall telephone sets of similar design and the one

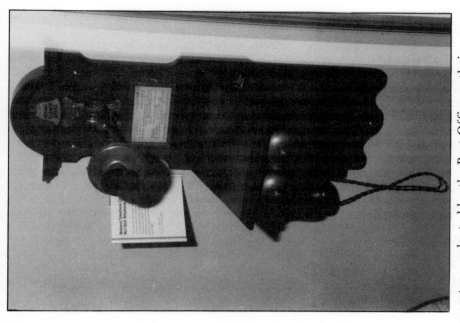

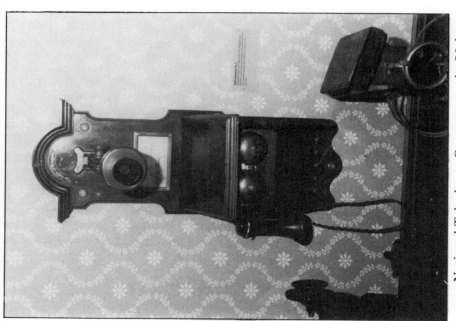

National Telephone Company early 20th century apparatus — adapted by the Post Office as their first standard wall set.

in use at Walton Street appears to have been National Telephone Company equipment.

Cannon Row had a wall set fitted and Bow Street a "Deckert" battery set with two ear pieces. Officers at Bow Street found it necessary to place a receiver at each ear making it impossible to write a message themselves. Peckham operated a similar instrument to that at Bow Street.

The Superintendent of each division was requested to report the pattern of instrument fitted in the Inspector's Office or Telegraph Office at their stations by 25th January, 1905. This enabled suitable writing tables to be installed where necessary for resting the new rough message book. Although the results of this survey are not available there is little doubt that instruments varied from one station to another.

Connection to the Public Exchanges

During the 1880s the United Telephone Company applied to have their system of telephones connected with the police in order that their subscribers could communicate direct with the stations. In December, 1886 a Metropolitan Police Board reported that 'the whole business of a station would be completely upset by acceding to such a proposal'. Both Sir Charles Warren and his successor James Monro were against the connections at police stations. Warren's observation on the U.T.C's request was to the point — 'the suggestion did not seem necessary' — and Monro in 1880 said, in reply to a similar application by the Company, 'the whole question has been fully considered more than once, the conclusion arrived at being that the adoption of the proposal was inexpedient'.

Although the applications were refused in respect of police stations there is evidence of a single exchange line into Scotland Yard in 1881. The United Telephone Company's List of Subscribers for September records '3536 Police — Metropolitan Police Station, Scotland Yard, Whitehall SW'. The company's 'Professional and Trades Classified Directory of 1885' shows the number still in existence. It is not clear to which department this exchange line was connected although the National Telephone Company's directory of 1898/99 clearly shows the Surveyors Branch at New Scotland Yard on the Gerard exchange (No. 3536). By 1901-1902 Surrey and Essex police stations in addition to the City of London stations are recorded in the directory. Buckinghamshire Constabulary, also bordering on the M.P.D., were on the exchange prior to 1906.

The earliest public call offices for telephoning appeared in 1884 and gradually the National Telephone Company increased their number. In the early part of this century public telephone kiosks in the streets began to arrive on the scene.

The Editor of the Daily Mail enquired in 1898 the reasons why there were no public telephone facilities for communication from the public to the police. The Commissioner replied in due course that the matter had been raised several times and emphasised the view that the whole business

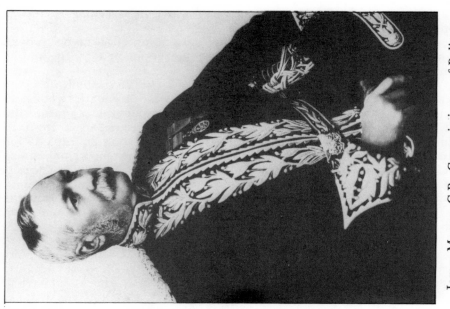

James Monro, C.B., Commissioner of Police, 1888 to 1890

General Sir Charles Warren, GCMG, KCB, RE, FRS, Commissioner of Police 1886 to 1888.

of a police station would be completely upset by acceding to such a proposal. The adoption of such a suggestion was considered neither necessary nor desirable. The Daily Mail duly mounted a campaign in an attempt to encourage the Force to become connected to the public exchanges.

The City Police, the Daily Mail of 15th November, 1898, observed in an article headed 'Our Telephone Crusades' were also loath to consider placing their stations on the exchange. The newspaper goes on to claim that the Metropolitan Commissioner had at this time, apart from an acknowledgement, failed to reply to a letter requesting an explanation as to why his Force were refusing to consider exchange lines complaining that, 'the sphinx has otherwise remained silent'. The article suggests that agitation to have the Force controlled by the London County Council, 'might well be fanned into flame again by the neglect by the Police of so obvious an accessory to the detection of crime as connection with the telephone exchange'.

The newspaper listed a number of Chief Constables who had testified as to the value of the facility and alleged that the London police, 'are hampering the operations of provincial forces, which have occasion frequently to communicate with them about criminal affairs, and have to employ means other than the telephone'.

An article in the paper on 3 December, 1898 said of the Force 'They have not got over their shyness of this new fangled instrument sufficiently to arrange yet to be on the public exchanges, so that communication between themselves and the public can be established; but they are making a step in this direction'.

The Daily Mail highlighted that the Metropolitan Police were the only office of importance which were not on the exchange. The 'Globe' is quoted as saying 'The telephone is used by many of the provincial forces and why the Metropolitan Police should be behind hand is nothing short of a mystery. Their remissness is apparently due to no more valid reason than an old-fashioned dislike of anything in the shape of innovation'. The Daily Mail emphasised that many private persons had telephones installed and available for use in the event of a burglary if only the police were connected to the exchange lines.

A letter from the Chief Constable of Portsmouth, A.T. Prickett, on 5th December in response to the Daily Mail article indicates that he considered the telephone of great value to his force when he wrote, '. . . it would be most difficult to particularise any cases where it had been of great service to the Police of this town. To be brief, I would say that in a very large majority of cases of crime the telephone has been of inestimable value in expediting the capture of criminals'.

On 23rd February, 1899 the newspaper announced that the eight stations in the City of London Police were to be connected to the public exchange but still the Metropolitan were showing no signs of movement towards the general use of the telephone. The newspaper even claimed that the police had declined their offer, the previous year, to pay the entire cost of putting all London police stations on the telephone for one year. Even a letter to the Home Office from the City Court of Common Council would not convince the Commissioner of the advantages of a connection to the exchange.

The following reply was sent by the Commissioner, Sir Edward Bradford, to the Home Office in answer to a question which had been raised in the House of Commons in 1899,

> "The Police stations in this District numbering 182 are connected by a system of efficient telegraphic communication which is entirely under Police control and which meets Police requirements. It has not been considered necessary to substitute any other arrangement. Moreover some years ago this office was connected with Public Telephone system when it was found that no material assistance was afforded whilst great inconvenience was caused by constant references on trivial and unimportant matters".

The Receiver, Richard Pennefather, decided in 1902 to have a connection with the General Post Office exchange but Bradford remained opposed to one for his own office. Similarly the Surveyor and Storekeeper were placed on the Victoria Exchange in that year.

Again in 1903 the National Telephone Company were pressing the Force to agree to connections with their exchanges. In a reply the Commissioner opposed the suggestion and referred again to the experiment which had been made in connecting Scotland Yard to the general exchange some years earlier which had proved embarrassing and had to be abandoned. Full details of this earlier installation have not been found.

When suggested that, as the City of London Police were on the public exchange, it would be suitable for the Metropolitan the Commissioner wrote that the conditions in the City differed from those in the Metropolitan area and the merits in one force would not necessarily justify adoption in another. Even when the experiment of placing the Force onto public exchanges was already underway the Commissioner was guarded about the outcome saying that 'any advance in this direction should be made with due circumspection. Only if connecting police stations with the public exchanges proved satisfactory to the public and not detrimental to police work would it be further extended'.

The prejudice by the police against the installation of the telephone was clearly on the grounds that it would increase work and be open to abuse and improper use by the public. When eventually, after continued pressure from Local Authorities, it was decided to place certain police stations on the public exchanges the Commissioner felt that police should only pay a nominal rate as their being on the system would encourage members of the public to become subscribers, particularly in outer areas, to the advantage of the telephone company. It does not appear that the company agreed with this view.

By 1905 the public telephone exchanges were well established and in the latter months and the early months of the following year pressure mounted, particularly by the justices at various magistrates courts throughout London, urging the Force to have telephones installed at police stations. The Borough Justices at Kingston passed a unanimous resolution, 'That it is desirable that all police stations situated within the area of the Metropolitan Police District should be supplied with telephones, not only to afford the public a sense of greater security, but to give them the reality of it, both by providing a deterrent to offenders, and an aid to their arrest, and that it is the opinion of this bench that the privilege is no more likely to be abused than is the similar privilege which obtains in respect of fire stations, and which has proved of so much advantage to the public welfare'. A copy of this resolution was sent to the Commissioner on 8th December.

A similar resolution was passed by the Justices of Croydon, Richmond, Mortlake, Staines and Epsom. At Wimbledon the Clerk to the Justices complained that when he wished to contact the police station he had to telephone to a private office near the station and ask for a message to be taken across. The Woolwich Chamber of Commerce passed a resolution in February, 1906 requesting that Woolwich Police Station be connected to the National Telephone Company's system. They complained of a case where a man died in the street and it took nearly two hours before the body was removed although the incident occurred nearby to places connected with the telephone. Another case of a man injured in the street resulted in a complaint that it took three quarters of an hour before the assistance of police could be summoned.

On 28th December, 1905 the Superintendent of 'V' Division, who had obviously been approached by the local justices on the matter, reported to the Commissioner, 'It seems to be the prevailing idea amongst the public and which is supported by the Justices as well as the local authorities that the time has now arrived when this system of easy communication (the telephone) with the police should be put into operation'. The Superintendent fully supported the introduction of the telephone on the grounds that the public who resided in exterior areas would have rapid communications in the case of fire, burglary or other serious offences.

Superintendents, required to report the desirability of stations in outer districts being connected with the public telephone, all, with the exception of the Superintendent 'P' Division, reported favourably on the suggestion. This Superintendent was of the opinion that it would lead to an increase of work for station officers and probably to complaints of inattention. He was concerned that telephone calls may be made during the investigation of an intricate charge or other important business requiring the attention of the station officer at the instrument. He, however, recommended a trial at Bromley Police Station situated in a good class neighbourhood with many of the inhabitants on the telephone.

'R' Division's Superintendent suggested that if stations were connected to the public telephone then the Divisional Surgeons, who were at that time connected directly by telephone to Blackheath Road and

Deptford, could be relieved of the personal charge for their instrument connected to the station. They would be able to enjoy the use of the public telephone as ordinary users.

The opinion of the Superintendent 'T' Division was that the introduction of the telephone would require the employment of a second constable on station reserve in order that messages could be dealt with efficiently and complaints avoided. The Superintendents recommended which stations on their divisions should be considered for installation of telephones and a list was drawn up.

Sir Edward Bradford had been quite obstinate, during his period in office, when it came to improving telephone communication. However, in March, 1903 Edward Henry became Commissioner and his period in office until September, 1918 saw rapid and widespread improvement in the Force telephone system. The Daily Mail were still campaigning for the cause in 1906. An article in the newspaper on 22nd February of that year reported that the official police view was that 'Cranks of all kinds would be ringing up Scotland Yard all day long; irresponsible people would play pranks, and Crafty Criminals would have opportunities of gaining information which they do not now possess'.

The Commissioner wrote to the Receiver on 27th January and 23rd February 1906 approving the connection, on an experimental basis, of the police stations at Bromley (P), Staines (T), Kingston, Richmond, Wimbledon (V), Croydon, Casrshalton (W) and Harrow (X) to the public telephone system. Superintendents were instructed to personally select the most suitable position for the instrument bearing in mind the necessity for the station officer to hear the bell. Rules for the guidance of Station Officers in the use of the instrument were published by the Executive Branch at Scotland Yard. (See appendix C)

Police Orders of 18th May, 1906 announced that Kingston, Richmond, Wimbledon and Ealing were connected to the public telephone. Harrow and Carshalton were delayed pending the opening of new public exchanges in those areas and Bromley and Staines, being served only by the National Telephone Company, also suffered delay. The annual rental for each line was £4 with a minimum yearly payment of £1. 10s for message fees. The arrangement with the Post Office involved keeping records of messages sent and strict limitations for official use only.

By August, Bromley had been placed on the National Telephone Company Exchange and Croydon on the public exchange. These were followed the same year by Carshalton and Barnet, and in January, 1907 Harrow was connected. A total of nine stations were then on the exchanges.

The experiment, clearly soon to be accepted as a necessity for police efficiency, resulted in both inner and outer divisions proving a requirement for the facility. Full introduction would require sufficient staff to operate the instruments and proper areas for them to be accommodated.

On 9th November, 1906 the Commissioner sent a memorandum to

129

the Receiver requesting that the following divisional stations be connected to the public exchange.

Hackney
Limehouse
Stoke Newington
Peckham
Blackheath Road
Albany Street
Hammersmith
Wandsworth
Brixton
Harrow Road
Kentish Town

(some were connected to the G.P.O. exchanges and others to the National Telephone Company exchange).

Additional places considered desirable at that time were —

'J'	Wanstead, Loughton
'K'	Ilford
'N'	Walthamstow, Waltham Abbey, Enfield Highway
'P'	Sydenham, Beckenham
'R'	Chislehurst
'S'	Hampstead, Edgware, Hendon
'T'	Twickenham, Teddington, Hampton, Sunbury, Bedfort, Hounslow, Brentford
'V'	Putney, Surbiton, Epsom
'W'	Mitcham, Sutton
'X'	Pinner, Uxbridge
'Y'	Highgate, Hornsey, Enfield

Annual rental for the above would be £358.5s.

A total of forty five stations were by August, 1907 connected including the majority of those mentioned above. On 17th July, communication had been established between New Scotland Yard and the Central Telephone Exchange (Telephone No. 14118 Central). By September of that year Marylebone, Lambeth, Tower Bridge and South Western Courts were on the public telephone system.

New communication facilities often required replanning of station accommodation to avoid disruption to staff with other responsibilities, this could be a lengthy process in itself. In 1905 the Superintendent at Kensington Police Station 'F' Division requested many building alterations to his station. He wished part of the waiting room to be converted into a Telephone Office ready for the reception of the telephone and telegraph instruments. These instruments were at this time housed in the Inspector's office at the station causing much inconvenience.

Kensington remained without public exchange lines in December, 1907 when the Superintendent requested that this be delayed until proper alterations were made to the building. He indicated that the installation of the facility would require the augmentation of three constables.

It took three years from the initial proposal to satisfactorily finish the work and not until 22nd July, 1908 was Kensington connected with the public telephone and the Telephone Office completed in accordance with the Superintendent's wish housing the communications staff and equipment. A report one year on indicated the considerable advantages of the system, both to the public and police, and the gradual increase in calls. In 1912 a telephone extension was linked to the reserve stables nearby.

A separate room, similar to that at Kensington, was recommended for communications at all new stations. This proposal in January, 1906 received a favourable response from the Superintendents of all divisions although some were concerned that the noise of the telegraph would render it difficult to hear what was being said over the telephone if they were in the same room. Some Superintendents were of the view that the room should be connected to the Inspector's office; the Superintendent 'P' Division felt that it should be a glass enclosed space in the Inspector's office in order that there could be proper supervision from the office.

By April, 1909 all outer stations were connected with the exception of some quiet stations where often there was no exchange. Progression towards some busy inner stations being placed on the exchanges followed; two receiving instruments would be a necessity at locations with a particularly high work load to enable simultaneous police and public calls to be handled. Divisional telephones were either fitted with continuous ringing bells or short ring bells.

Installation of the public telephone proceeded over the years that followed and in 1913 of the 199 stations only thirteen were not on the system. Even as late as 1917 two minor police stations remained unconnected to the exchanges.

Superintendent Froest of the Central C.I.D. requested a telephone at his home in order that his staff could communicate with him. In August, 1909 his house at Streatham Hill was connected to the National Telephone Company exchange.

In May, 1910 Home Office authority was given for each divisional Superintendent to have his own separate telephone at the divisional station which could be switched from police to public lines. In 1914 the Superintendent 'H' Division's home was connected to the public exchange at a cost to the Police Fund and other divisional Superintendents followed. Not until 1920 was authority given for the offices of Chief Inspectors and divisional clerks to have the telephone.

The National Telephone Company reserved the number 200 for each station where possible. There were connection problems on 'T' Division between stations as both the G.P.O. and National Telephone Company systems operated in that area.

In 1911 the National Telephone Company lines were taken over by the Post Office requiring many instruments in stations to be changed.

Problems of cost arose as the Metropolitan Telephone Area did not align with the Force area and often it was necessary to make a trunk call to ring another station. The G.P.O. declined requests by the Force to align the areas. The first automatic telephone exchange opened at Epsom in 1912.

Northwood Police Station was connected to public system in 1913 as a result of requests from residents. As the station closed at night an extension, placed in the private quarters of resident police officers, allowed them to be called in an emergency.

A complaint from a man who at 4.30 a.m. one night had been refused permission to use a police telephone to call a nurse to his expectant wife resulted in a change of regulations in 1918 thereby allowing the public to use the police telephone in a special emergency.

The general introduction of automatic telephone exchanges in 1924 led to four figure numbers being used within a ten mile radius of Oxford Circus. A proposal that a 'Police' number '1111' should be allocated at various exchanges to be advertised prominently in the London Telephone Directories for the benefit of the public, was gradually introduced. The number '1111' continued until 1936/7 when, due to technical problems, it was revised to '1113'. This new number was not used exclusively as small country exchanges still did not exceed three figure codes and in some areas more than one police station was served by one exchange. The Post Office objected to '1212' being common to all police stations.

The Commissioner's Office, eventually connected to two public exchanges City and Victoria (City 400 and Victoria 9040), by 1917 saw the number of incoming and outgoing lines on these exchanges increase. On 17th June, 1918 a new telephone switchboard, staffed by three female operators supplied by the London Telephone Service for employment at Scotland Yard (two were always present), was in operation. These women worked the switchboard between 9.30 a.m. until 6 p.m. daily, except Sunday. In July, 1918 a printed list of internal extension numbers was issued and circulated throughout the Force.

Prior to the introduction of the new switchboard two constables were employed in the Telephone Room at Scotland Yard, one attending to calls and the other writing out and transmitting messages. In 1919 authority was given to retain one constable in support of the three female telephone operators. On 7th October, six additional telephone lines were connected from the Victoria Exchange to the switchboard at NSY due to a rail strike. They were not removed.

By 1910 the senior officers were requesting the removal of the under used telegraph machines from their homes. The Assistant Commissioner, F.S. Bullock, requested that the Receiver take over payment of his public telephone instead of installing a private telephone wire to Scotland Yard. Home Office approval was given in January, 1911 to establish direct telephone communication, for official purposes, between Scotland Yard and the town homes of the Assistant Commissioners, unless they already had exchange telephones in which case the Receiver would take over the charges for official calls.

In 1913 Macnaughton, the Assistant Commissioner, retired and was replaced by Mr. Basil Thomson. It was agreed that Mr. Thomson would not have a private line into his home but a public exchange telephone instrument would be regarded as rented for police purposes along with an extension line to his bedroom. The annual rental amounted to £14 plus £1.10s for the extension.

The more economical message rate provided by the telephone company, was used in preference to the unlimited rate.

The 14th April, 1932 at 5.30 p.m. saw the incoming telephone service transferred to the new Whitehall Automatic Exchange. The world famous number 'Whitehall 1212' came into being. The outgoing service remained on the Victoria Exchange. Dorothy Annie Nye, seconded by the Post Office to take charge of the Whitehall 1212 Private Branch Exchange (PBX) received the BEM for her services before her retirement in the 1950s. The author met her before her death in 1985 and she said that she became known as 'Miss Whitehall 1212'.

As the telephone facilities in divisions increased the installation of switchboards became a necessity. The Post Office supplied switchboards to the police designed, in conjunction with Messrs Ericsson Telephones Limited, to meet the special requirements of the service taking into account the new call box system. The switchboard model PA101, introduced in 1932 for police use, was modified to meet the individual needs of the Metropolitan Police. This unit, produced in three sizes, had three panels, the first and third for police box terminations and the centre for normal PBX circuits.

In 1935 a model PA150MP, produced especially for the Force, incorporated improved circuits and design. This modified version of the standard police switchboard (PA150) was necessary in part due to the Force only requiring a single telephone at police boxes unlike the provincial forces where separate instruments for public and police use were normally installed.

T.G. Morris in his article 'Police Telephone Systems' which appears in the Post Office Electrical Engineers Journal of October, 1937 provides a comprehensive technical description of police switchboards in the 1930s. He sums up well the requirements of an efficient police telephone system at that time as follows —

'(a)   absolutely reliable
(b)   simplicity in operation
(c)   instantaneous fault indication on all lines terminating on street units
(d)   facility for the operator to set up a mass call to street points in the shortest possible time
(e)   visible and audible signals to street telephones'

By 1936 the new Ericsson switchboards were being introduced on 'T' Division requiring a proper training programme to be carried out on equip-

Colonel Sir Edward Bradford, Bt., GCB, GCVO, KCSI, Commissioner of Police 1890 to 1903

Sir Edward Henry, Bt., GCVO, KCB, CSI, Commissioner of Police 1903 to 1918.

ment containing up to twenty exchange lines and sixty extension keys. It was decided to train twenty-four men from each station in the operation of the equipment along with the Creed teleprinter. New switchboards with audible calling and visual ringing off arrangements were ordered from the GPO in 1937. These new boards accommodated incoming lines from police boxes without requiring any modification.

Although by 1936 a number of senior officers had already been supplied with modern hand microphone telephones, in May the Receiver agreed that all officers of Superintendent and above should have their pedestal type telephones replaced in their offices.

Private wires continued as a means of internal communication between Scotland Yard and divisions. The introduction of police boxes extended the network extensively in the 1930s. Resulting from difficulties experienced in passing information rapidly in connection with meetings, demonstrations and processions in 1933, the District Commander's Office of No. 1 District was connected to Chief Superintendents' offices. Three years later the facility was extended to the other three Districts and by 1940 the District Commanders were connected to the C.O. switchboard.

In January, 1936 a review of the 'R' Division telephone communication was carried out by the District Communications Officer, Sergeant McAndrew. The divisional headquarters at Blackheath Road, although fitted with a modern Ericsson switchboard, had no direct communication with sub-divisions. East Greenwich, still managing with a very old single cord wall instrument, one exchange line and one extension line, was recommended for a switchboard. Many other stations on the division had obsolete equipment and a complete reorganisation of the system was essential.

The telephone had been introduced initially in a piecemeal fashion without any organised approach. The reluctance of the Metropolitan Police to accept the modern technology of the day until the early part of this century is emphasised in this chapter. Particularly determined to avoid anything which would give the public easy access in an emergency was Sir Edward Bradford, although reputed as a very good Commissioner, he remained convinced that the telegraph provided everything that the Force needed. The force for change, so great by the time Edward Henry took office, left the new commissioner with no alternative but to improve the system of communication. The unwillingness to move with the times can be appreciated to a degree as the telephone was to change forever the relationship between the police and the public to one where the public expected far more from the Force.

CHAPTER IV

CONTACT FROM THE STREETS – POLICE BOXES AND BEFORE

A rapid response to information concerning suspects of crime could only be achieved by finding a method of passing that information quickly to the officer on the beat. As John Fielding proposed long before the Force was formed 'quick notice and sudden pursuit'.

The fixed point boxes which were used by the Force by the 1870s were not in communication with the station although as early as 1876 Superintendent Digby of 'V' Division was suggesting that they should be connected to the telegraph system. A telegraphic call point system, patented by the Exchange Telegraph Company, was in use in London clubs and the Houses of Parliament by 1874 to summon cabs or messengers. Domestic subscribers were provided with an automatic signalling instrument connected to the nearest Call Station of the Company. At the press of a button it was claimed that a messenger, cab or policeman could be called.

By 1880 Metropolitan Fire Brigade stations were connected to call points located at pillar and wall letter boxes. There were forty such alarms linked to Westminster, Clerkenwell, Whitechapel, Kennington Lane and Southwalk Fire Stations. At this time no similar alarms were available for police communication although in 1884 a fire alarm post at Walton Street Station (B) was convenient for police use. Fire alarm posts had by 1886 increased to 347 and the locations of new installations were regularly published in Police Orders. They were of much value to the constable on the beat, as well as the public, when he required the assistance of the brigade. In 1883 it was proposed that police stations should keep keys to the posts.

A police box system was put to practical use in Boston in the USA in 1886 known as the Wilson Public Safety System. The Commissioner of that city described it as 'the most valuable improvement that has so far been introduced into the police department'. At this time Scotland Yard was inundated with applications from inventors and companies offering to demonstrate various signalling devices although only two systems, both American, were seriously considered by the Metropolitan Police.

On 25th March, 1888, during Sir Charles Warren's Commissionership, nine iron 'Street Call Boxes' were taken into operation in the Islington sub-division. These boxes, already in use in America, were invented by a William Rust and produced by the Public Safety Signal Association, 64 Cannon Street, EC. The inventor paid all the expenses for installing and maintaining the boxes in addition to defraying the cost of a van, 'ready horsed', with driver from 3 p.m. to 1 a.m. each day at Islington Police Station.

The boxes, measuring 21 inches by 14 inches by six inches, were supported on a wooden platform. They were fixed in the streets and connected to a receiving instrument at Islington Police Station where messages were recorded automatically on slips of paper showing the exact time of receipt. An important signal from the call box for the ambulance or to speak to the officer on duty were made known by a bell ringing in the station. Unimportant calls were reported on paper and no bell rang. A constable on the beat opened the box with a key and called the attention of the central station by fixed signals.

In conjunction with the call box system the horse wagon (containing a stretcher) remained at the station for conveying prisoners. On receipt of a call the wagon would be driven to the scene by the civilian driver accompanied by two constables. One constable would replace the officer from the beat while he dealt with his prisoner at the station. In the early days the van was sent out daily to answer calls for assistance.

Unfortunately the telephone proved to be of little use during the day although working well at night. Telephone signals were poor due to induction currents and traffic noise although the automatic indicator operated efficiently. A bell fitted to the call box was the subject of complaints that it could only be heard by an officer nearby.

The Inspectors at Islington reported favourably on this system which they said had a 'deterrent effect on the rougher and more violent class of prisoner as police officers could quickly obtain assistance'. Similarly it gave officers more confidence knowing that assistance could easily be obtained. The inhabitants of Islington appreciated the boxes as they also gave them a feeling of security.

Some residents of the area were supplied with 'citizen keys' which, when inserted and turned in the lock of the call box, alerted the station. The key could not be removed until an officer attended and opened the box.

The cost of the horse, van and driver was £3 per week which Rust agreed to continue paying along with the maintenance of the boxes, until 31st August, 1889. He asked to be relieved of the cost after that date in the event of the system proving useful to the police. The Commissioner agreed, with Home Office approval, to finance the facility from 1st September, with a recommendation that the number of boxes be increased to 25 in the sub-division. Satisfactory trials in this area would, it was felt, eventually lead to an extension to all suburban areas.

The boxes priced at £30 were each connected to the recording apparatus costing an additional £50 or £60. The annual rental of £5 was inclusive of this apparatus at the police station and the cost of the GPO wires amounted to £7 per mile. Over and above was another £150 each year for the horse, van and driver. Citizens paid a small annual charge for keys to the boxes. The total cost for 1890/91 was £349.0s.1d and for 1891/92 £388.19s.4d.

Before going ahead with the extension of this system the Commissioner, James Monro, considered that a visual signal on the box was absolutely essential if it was to be of practical use to the Force. Although the inventor undertook to develop such a signal it never materialised.

Suggestions that the boxes could be used in co-operation with the local authority as fire signals do not seem to have been implemented. Mr. George Parker, the Superintendent of the Bootle-cum-Linacre Fire Station alleged in September, 1889 that the system infringed his patent taken out in May, 1888.

The agreement that the G.P.O. would provide a radial system of wires at the cost of £365.5s per annum for 25 boxes was preferred to a less efficient but cheaper circular system. The estimated total cost including boxes, an ambulance and horse and driver amounted to £645.5s. Never completed, by August, 1892 the horse and wagon were discontinued with a recommendation that a cab should be hired when necessary. By the end of 1893 the neglected system was in a poor state of repair. Early in 1894 the contract with Mr. Rust, who had by then returned to America, was closed and the posts were removed from the streets of Islington by the parish authorities although Rust had asked the police to retain them without charge.

Superintendent Sherlock in charge of 'N' Division observed that the facility had resulted in no saving to the Police Fund. The van did, however, ensure that a constable dealt with a prisoner much more rapidly thereby allowing him to return to his beat sooner. Normally a prisoner would require two constables on foot to take him to the station (one from a neighbouring beat) whereas the van made this unnecessary.

In March, 1888 the attention of the Sir Charles Warren, the Commissioner, was called to a system of signals by the American Trading Company, 99 Fenchurch Street, who requested an interview to explain the invention patented by Brewer and Smith for the 'simplifying of police intercommunication and visual signalling'.

On 2nd January, 1889 Mr. Otto Friederici, the Chairman, reported on behalf of the National Signal Company, 58 Lombard Street, EC1 the arrival of the specimen signals in this country and offered to fix them free at any locations selected by the Commissioner. In February of that year the Superintendents of 'N' and 'H' Divisions attended the office of the Company for a presentation of the system. They reported it to be superior to the system in use in Islington and Friederici forwarded a report from engineers, Woodhouse and Rawson, on its advantages. At first the police declined an offer to fit the system pending completion of the evaluation of the Islington boxes.

In March, 1890 the Morgans Automatic Visual Police Signalling System, as it became known, on display at the Westminster Palace Hotel in London, was seen by all divisional Superintendents who, apart from the Superintendent 'P', reported favourably. The new Commissioner, James Monro, concerned that there may be difficulties in introducing this system while Rust's was still in use, referred the matter to the Receiver who envisaged no problem. The system also consisted of a number of street posts connected to a central police station. A post

The Exchange Telegraph Company, Limited.

HEAD OFFICES : 17 & 18, CORNHILL, E.C.

TELEGRAPHIC CALL SYSTEM.

TO HOUSEHOLDERS.

CALL STATIONS

For the due administration of this system, as adapted to domestic purposes, and for the protection of householders against

THIEVES AND FIRE

Are now being established throughout the metropolis, with a continuous

DAY AND NIGHT SERVICE.

Subscribers thereto are furnished at their houses with automatic signalling instruments occupying but a few cubic inches of space and telegraphically connected with the nearest call station of the Company, which in no case is more than a quarter of a mile (or three minutes of time) distant, by the aid of which, and the simple pressure of a button, they may call a

MESSENGER, CAB OR POLICEMAN

AND GIVE THE

ALARM OF FIRE,

While many other calls indicating the requirements of a household may be arranged for.

TERMS:

Four Guineas per instrument, per annum, payable in advance.

Messengers, when employed, sixpence per hour. Cab calls twopence. No money received by messengers, accounts being rendered quarterly for payment. Instruments, wires, &c., fitted and kept in order by the Company, free of all charge to subscribers.

Subscribers wishing to discontinue the use of an instrument, can do so by giving a quarter's notice in writing to the Secretary. For full particulars of the Call system, see pamphlet, which may be obtained from the Secretary.

NOTE.—The Company will in no case be liable beyond the sum of £10 for any loss or damage that may occur during, or in course of, the engagement of any Messenger.

Applications for instruments should be made on the reverse, and be forwarded to the Secretary, at the above address, where all inquiries will be attended to, and the system be seen in operation.

Max. Goldfinger,

General Manager of the European Lock & Time-lock Company.

WESTMINSTER PALACE HOTEL.

Exchange Telegraph Company publicity.

contained an automatic indicator dial and a telephone for conversation. The policeman on the street would open the box and select a message printed on a dial inside such as 'send officer', 'wagon wanted' and other appropriate messages. A similar instrument at the central station would receive the message and action would be taken accordingly.

Mr. Friederici observed in his published paper on the system, 'It is right enough that telegraphic communication exists as between Scotland Yard as head office and various stations, and vice versa, but the individual policeman of today is exactly in the position of his 'confrere' of 50 or 100 years ago. He is at the mercy of marauders, burglars or riotous mobs, and to call for assistance he must have resource to a whistle or rattle, summoning assistance if lucky, otherwise giving loud and timely notice to perhaps the very men he wishes to surprise'.

In May, 1890 the agents for Morgan's Automatic Electric Signal offered to install the system as an experiment in the Metropolitan Police District at the Company's expense. However, before coming to a decision the Home Office wished to know the success of the Islington system. They required to know the frequency of use by the police or public, the satisfaction afforded to the public and the saving, if any, to police funds. From the generally favourable report received from Superintendent Sherlock of 'N' Division observations along these lines were forwarded to the Home Office.

Not until August, 1891 did the Home Office approve use of the system experimentally in the Brixton Division for one year without any cost to the Police Fund. At the end of the year the Commissioner could either terminate the arrangement or take over payment. Agreement was reached to install the receiving apparatus at Brixton Police Station, then on 'W' Division, along with 10 lamposts at various places throughout the sub-division. The cost to the Company was £20 for each post although, if the Force could be persuaded to purchase over 500 posts, the cost would reduce to £10.

The posts were sited at the following locations in the division, agreed by Major Gilbert, the Chief Constable of the District and Superintendent Lucas —

1. Acre Lane/Brixton Road
2. Cornwall Road/Brixton Hill
3. Herne Hill Point
4. Loughborough Junction Point
5. Loughborough Road/Brixton Road
6. Prima Road/Clapham Road
7. Swan/Electric Railway
8. Dorset Road/Public House
9. Bedford Road/Clapham Road
10. Atlantic Road/Coldharbour Lane

The National Signal Company were confident that their system would be taken over permanently by the police and in March, 1892 the

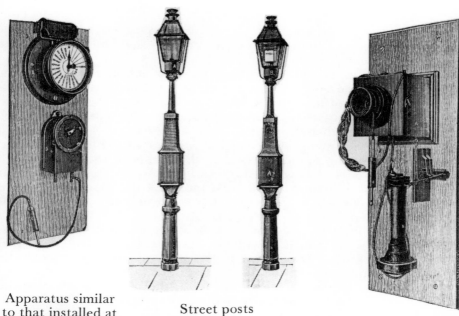

Apparatus similar
to that installed at
Brixton Police station
(above, below, top right)

Street posts

Interior of post

National Signal Company system of police posts installed on Brixton
Division — 1892 to 1894.

trial in Brixton commenced.   There had been some delay due to the Post Office having problems with way-leaves.   Rust was concerned about his contract and asked for the new system to be tried alongside his thus providing a fair comparison.

At the station, in addition to the telephone and indicator, a facility existed which, when operated, altered the street lamp to show red.   This indicated that the officer on the beat was wanted.   These lamps were normally at a road intersection which ensured that the maximum number of officers could see them from their beats.

There were many other complex features incorporated into the equipment.   A gong sounded when a call came in to the station and a pointer on a receiver dial indicated from which post the message had been routed.   Another pointer on the dial indicated the type of assistance required by the person at the post.   It was possible to place up to 100 posts on the system.

The transmitter at the station also incorporated a dial with pre-determined messages which would be reproduced on the receiver dial at the selected post.   Depending on the post required a plug would be inserted into a numbered hole.

The system included a Morse receiver at the station which could be operated by a small instrument carried by a constable in his pocket and inserted into the lampost equipment.   This method automatically regis-tered the constable's number on paper tape on the receiver.   He could also use the telephone apparatus if he wished.

Before closing the door on the lampost equipment the constable would, by the means of a metal rod, extinguish the light.   The citizen's key when inserted into the box, although not opening the door, would send a signal to the police station.   In return the station would cause the red gas or electric light to operate on the lampost thereby attracting the attention of the man on the beat.   Whether all the available features were actually used in Brixton is not clear.

An interesting additional recommendation by Frederici was to fit an instrument in private houses — 'Let one of them be attached to the wall at the head of one's bedstead, and let it be connected with the central station.   When occasion arises that the householder, finding himself in danger, would like to call up the Police, he simply (without getting out of bed) turns the pointer to "burglary here" or what not'.   This feature was not introduced.

A comparison between the two systems found that the lack of a visual indicator on the Islington boxes to attract the attention of a const-able at a distance proved a positive disadvantage.   The verbal communic-ation not being heard well did not arise on the Brixton system which relied mainly upon the coded messages.   The visual indicator on the Brixton lamposts also appear to have been satisfactory.

Although efficiency and effectiveness of the police probably improved the Force were motivated by financial saving which neither of the systems provided.   The Commissioner, James Monro said, 'it is the Constable who is required not the signal box'.   Some saving however was envisaged in the reduction of supervising officers by allowing constables to be instructed to 'report in' from boxes at regular intervals, but this did not sway those in authority to accept the concept of street communication.

By February, 1893 the National Signal Company's system had been handed over to Mr. Siemens who was informed by the Assistant Commissioner, Charles Howard, that it would not be adopted by Sir Edward Bradford, the Commissioner. Siemens asked for the system to remain in place for a three month period in order that it could be seen by all divisional Superintendents. This was agreed and, of those who examined it, eight were of the view that it provided no practical use to the Force. The Superintendents of 'J' and 'K' considered that it would require an increase of staff on reserve duty at the station and the officer in charge of 'N' stated that the inability of PCs to keep the alarm posts in view or to visit them frequently made them of limited value. In March the reports were referred to the Chief Constables, and Monsell and Dean recommended that a better plan would be the installation of shelters with telephone links. Trials at Cricklewood and East Ham Gate were proposed. By the end of 1894 the system at Brixton was removed and apparently never used again.

In November, 1891 a Mr. Frank Stuart of Twickenham requested permission to install his system of Telephone Police Signals between Charing Cross and Trafalgar Square and Bow Street, King Street and Vine Street Police Stations. Offered again on trial free of charge to police, Stuart's system had been used (without a telephone) as street fire alarms in several cities in the country including the Ealing area at this time.

Campbell Swinton, Electrical Engineers, were requested by the Receiver, Richard Pennefather, to examine Stuart's system on behalf of the police. (Incidentally, Swinton was the engineer who gave Marconi his letter of introduction to William Preece, Chief of the Engineering Department of the G.P.O. when he arrived in England). These engineers also looked at the system in use in Brixton and advised the Receiver that the Commissioner should decide independently upon a police requirement without the intervention of any inventor. This would allow a manufacturer to be approached with a clear specification. Stuart's system was never installed for police use.

In July, 1897 another police patent signal system, brought to the notice of the Commissioner and known as the 'Davis Signal System', had been in use in Liverpool for over a year. Two hundred were operating in that city with an intended increase to 500. The following year the 'Gamewell Police Alarms' were offered to the Force but this system did not even compare with the National Signal Company apparatus for efficiency. John Gamewell contributed a great deal towards fire alarm and signal box technology in the United States and his systems were used there extensively. Neither of these apparatus were adopted by the Met.

Consideration had been given in the 1870s to establishing telegraphic communication between fixed point boxes and police stations. In 1893 the Receiver looked again at the question, but the designs of fixed point boxes were considered too elaborate. A Board in December, 1898 advocated 'the judicious extension of Telephone Boxes'.

Resulting from a murder which occurred at Muswell Hill a resident, concerned about his safety, requested that his home be put in direct telephonic communication with the local police station. The Commissioner feared that by allowing such a request an influx of such applications would follow. A decision was therefore made to pursue a policy siting of fixed point boxes with telephones on main thoroughfares which the residents could use in an emergency.

On 28th March, 1896 the Commissioner, Sir Edward Bradford, requested the Receiver to supply a design for a shelter box to be used at fixed points 'large enough to permit of the Constable standing within it with the door closed to use the Telephone Instruments'. It was agreed to locate such a box experimentally at the corner of Cricklewood Lane and Edgware Road with telephone line to West Hampstead Police Station.

Home Office approval, given in September, for the outlay of £20 to purchase the box and another £13 per annum for telephonic communication, allowed an evaluation of the system to go ahead. If wheels were provided on the box the cost rose by an additional £4. A trial of six months, with a report of the results after that period, was accepted. The Hendon Urban District Council gave approval and the National Telephone Company agreed a contract for fixing a telephone link at the site.

The early life of this first telephone box was plagued with problems. On 9th January, 1897, although placed in position on that day, difficulties arose in arranging the telephone connection to West Hampstead. The Midland Railway Company complained that the box obscured the sign indicating the way to Cricklewood Station. By June, however, the Post Office had fitted the telephone line at the cost of £20 and it went into operational use.

There were complaints from constables that they could not hear the bell of the telephone and consequently an indicator was fixed outside. Once fitted the indicator did not work properly: it dropped down at the wrong time and could not been seen at night. A larger indicator disc and lamp were therefore supplied capable of being seen by the constable on the fixed point 40 yards away. A request was also made for a more satisfactory lamp to illuminate the inside of the box.

In May, 1899 the County of Middlesex notified their intention of taking over the land for a tramway; the Receiver objected on the grounds that no other suitable place existed for the box. On 21st August, 1900 Messrs F.G. Lockhart and Co., Coal Merchants, offered £5 towards the cost of removing the structure as it obstructed their office. In 1905, after the frontage of the building had been moved back, the box was resited after which its rather stormy life settled down.

In 1899 another attempt to introduce an extended box system failed to materialise. The view that boxes should be linked by telegraph to the station remained popular.   However, after the successful trial at Cricklewood, similar boxes were agreed that year for East Ham Gate, Ladbroke Grove, Portobello Road and Wornington Road; it is not clear whether the latter two were ever erected.

Superintendents Davis and Mulvany visited Liverpool the following year and reported on the signalling system in use there.   As a result the extension of the telephone box system, the forerunner of the well known concrete police box, moved ahead.   The Liverpool system, operated by both police and the fire service, used the same men, horses and waggons for police and fire purposes.

Fixed points had normally been located in isolated or 'disorderly' districts and at Hackney Carriage Standings to meet public demand for more protection.   Approval for fixed point telephone boxes to be installed, in addition to those locations already mentioned, at Childs Hill, Nunhead, Muswell Hill, West Molesey, East Wickham, Crayford, Wealdstone and Seven Kings was given.   Superintendent Davis and Mulvany recommended that efforts should also be directed into perfecting private communication between stations.   Small white disc indicators, similar to that on the Cricklewood box, were displayed on the boxes which dropped down to signal that the officer on duty at the fixed point was required.

The years from 1900 saw the gradual increase of boxes in outer areas.   In July, 1900 a police telephone box provided a valuable facility at Walton Road junction with New Road with a connection to Thames Ditton Police Station.   This was abolished in 1903.   On 29th August, 1901 Home Office approval provided for the 'establishment of a telephone box at Claygate with communication to Ditton Police Station, and an augmentation of three police constables to provide for continuity of duty at the fixed point'.   With the blessing of the local authority the box was to be located near the Hare and Hounds Public House.

Authority, given in 1904, allowed the purchase of a fixed point box to be held in reserve and available for immediate use wherever required.

In 1906, as a result of pressure from the residents of Norbury, due to the number of burglaries in the area, telephone communication was established between a fixed point box at Norbury Railway Station and Thornton Heath Police Station.   Approval followed for a box to be erected at George Lane, Woodford with telephone connections to Woodford and Wanstead Stations.   This location allowed the officer to see for some considerable distance along the roads adjacent to the box.

On occasions the boxes were subjected to complaints of obstruction. In 1911 the one at New Cross Gate had to be moved to erect a tramway shelter.   Opposed by police on the grounds that there would be a temporary disconnection of the telephone line to the station, the work still went ahead with the box being re-erected later.   The County Surveyor of the Surrey County Council complained in 1912 that the box at Ewell constituted an obstruction.

There is evidence that officers had access to other street communications (some mentioned in the previous Chapter) as with Bushey Urban District Council which agreed in 1914 to police having the keys of their alarm posts from where they could telephone the police station in an emergency. Obviously there were advantages in having the boxes in well illuminated locations and 1914 the Coulsdon Parish Council made arrangements for the gas lamp near the Smitham Fixed Point Box to be kept alight until daybreak. The constable on duty extinguished it.

By 1907 fixed points (FP) with telephone links and police telephone boxes (TB) were located as follows:-

K	Barking	—	East Ham Gate	(TB) — Abolished 1905
K	West Ham (1905)	—	Leytonstone Road	(FP)
K	East Ham (1905)	—	Barking Road	(FP)
K	Forest Gate (1902)	—	Barking Road	(TB) — Abolished 1905
K	Ilford	—	Cameron Road Seven Kings	(FP)
N	Stoke Newington	—	Stamford Hill	(TB)
N	Stoke Newington (1903)	—	Manor House, Green Lanes	(FP)
N	Chingford (1902)	—	Winchester Road, Highhams Park	(TB)
P	West Dulwich (1904)	—	Dulwich Village	(FP)
P	Peckham (1905)	—	New Cross	(FP)
P	Peckham	—	Nunhead	(FP)
P	Catford (1905)	—	Bell Green	(TB)
P	Farnborough	—	Orpington	(FP)
R	Blackheath Road (1905)	—	New Cross	(FP)
R	Bexley (1903)	—	High Street, Bexley	(TB)
R	Bexley (1902)	—	Crayford Bridge	(TB)
R	Bexley (1902)	—	High Street, Welling	(TB)
R	Lee Road (1906)	—	Kidbrook	(TB)
R	Eltham (1904)	—	Mottingham	(TB)
R	Plumstead	—	Abbey Wood	(TB)
S	West Hampstead (1897)	—	Cricklewood	(TB)
T	Bedfont (1904)	—	Feltham	(TB)
V	Wandsworth	—	Earlsfield	(TB)
V	East Molseley (1903)	—	West Moseley	(TB)
V	Ditton (1902)	—	Claygate	(TB)
V	Richmond (1903)	—	Kew Gardens Rd.	(TB)

W	Kenley	—	Foxley Heath, Purley	(TB)
W	Thornton Heath (1906)	—	Norbury	(TB)
X	Harrow Road	—	Ladbroke Grove	(TB)
X	Hanwell	—	Southall	(TB)
X	Harrow	—	(S) Wealdstone	(TP)
X	Harlesden (1903)	—	Wembley Railway Station	(FP)
Y	Southgate (1905)	—	Palmers Green	(TP)

(* Dates in brackets show year of installation where known)

An Observation Box, erected in Hyde Park in 1909, was used by police officers during demonstrations in the park. This box, fitted with a direct line to Scotland Yard, also had extensions to Hyde Park Police Station, Marble Arch and the box at Speakers Corner. Access was gained to the box by means of an iron ladder. Its removal in the 1930s saw the replacement by a far more substantial building fitted with a proper switchboard and more extensive communication facilities.

Arrangements were made in 1920 for copies of Informations and Police Orders to be supplied to all fixed point boxes in outer station areas where men paraded on and off duty at the box. In 1924, following a Police Federation Branch Board resolution, permission was given for the boxes to be used by constables on the beat to take their refreshments on the distinct understanding that abuse of the privilege would lead to its withdrawal.

Between 1900 and the 1920s the number of boxes with telephone communication to their nearest police station increased to almost sixty on the outer divisions. Fixed point boxes were cleaned by station cleaners at nine pence per week with an allowance of two pence a mile for travelling.

A Board was deputed by the Commissioner in 1914 to report on 'a suggested system of street telephone and visual signal boxes for use by Police in communicating with the stations.' The report stated that the provision of such instruments (£25 plus installation costs) was too costly considering the amount they would be used. Alternative suggestions were made by the Board but the Commissioner, Sir Edward Henry, decided against the ideas.

In 1919 the question of street telephone boxes arose again. It was not thought necessary at that time to increase the numbers available on outer divisions, as they were unlikely to be used sufficiently to justify their erection. Boxes on inner divisions were not considered to be a requirement.

Due to the number of meetings held at Trafalgar Square the requirement for a police box with communication to Cannon Row was put forward in May, 1919. There were objections to the erection of such a

The Trafalgar Square Police 'Box'.

structure and not until 14th April, 1921 did a box appear in the subway to the tube station. Private telephone lines were connected to Cannon Row Police Station, Great Scotland Yard and New Scotland Yard thereby giving police officers the ability to summon assistance should an emergency arise. In March, 1928 the box was replaced by a facility in the existing stone pillar located in the south east corner of the Square. This involved 'hollowing' out the circular pillar thereby not interfering with the architectural design of the Square. The existing lamp remained in position on the top of the 'box'. The cost of the work amounted to £479 9s.3d., and on 25th March it was satisfactorily used for the first time during a meeting.

The Chief Constable of Sunderland forwarded in 1924 to the Metropolitan Police an account of the police boxes working in his city and suggested that a system of this type would be of value in the Metropolitan Area. He was informed of the Force's experiments over the previous thirty years and that the system was considered unsuitable for the Metropolis.

The Commissioner, Sir William Horwood, said in reply to a question raised in the House of Commons in 1927 that an extension of the police box system would be expensive and could not be justified unless accompanied by a reduction in establishment. This he felt was highly undesirable at the time.

On 5th April, 1928 the 'Building Committee' of the Metropolitan Police presided over by Chief Constable H.D. Morgan produced a report outlining a new scheme for policing. This proposed scheme included changes in the duties of Inspectors to ensure the availability of one on each sub division for each shift, along with the provision of two light cars and one van. The Committee also recommended that 'a Police telephone box be erected at a junction of two or three beats, or at, or near a fixed point, so that it will be available for use by supervising officers and two or three PCs whilst on ordinary duty'. The boxes were also intended to be used by the public and the report said that the well-known jibe that a policeman can never be found when he is wanted would be dispelled.

On 27th August, 1928 Home Office approval was given for an experiment of the new scheme on Richmond and Wood Green sub divisions. The siting of the boxes took some time to agree with the local authorities concerned, and Richmond were at first completely opposed to the scheme. Certain of the boxes for Richmond were placed in Barnes where the council was more reasonable in its attitude, although there were strong objections from both councils to boxes being placed on the commons for fear they would be a blight on the area. The six local authorities for the Wood Green area accepted the scheme with little difficulty.

In 1929 Mr. G.M. Trench, the Surveyor to the Metropolitan Police, and Superintendent Abbiss visited Sheffield, Manchester, Salford, Nottingham and Birmingham to inspect and report upon the installation and operation of the police telephone box system in those cities. They found that in Sheffield the introduction of the boxes had enabled the

Force to be reduced from six to four divisions and to close eight stations. The boxes contained a wash basin and regular water supplies, and were used for taking refreshment by officers.

Salford was wholly policed by the use of boxes where were in effect 'miniature stations'. They were 5 feet square and large enough to house a bicycle. Manchester Police were in the process of installing their box system predicted to revolutionise policing in that city. Birmingham and Nottingham were at that time using fire telephone alarms in emergencies whereas Nottingham had a small number of their own timber built boxes.

The Chief Constable of the cities visited were of the opinion that the necessity for augmentations to their Forces to cope with the increase in police work had been reduced. There had also been savings in that the need for new buildings had been obviated and some older stations were given up.

As a result of the visits the Surveyor and Superintendent concluded that a police telephone box system was sound in principle and would result in a higher standard of efficiency in the MPD providing that its framing suited the special requirements of the Metropolitan Police. They were of the view, however, that officers should continue to parade at their station for duty.

The object of the telephone box was outlined as follows:-

For Police

(i)   To communicate information to or obtain advice, information or assistance from the station and for dissemination of urgent information and messages requiring immediate action.

(ii) To report to the station at prescribed intervals.

(iii) As a place in which sergeants and constables will take their refreshments during prescribed periods.

(iv) To prepare, when necessary reports of occurrences.

(v)   For emergency signals from the station.

For the Public

(i)   To obtain immediate communication with, and, if necessary, prompt assistance from 'Police'.

(ii) To make enquiry or obtain advice on any matter within the range of Police Duty.

(iii) To obtain assistance in cases of urgency for humanitarian or other legitimate purposes.

The box, erected in or near each beat, had a direct private wire to the sub-divisional station with the ability to obtain a connection to any other police station or box or to the ordinary telephone network. Members of the public could make calls from outside the box by gaining access to the cupboard containing the telephone. Only police officers were permitted to enter the box by use of a special key which every officer was required

Morris Commercial Police Van operating with the
new Police Boxes, 1929.

Ickenham, Middlesex — activity at the Police Box, 1936.

to carry.

The boxes contained, in addition to the telephone, a stool, small cupboard, desk and drawer, a box diary, first aid kit, fire extinguisher and electric heater. When 'ringing in' from a box the constable or sergeant was to report, "Beat No . . . . . . PC 99 SMITH, Box No . . . . . . all correct". The station operator was to reply "All right PC 99".

The cost of building and equipping a police telephone box in 1931 is detailed below:-

POLICE TELEPHONE BOXES

	£.	s.	d.
Box Complete	43.	0.	0.
Site Preparation, average,	2.	10.	0.
*Electric light installation, average	3.	13.	1.
£1. 18. 6. £1. 14. 7			
Electric External Waring Light fitting,			
19/6d. 11/6d.	1.	11.	0.
Electric Radiator,		11.	0.
Engineering labour on above, average,	2.	0.	0.
Electric Relay between internal warning)			
light and telephone)	1.	0.	0.
G.P.O. charge for fixing last,		5.	0.
"Police" plates, 4 @ 6/-	1.	4.	0.
Public notice		2.	6.

£55. 16. 7.

*(Exclusive of cable
charges by Electricity
Supply Companies.)

Furniture etc.

	£.	s.	d.
Lino		4.	0.
Hat & Coat hook,		1.	6.
Number Plate,			4.
Stool,		8.	6.
Fire Extinguisher)			
& Bracket)	1.	15.	0.

2. 9. 4.

| Labour on above, | | 12. | 6. |

3. 1. 10.

| Brush and Dusters, say, | | 1. | 6. |

£58. 19. 11.

'Ringing in' from the Police Post.

'Ringing in' from the Police Box.

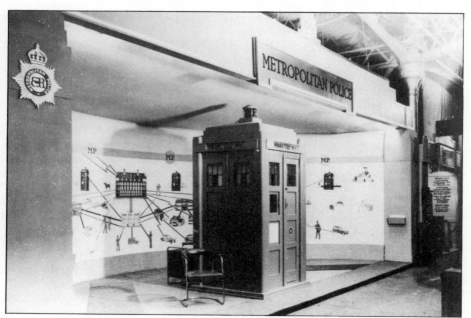

Olympia Exhibition Hall — the Police Stand at Radiolympia, 1936.

On Monday 2nd December, 1929 the experimental scheme of 22 boxes were made available for general use in the Barnes, Kew and Richmond districts of 'V' Division backed up by a van at the station. The boxes were blue in colour with the word 'Police' on the side and a red signal lamp on the top. The flashing light indicated to the officer on the beat that he was required by the station officer. The lamp had a fog pentrating beam. The national press heralded the arrival of these blue structures with such quotes as 'this is bad news for the crooks of London's underworld. They will soon be out of business.' Crime in the Richmond area, it was claimed, decreased as a result of the instant communication provided by the police box through criminals avoiding the area. The Morning Post called the boxes the 'new arm of the law' and the Daily Telegraph referred to them as 'mouse traps'.

The boxes in Wood Green were introduced in January the following year and from then on gradually throughout the Metropolitan Police District. The rest of 'V' Division (Wimbledon, Kingston and Wandsworth sub-divisions) were all in operation by April 1931. Sutton sub-division (W) was operating the system in November, 1931, followed by Wallington, Croydon, Norbury and Streatham (Z) early the next year. Tooting and Balham sub-divisions (W) were completed in July, 1932 and by that year 122 boxes were in use throughout the Force compared with 104 in 1931.

The Police Federation complained in March, 1933 that the heating in the boxes was inadequate. Consequently the 80 watt heaters were replaced with 250 watt models later that year. There were complaints that the new concrete boxes were much colder than the wooden ones and unsuitable for taking refreshments.

In September, 1932 the Metropolitan Constables Branch Board of the Federation passed a resolution requesting the removal of the police box at Wornington Road, on Harrow Road Division on the grounds that it was located near a public urinal which overflowed and caused an unpleasant smell. Although the removal of the box was not at first approved, officers were no longer required to take refreshments in it. The Superintendent of 'X' Division would not accept that the wind was causing the smell and blamed the officers for smoking in the box; notwithstanding this view the box was removed to Ladbroke Grove on 22nd December. The new box system was completed on this division in May, 1936.

By May 1933 there were a total of 170 of the new type of box with 51 of the old type fixed point boxes adapted to the new system. A total of 2,461 calls were passed by the public from the boxes during that year. The number had increased to 575 by the end of 1936 with an annual call total from the public of 8,330. The system required the fitting of more sophisticated switchboards (described in the previous Chapter) in police stations to handle incoming and outgoing messages.

The doubts about police ability to respond to an emergency were tested by the sub-divisional Inspector at Edgware when he allowed the Mayor of Hendon to call police from a police box indicating that a smash and grab had just occurred. Two police cars arrived on scene within two and five minutes respectively. The police crews did not appreciate this exercise in checking their efficiency.

A separate system where the traffic signal posts at St. Giles Circus, Bernard Street, Marble Arch, Orchard Street, and Frier Street were fitted with small iron boxes containing telephones with a switchboard in a control box at Oxford Circus was also in operation. There were lines connecting the control box to Marylebone Lane and Marlborough Street Police Stations. These boxes were little used and, in fact, some of them could not be opened as they had been painted over so many times.

The Force were promoting their new crime fighting system on a stand at the Olympia Exhibition Hall's 1936 Radiolympia Exhibition. Pamphlets, outlining how the boxes were in the street for the benefit of the public, were distributed to a total of 80,000 people. This publication also advised the public, requiring immediate assistance when no box was nearby, to telephone 'Whitehall 1212 — Information Room'.

Sergeants were employed on the stand, displaying a police box connected to Hammersmith Police Station, accompanied by specially selected constables from the Communications Branch to answer calls from the public. Throughout the Exhibition between 26th August and 5th September the public made a total of 1,456 calls from the box. They were asked for their suggestions to improve the efficiency of the system and were generally impressed by the stand which created a great deal of interest as many had previously thought that the boxes were only for police use. The box provided a practical facility at the Exhibition for reporting persons ill and property lost or stolen.

Between 30th March and 24th April the following year a similar police stand, taken at the Olympia Ideal Home Exhibition, again showed that the public were not aware that the boxes were for their use. The female visitors had a fear that if they used the telephone 'a gruff police-man would snap their heads off' at the police station. During this exhibition a total of 6,510 calls were made to Hammersmith Police Station and 140,578 pamphlets were distributed. This stand continued as a feature of the exhibition until the outbreak of the war.

By the end of 1937 boxes in the Force totalled 703 and in the more congested areas telephone posts were erected. During that year and in the early months of the following year many of the inner divisions were completed. Even though the box system had been given extensive publicity a noticeable reluctance to make full use of the service still existed.

The blue concrete police box remained an important feature of Metropolitan Police communications until superceded by the intro-duction of the personal radio in the mid 1960s. Police telephone posts remain in use with the City of London Force as does one at Piccadilly Circus, although the year 1988 witnesses the City giving up all but two of its 65 distinctive blue pillars.

The police boxes, coupled with the introduction of a van and two

Use the Blue Boxes

in connection with :—

Crime.
Housebreaking.
Burglary.
Larceny.
Stolen Property.
Unattended Houses.
Suspicious Characters.
Suspicious Noises.

Accident.
Fire.
Ambulance.
First Aid.
Persons Missing.
Animals Lost.
Animals Found.

Complaints.
Rowdyism.
Traffic Blocks.
Information.
Routes.
Advice.

M.P.-250M.

HELP THE POLICE
TO
HELP YOU

RADIOLYMPIA, 1936.   Stand 100.

POLICE TELEPHONE BOXES

All these boxes are painted BLUE.
Calls to Police may be made from them FREE.
They exist in all outer districts of the Metropolis.

Any call from them will receive immediate response.
Transport is held available to deal with urgent calls.

Open the cupboard door and lift the receiver.
Never hesitate to use these boxes—no matter is too trivial.
Calls will be passed on to wireless cars when necessary.
Every box is a means of helping Police to help you—Please use them.

If you require assistance urgently when no Police
Box is available, use ANY telephone and ring:

"WHItehall 1212—Information Room."

Police Box publicity, 1936.

cars for use at each sub-division, were really the beginning of a planned 'fast' response to calls from the public. The system, introduced initially some years before Information Room commenced operation when wireless communication rested mainly with Flying Squad vehicles, and came at a time when the public's expectation of the police service reached greater proportions. Motor vehicles, increasing in number, were being stolen and used in the commission of crime making more efficient methods of communication essential in combatting these trends.

CHAPTER V

REALISING A RAPID RESPONSE – WIRELESS, INFORMATION ROOM AND 999

Guglielmo Marconi demonstrated his wireless telegraphy apparatus to the Post Office in 1896 and was given official support for trials of the system on Salisbury Plain. A recommendation that the Post Office should purchase Marconi's patent did not receive approval from the Treasury. Consequently in 1897 the Wireless Telegraph and Signal Company was formed to develop the apparatus commercially and by 1900 experiments with telegraphy on naval vessels were being pursued; the name then changed to Marconi's Wireless Telegraph Co. The East Goodwin lightship had successfully used Marconi equipment to send out a distress signal after a collision at sea the previous year, but the message that proved the true power of wireless was the single letter 'S' sent in Morse code, across the Atlantic from Cornwall in December 1901 and received by Marconi in Newfoundland.

A Wireless Telegraphy Act of 1904 prevented the operation of wireless telegraphy without a licence issued by the Post Office, which in 1909 took over the main shore wireless stations although very few ships were, at that time, fitted with such communication facilities. Marconi had set up the Marconi International Marine Communications Company in 1900 for the production of maritime wireless.

In 1864 Inspector Richard Tanner had pursued the murderer, Franz Muller, across the Atlantic after the killing of Mr. Briggs on the North London Railway, without the aid of any communication. Tanner boarded a faster ship and reached New York before the suspect. In 1910 the similar pursuit, by Scotland Yard, of Doctor Hawley Harvey Crippen for the murder of his wife, Cora, (known also under a stage name of Belle Elmore) was to prove the immense value of the wireless to police work.

As a result of friends becoming suspicious about the disappearance of Cora, Detective Inspector Dew went, on 8th July, to Hilldrop Crescent, Camden where he saw Crippen in the house with Ethel Clara Le Neve, his typist, who had been known to him for many years. Dew informed Crippen of the reason for his visit and a statement was made to the officer falsely indicating that his wife was still alive. The day after the interview Crippen and Le Neve left Hilldrop Crescent and when police visited the house again on 11th July their disappearance was discovered and a search of the premises commenced. On 13th July the remains of Mrs. Crippen were found in the cellar and the murder hunt began.

The descriptions of Crippen and Le Neve were circulated to police forces throughout Europe and America over the cable telegraph service. On 14th July the S.S. Montrose sailed from Millwall Docks, Henry George Kendall, the Commander of the vessel, having been supplied with a description of the wanted couple by Thames police officers, Detective

Stockholms Polis

Torsdagen den 21 Juli 1910

Polisunderrättelser

N:o   83

Aftonbladets tr., Sthlm.

Under inseende af Stockholms Polisstyrelse utgifna för rikets Polismyndigheter.

Hawley Harvey Crippen.

Ethel Clara Le Neve.

Crippen's handwriting   39 Hilldrop Crescent.
        Feb 9/10

Dear Miss May

     Illness of a near relative has called me to America on only a few hours notice, so I must ask you bring my resignation as treasurer before the meeting today so that a new treasurer can be elected at once. You will appreciate my haste when I tell you I have not been to bed all night, packing and getting ready to go. I

Le Neve's handwriting
     39 Hilldrop Cres

Dear Sir

     Am so sorry dear to disappoint you to day, have been called away will write you late my love dear. to you all & kisses

From
    your loving
      Ethel

Sergeants Arle and Barclay, the previous day.   The ship sailed first to Antwerp from where it set sail for Quebec and Montreal on 20th July. There were a total of 266 passengers on board when she sailed and before leaving Kendall purchased a continental edition of the Daily Mail which contained photographs and descriptions of Crippen and his companion. As the journey progressed Kendall became suspicious about two of his passengers, one of whom (Le Neve) was travelling dressed as a boy and both were using the name Robinson.

By 22nd July Kendall had satisfied himself, after a conversation with Crippen about sea sickness amongst the passengers, that he was the Doctor.   The Captain kept quiet about his suspicions, apart from informing his Chief Officer, Alfred Sergeant, and at 3.35 p.m. on that day he sent the following telegram over the ship's Marconi wireless —

"To Peirs Liverpool.
3pm G.M.T. Friday 130 miles West Lizard have strong suspicions that Crippen London Cellar Murderer and accomplice are amongst saloon passengers moustache taken off, growing beard accomplice dressed as boy, voice manner and build undoubtedly a girl both travelling as Mr and Master Robinson.

Kendall".

The Marconigram was passed to the Liverpool City Police who in turn forwarded the information immediately by telegram to New Scotland Yard.   The Liverpool Police booked a passage for Chief Inspector Dew on the steamer S.S. Laurentic, which was due to sail for Quebec on 23rd July at 6.30 p.m., and telegrammed the arrangements to London.

Kendall continued to keep his suspects under observation and, as he became fully convinced of their true identity, sent another Marconigram to Liverpool from mid-Atlantic and a report to London on the S.S. Montezuma for his ship's owners in Liverpool.

Dew sailed for Quebec and on his arrival in Canada on 30th July a telegram was sent through the Direct United States Cable Company Limited —

"Father Point Que 12 (Via Direct Cable)
Handcuffs London;
Arrived Rimouski Montrose expected Saturday cable any information
Father Point.
Dew".

The Chief Inspector kept in touch with Kendall on the Montrose by wireless and arrangements were made for the ship to be boarded.   In fact, the Captain sent three messages to Dew on 29th, 30th and 31st.   On Sunday 31st July, Dew boarded the ship dressed as a pilot and, accompanied by Canadian officers, arrested the two suspects.   A series of cables were then sent to London in confirmation of the arrests and eventually the couple were escorted back to England where they were charged.   This case really caught the public imagination and the value to police of wireless could not be underestimated.

The newspapers were being used to assist in tracking down criminals but not until the early 1920s were the British Broadcasting Company available to assist police by broadcasting to the public urgent requests for witnesses in accident cases, tracing missing persons and similar appeals. In 1923 Charles Reith, managing director of the BBC, wrote to the Commissioner requesting that instructions be given to Superintendents to ensure the proper use of the facility. An example of the value of these broadcasts appeared in November, 1923 when a police officer was knocked down and seriously injured by a tramcar. Through the BBC broadcasting an appeal, a witness was traced and the driver subsequently prosecuted.

Superintendents in charge of divisions were advised of the value of BBC broadcasts and a procedure was set up for submitting requests through Scotland Yard. In view of the large number of applications for access to the system in respect of missing persons it was accepted initially that Scotland Yard would also handle those received from the provinces.

Agreement was reached that urgent messages in relation to crime, where a criminal had escaped from the scene and a good description had been obtained, could be suitable for broadcasting, although the facility does not appear to have been used for this purpose to any great extent. The pursuit of Samuel Furnace, for the murder of Walter Spatchett at Camden Town on 3rd January, 1933 involved the use of a news report on 9th January, which gave the description and requested the public to provide information to police if they had any knowledge of his whereabouts.

Evidence indicates that the Metrpolitan Force did not use the BBC extensively for any purpose, although the Company had expressed concern about the number of police messages. In 1928 for instance there were only 18 missing person appeals (one successful) 25 accident appeals (20 successful) and five appeals to trace relations (one successful) and by 1930 the overall figures had decreased.

The fire brigade were experimenting, as early as 1900, during the construction of their new station at Streatham, with Marconi equipment from a street caravan in the area to a temporary fire station. The following year saw Marconi assessing his earliest mobile equipment fitted, along with the cylindrical chimney like aerial, to a Thorneycroft Steam Bus. More than ten years were to pass after the Crippen success, however, before the Metropolitan Police pursued wireless as a means of improving their efficiency.

Prior to 1920 all engineering work in the Force rested with the Architect and Surveyor in charge of the Surveryor's Department. In that year Gilbert Mackenzie Trench succeeded John Dixon Butler in this post and the department was divided into five sections, one of which concentrated on engineering. Major Thomas Vittey, formerly employed with the Royal Air Force, became Assistant (Engineering) Surveyor with responsibility for the engineering section assisted by George Wootton, renowned for his many experimental projects and credited with inventing and producing the first electric lantern to be used by police. By 1922 the engineering section, removed from the control of Trench, became Major Vittey's overall responsibility with his appointment as the Engineer, working directly to the Receiver, with Wootton as Assistant Engineer.

In 1923, Harold Charles Kenworthy, who was to become the leading figure in wireless experiments within the Force, joined the Engineering Branch on loan from the Marconi Company becoming, six years later, a permanent member of Metropolitan Police Receiver's staff.

Thomas George Cole explained, when interviewed by the author in 1987, how he had been recruited into the wireless section in the early 1920s as a constable. Cole remembers seeing Kenworthy fitting a wireless set to a car at Scotland Yard and expressing to him his interest which he had developed during service in the Royal Navy. Kenworthy welcomed this experience and enthusiasm and Wootton obtained authority from George Abbiss, the senior police officer, to employ the young constable in the section.

Cole praised highly the ability of Kenworthy and Wootton as engineers and much of the credit for the advances in police wireless communication must be attributed to Kenworthy's early experiments, assisted by other junior engineers and constables with a good wireless background. George Farrand is remembered by Cole as one of those engineers. The wireless section of the Metropolitan Police has remained until the present day a very independent and efficient section employing many innovative and experienced engineers.

An expenditure of less than £30 had been incurred by the Engineering Branch prior to 1922 for experimental purposes, investigating the possible future use of wireless telephony (speech) or telegraphy (Morse) by police; receiving apparatus had been the only equipment used. The engineers occupied two rooms on the fourth floor at Scotland Yard where the early experiments building transmitters and receivers commenced.

In May, 1922 Major Vittey submitted his proposals for trials in the use of wireless for the detection of crime and circulation of information. He suggested the erection of a sending and receiving station at New Scotland Yard at the top of the Receiver's building (known as Scotland House), 'in a part of the tailor's shop, which was as near the roof as possible'. The recommendation to erect two aerials involved locating one on the chimney which passed through the tailor's shop. The estimated cost amounted to £360. Additionally it was proposed to fit a Crossley car, of the type used by the C.I.D., with wireless and associated equipment at a cost of £180 capable of sending telephonic messages up to 20 miles. In fact this proposal would allow the sending and receipt of messages from and to a car anywhere in the Metropolitan Police District.

On 24th May, the Receiver, John Moylan, wrote to the Commissioner outlining the proposals and expressing doubt about the value of Vittey's recommended experiment. He suggested that someone should be

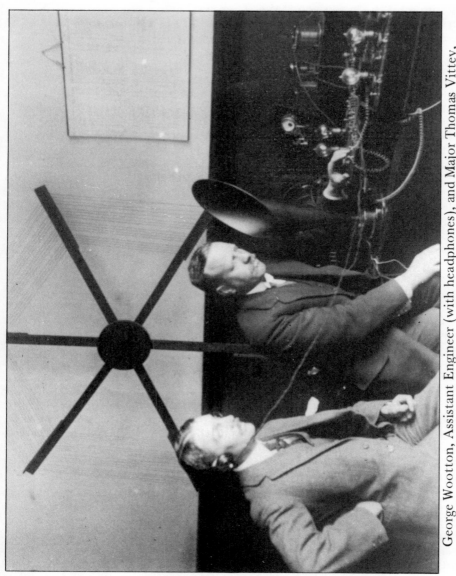

George Wootton, Assistant Engineer (with headphones), and Major Thomas Vittey, the Engineer of the Metropolitan Police, in the Wireless Room, c.1922.

sent to Paris to examine the wireless system used by the police in that city.   Although doubtful about the value, Moylan did make application to the General Post Office for the allocation of two wavelengths for experimental purposes and the Commissioner, Brigadier Sir William Horwood, expressed the view that the trials should proceed saying, "in my opinion we cannot afford to be left behind".

Later that month Inspector Bannon, the Special Branch officer in the Bureau de Controle Britannique, was directed to discuss the value of the wireless with the French police, in respect of C.I.D. work and traffic control.   At the request of the Commissioner he also looked at the Belinographe used to transmit photographs over the telephone.   Inspector Bannon reported back on the 2nd June, that no practical value had been gained by the French police from wireless telephony for criminal investigation.   However, it had benefits for keeping headquarters informed about political demonstrations in the city which were at that time illegal.

The French police used an aeroplane, fitted with wireless telephony equipment, circling the city when demonstrations were anticipated in order that they could identify trouble spots and reserves of officers could easily be sent to the scenes.   In addition they used two vans fitted with wireless telephony.   Although wireless in the Paris Force was still experimental they were considering its use for long distance messages and could see the future value for communication with London, Brussels, Berlin and the other main cities of Europe.

Between 9th and 13th June, Major Vittey visited the Paris police and, with Inspector Bannon, gained a great deal of information about their system.   Vittey, although interested from the engineering and scientific view, was not convinced that radio telephony was of any great value to the police.   He felt, however, that the Force should keep abreast with the new technology and pursued the recommendation that a Headquarters Wireless Station, similar to that seen in Paris, should be established.

Vittey also visited Monsieur Belin's works at Rueil to examine the Company's photographic transmitter.   He reported that at that time he could see no practical value of the machine to the Metropolitan Police. Interest had also been shown by the C.I.D. in using the machine for transmitting fingerprints although the Paris police had not, in fact, at that time used the Belinographe.   (a machine of this type is displayed at the Science Museum in London).

On 26th June, a meeting was held, which included participants from the G.P.O. and Home Office, and Moylan, Vittey and Wootton, who discussed the future use of wireless for communication in the Force. That year experiments were carried out between Marconi House and a Crossley tender fitted with a transmitting and receiving set.   Although transmissions to the tender were satisfactory those from it were not.   The agreement followed with the Marconi Company that they would install an experimental transmitter in the room at the top of New Scotland Yard for communication with a vehicle.   By the end of the year the contractor,

The wireless tender used at the Derby Race Meeting, Epsom from 1923.

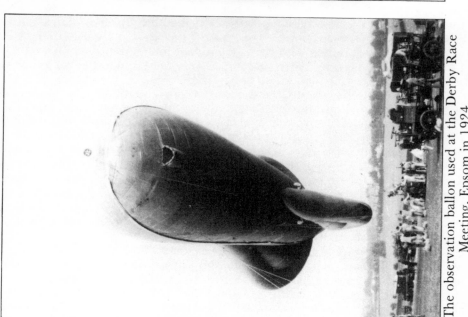

The observation balloon used at the Derby Race Meeting, Epsom in 1924.

J.W. Gray and Company, had almost completed the aerial masts.

The Home Office approved an expenditure of £1405 on the scheme and in June, the following year, the Commissioner considered fixing wireless to three additional Crossley tenders from the establishment of forty. A special wireless body was already under construction at Barnes Garage, far more substantial than that on the existing experimental vehicle.

The aerials, in due course erected on the roof of New Scotland Yard, consisted of steel masts and four wires each with a horizontal span of 100 feet.   The Crossley van supported an aerial consisting of five parallel wires mounted on adjustable arms attached to the roof of the vehicle which could be adjusted from inside.   These early experiments used telephony (speech) and, apart from considerable interference from aircraft, boats, trains and motor cars, were reasonably satisfactory.   Telephone and telegraph wires often screened signals as did buildings with an internal steel construction.   A repetition of figures and names used in messages were necessary which resulted in slow transmission and reception.   Later experiments with telegraphy, using the same equipment, proved much faster with interference of less concern to the operator receiving Morse signals.   The huge aerials on the roof the van led it to become known to the 'villains' as a 'Bedstead'.   Fortunately by 1926 they were abandoned and replaced by less obvious aerials.

Traffic congestion at special events caused difficulties of control for the Force; any answer to improve the situation would be welcomed. The Derby at Epsom was one such event where various methods of observation had been tried including an airship with an observer who could view the congested roads without being able to communicate that information to the ground.   On another occasion in 1921 an R.A.F. aeroplane with a police observer, again had no communication which meant it had to land in order that any instances of congested roads could be reported.

The Deputy Assistant Commissioner, Percy Laurie, was in charge of operations when, in June, 1923, a tender with wireless communication was first used at Epsom and, apart from the wireless operator, George Farrand, who suffered from exposure to exhaust fumes, it appears to have been a successful exercise.   There was atmospheric interference as would be expected in early experiments.   In addition to the tender, observation was kept by police in an aeroplane fitted with radio telephony in communication with the officers on the ground.   The controlling station was at Scotland Yard with the fixed station at the race course.   Information could be passed to motor cycle patrols, although not by radio, to deal with traffic problems.

Laurie's favourable report on traffic control and wireless recommended that at future such events there should be four strategically placed tenders providing more effective cover.   As an airship was considered too expensive he suggested an observation balloon to view the traffic as an alternative to the aeroplane which had moved too quickly.   The Commissioner, Horwood, also very satisfied, expressed his gratitude for the work of Vittey and Wootton at the event.

The 1924 Derby saw aerial observers in a captive balloon assisting with traffic control. The balloon was in telephonic communication by cable with the ground and, on receipt of a call regarding congestion, either despatch riders would be sent to the spot or a message would be passed by wireless to a specific point. The wireless vehicle was manned by constables trained in Morse. Again in 1925 the use of wireless was reported as a great assistance at the event.

Arthur Bassom, Director of Traffic Services for the Force, was, unlike other senior officers, unimpressed by wireless at these events. In 1923 he had been in the aeroplane and subsequently the tender and the following year in the balloon after which he said, 'My considered view on the wireless in 1924 was that it was not effective for the purpose for which it was intended'. Declining to use it for the opening of the Wembley Exhibition or the Football Final he said, 'I confess I am at present unable to indicate any use to which the tenders might be put for traffic purposes'.

Mr. Cole recollects being present during the 1920s at the Races with two wireless vehicles, a blue van, call sign GCN and a Crossley Tender, call sign GTA. He described how Superintendent Bassom of B.3 Branch, was up in the balloon keeping observation when he suffered 'sea sickness'.

The G.P.O. wrote to the Receiver on 27th October, 1923 informing

Wireless tenders in use by the Metropolitan Police — Derby Race Meeting, Epsom — 1924.

him that there was no objection to the Force using a specific wavelength (265) although they would not agree to its exclusive use by police Neither would they agree to the use of a second wavelength unless there were special circumstances. The wireless sets at New Scotland Yard had been constructed for two wavelengths (265 and 730); the view was that to be limited to 265 would seriously affect efficiency. As a result of correspondence with the Post Office the police were told to look for another 'quiet wavelength' on which they could operate.

On 10th January, 1924 a quotation of £160 was received from Marconi's Wireless Telegraph Company Limited, Marconi House, The Strand, WC2, for the purchase of equipment already on loan and installed at New Scotland Yard, to be used as a spare wireless set. Expenditure on wireless from October, 1921 until August, 1925 totalled £2,631. The Crossley Van and wireless equipment cost a total of £1,275 and fitting the Headquarters Wireless Station amounted to £805.

On 16th May, 1924 the Postmaster General formally authorised the Force to set up a wireless telegraph (Morse) sending and receiving station at New Scotland Yard and a mobile sending and receiving station on a tender or lorry used in the Metropolitan Area. Authority was also given to use the second wavelength for transmission from the Yard. The Post Office authority stated that "normally, no transmission shall commence without listening-in on the wavelength to ascertain whether the proposed transmission is likely to interfere with any other station".

Lt. Col. Sir Percy Robert Laurie, KCVO, CBE, DSO, later Assistant Commissioner, Served with the Force 1919 to 1936.

Prior to 1924 the call sign 6SY, allocated to Scotland Yard, led to a number of complaints and requests for a change to one with less sibilance. NSY or CO (Commissioner's Office) were sought but with neither available, Scotland Yard became GSY and the mobile GCN. The fees for the permit were £5 per station for the first year and £3 per year thereafter.

The Flying Squad was born in September, 1920 with the purchase of two Crossley tenders for C.I.D. use. These were large, heavy vehicles with van type bodies; their tyres were very narrow and they had no front wheel brakes. They were, however, very reliable. One vehicle patrolled north of the River and the other south. A major difficulty in the early days, before wireless, was that any communication with Scotland Yard had to be made by stopping the vehicle in order that one of the crew could telephone for instructions or information.

Experiments had proved Morse to be far more successful than wireless telephony and from September, 1923 three constables, recollected by Mr. Cole to be PC Archie Pross from 'D' Division, PC Edgar Brown from 'A' Division and himself from 'P' Division, were employed on wireless duties. This establishment increased to five in 1925 (on Cole's account now included PC Paddy Griffin and PC Harry Sidle) when the C.I.D. began to use telegraphy. Two men were employed on two watches (0800 to 1600 and 1500 to 2300). In March, 1925 a total of nine constables were covering the two Flying Squad tenders which had by then been fitted with wireless. Resulting from the General Strike the number increased to twelve in order that short wave transmissions could be monitored. This caused the Receiver to question the authority for such employment of constables in view of the expenditure involved. The officers in these early days were mainly ex-Royal Naval wireless telegraphy operators already skilled in Morse code. Brown and Pross, however, were ex-Marconi operators from civilian ships.

The twelve pioneers attached to the Wireless Branch in August 1926 were:-

PC.625 'B' ALDRIDGE
PC.611 'A' BROWN
PC.339 'P' COLE
PC.761 'T' GRIFFIN
PC.766 'J' HARVIE
PC.377 'W' HEATH
PC.561 'Y' JOHNSON
PC.485 'B' SIDLE
PC.366 'J' STEPHENS
PC.549 'L' TURNER
PC. 66 'D' WALKER
PC.687 'K' WORSFOLD

Cole claims that he originally suggested to Kenworthy that wireless could be used for Flying Squad work and went to see the then head of

169

the Squad, Detective Chief Inspector Cooper, explaining to him how information regarding stolen cars could be passed to his vehicles. Mr. Cole went on to describe one of his early experiences in communicating with a 'Flying Squad van'. "It was agreed that two C.I.D. vans, really they were ex-ambulances used by the Flying Squad, should be fitted with wireless. We couldn't make the C.I.D. understand that they didn't have to stop to receive a message. One day I was up in the main receiving room when a squad man phoned up and said 'could you get a message very urgent to a car with Police Sergeant Tom Minter on board'. I transmitted the message for Minter to telephone the Yard immediately. The vehicle was operating in the Catford area and he got the message with no difficulty and phoned in. He then picked up his Inspector and went to Doncaster on this murder job. The C.I.D. began to realise then the value of the wireless".

He explained, "We were experimenting all the time taking sets to pieces and putting them up on the 4th Floor of the old building on the Receiver's side. We used to put our own aerials up on the 4th Floor, but Edgar Brown, the Marconi man, could not face heights. The chimneys on the roof were very large and square and you could walk across them. Kenworthy used to test the receivers we made by dropping them on the floor, from the bench. If they still worked then they were O.K."

During the last three months of 1926 twenty five messages were transmitted from Scotland Yard to the Squad vans. In a recorded example in November, 1926 a suspect, seen entering a house on 'S' Division, led the police officer who attended the scene to telephone Scotland Yard from where a wireless message was sent to a C.I.D. van. The van attended resulting in the arrest of the house breaker.

The first wireless sets used by the Squad were bulky with the aerial leading into a 'biscuit box' tuner. A code, devised to identify streets and districts by numbers, obstructed unauthorised persons picking up police messages. Inside aerials could be used with Morse making the vehicles less noticeable and, of course, lessening the danger from the protruding frame previously fitted. A note frequency oscillator increased the range from about 15 miles to 100 miles.

The International Radiotelegraph Convention of Washington in 1927 allocated to the police new frequencies on which they were required to operate. A new ½ kilowatt transmitter installed at New Scotland Yard met the Convention's requirements.

By the end of the decade it was clear that the police were to pursue wireless as an essential form of communication and during a Conference held at the General Post Office in November 1928, attended by representatives from the Force and the Home Office, the limited availability of wavelengths was emphasised by the GPO. The need for police forces to limit their wireless requirements to purposes which could not be provided for by other means was highlighted. Agreement that four spot waves in the 140-150 metre band (which included 145 metres then being used by Scotland Yard) would meet the requirements of London and the provinces for communication with motor vans was reached. These four waves would, as far as possible, be protected from interference and use of others for police purposes would be discontinued once there had been an opportunity to alter the apparatus in the ten existing vans. The call signs GSY and GSZ and the full series from GTA to GTZ were issued solely for police. A numerical suffix could be used after the letters to identify a vehicle in a particular group. Discussions and correspondence in respect of radio frequencies continued during the 1930s between police forces and the Home Office.

During the meeting of delegates at the Criminal Police Congress in 1923 in Vienna the International Commission of Criminal Police, the forerunner of Interpol, was formed providing co-operation between member countries on criminal matters.

In July, 1927 in Amsterdam the members of the Commission agreed to fix an international police wireless service. This network, first set up in 1929, was interrupted during the Second World War and reconstituted in 1946. From 1928 the Assistant Commissioner (Crime) headed the United Kingdom delegation at the Commission meetings.

In a report from Kenworthy to Wootton in 1925, suggesting the linking up of the British Isles in a national system of police communications, he recommended the use of telegraphy over telephony. Kenworthy indicated that telegraphy, more accurate, faster and cheaper, was also less liable to interception if skilled telegraphists were used. Telephony could be listened to by persons owning domestic receivers. A suggestion put forward by Kenworthy for communication throughout the country does not however appear to have been implemented.

In 1926 additional Marconi equipment, purchased at the cost of £516. 13s. 5d. by the Force, was used in secret surveillance work listening in to foreign stations passing information over the shortwave. Prior to the Second World War this specialist work was transferred to a new wireless receiving station at Denmark Hill in south London along with nominated constables. By 1940 one station sergeant, three sergeants and thirty three constables were employed at the wireless station with twenty eight of them paid through the Foreign Office for wartime eavesdropping on enemy broadcasts.

In March, 1928 the divisional Superintendents were instructed to submit to Scotland Yard the names of constables, with not less than twelve months service, who were experienced in wireless telegraphy. Of the names sent forward twenty three were selected to attend an examination and the twelve who passed were loaned to the Wireless Telegraphy Department. All operators were found from the uniform branch, although a few C.I.D. men were tested but 'their knowledge was found to be non existent'. It was considered impossible to train anyone to be efficient in Morse after the age of 25 therefore limiting potential candidates from the C.I.D.

The officers selected for the section in 1928 were:-

PC.303 'A' HAWKINS
PC.444 'A' HOBSON
PC.698 'B' BAILEY
PC.420 'B' DAWKINS
PC.124 'D' CRAWFORD
PC.378 'G' FRANCIS
PC.409 'J' LOVEMAN
PC.583 'J' WOOLVEN
PC.795 'K' JANES
PC.172 'L' PREECE
PC.177 'L' HOLLAND
PC.295 'X' ABEL

By December, 1928 there were a total of 26 constables employed on wireless duties throughout the 24 hours — ten as operators on the four Flying Squad vans and six Lea Francis cars, six at Headquarters and four on the interception of messages for the Home Office. The remaining six officers were relieving those on cars. By 1930 five tenders were equipped with receiving/transmitting sets, and of a further twelve Flying Squad cars, seven had receiving apparatus, and five were without wireless.

The considerable amount of overtime worked by wireless operators caused concern to those in authority. In 1932 Squad operators were instructed to parade ½ hour before duty and not one hour before as they had previously. This attempt to reduce overtime did not succeed and by 30th September, 1933 the thirty eight operators had a total of 6,881 hours outstanding. In December approval was given for five shillings each week to be paid to W/T operators when they were employed on Flying Squad vehicles in lieu of overtime. No such allowance was paid when they were working at the Wireless Station.

Arrests by the Flying Squad increased from 176 in 1925 to 515 in 1929 about 75% resulting, it is claimed, from wireless calls. In 1932 the nineteen operational police vehicles fitted with wireless were all allocated to the Flying Squad. They included three vans and one Bentley saloon car with transmitting and receiving sets and fifteen other cars with receiving sets only. The two additional vans used for experimental wireless work also had transmitting facilities.

The difficulty with Morse, as already indicated, was the requirement for extensive training of operators without previous experience in the armed services in reading or transmitting the code.

The reasons for fitting cars with transmitters in addition to receiving facilites were given as:-

a. To permit close co-operation in the arrest of criminals e.g. a Squad car chasing a criminal can call another car.
b. To assist in crime detection and prevention e.g. a car, already engaged in chasing a criminal which notes anything suspicious on route can report it to CO without delaying the chase.
c. To enable best use to be made of available forces e.g. reporting their

position periodically in order that the most appropriate car can be called to an incident.

d.   To assist traffic control during processions e.g. by means of vans stationed at local points on the route.

An estimate of the cost of such apparatus for each vehicle amounted to about £150 plus installation. Due to the expense and likely congestion and confusion on the air, the fitting of all vehicles with the facility to transmit Morse was avoided.

By the early 1930s the improvement in effectiveness of the Force's fleet of cars, by fitting them with communication facilities, was under consideration and a decision was needed on whether telephony suited police purposes albeit slower and less accurate than telegraphy. Discussions between the Commissioner and Assistant Commissioners even gained the support of the Assistant Commissioner (Crime) for telephony although more liable to interception than Morse. Agreement was reached to go ahead with experiments thereby ascertaining whether 'the expenditure would be justified having regard to the probable results'. Telegraphy required far less power and could operate effectively on half a kilowatt unlike the rival system.

Clearly a decision was needed quickly on whether the Force could move towards the extensive use of telephony. The ideal would be to provide all crews with the ability to send and receive messages. The general view was, however, that only a certain number of cars should have the facility to both transmit and receive whereas far more would be able to receive only. An idea that certain cars, known as 'Contact Cars', would have the 'transmit' equipment did not receive the Commissioner's support.

Lord Trenchard, the Commissioner, considered that all patrolling cars, including C.I.D. and Traffic Control cars, should in time be fitted with receiving apparatus. Such a move could not be approved until a proper investigation into the expenditure, efficiency of the equipment and value to the Force of a new wireless station had been assessed. Trenchard's genuine interest in wireless and modern technology provided Cole with recollections of taking him out in a police car for a full tour of night duty to examine the effectiveness of the system.

Initially suggested for telephony was the setting up of a central broadcasting station at Imber Court followed by a later proposal for three smaller transmitting stations at Wood Green, Barnes and Lewisham each covering a six mile radius with nothing at Imber Court. Messages would be sent by land line from Scotland Yard to the transmitting stations where staff would not be required.

During January and February, 1933 tests were carried out in conjunction with the Royal Air Force, who supplied a mobile transmitting station located at St. Anns Road Police Station, Tottenham and later at Kew Police Station. A mobile receiving station patrolled the streets along with two ex-Flying Squad cars. The transmitting station, known as

1930s Bentley Police Car — 'M.P' sign in Windscreen.
Fabric top suitable for an aerial.

1936 — Metropolitan Police Car — Wireless operator in the back seat.
Aerial concealed in the roof.

'Humming Bird', was manned by the R.A.F. personnel and the receiving vehicles by the police officers. The experiments were directed by Mr. Kenworthy. Signals could only be relied upon up to two miles from the transmitter and, even in that area, they were often bad. From St. Anns Road, communication could not be received at all in the West End or City areas. Transmissions were affected by electric flashing signs, Neon lights, bus ignition and movement of tramcars.

The operators carrying out the experiments experienced signals ranging from the very weak to a maximum strength causing 'a very hurtful shock to one's eardrums'. The index numbers of cars and place names were often misheard and a message took four times longer to transmit than by telegraphy.

The advantages of telegraphy over telephony were emphasised again by these rather unsatisfactory results:-

(a) Messages were capable of receipt practically anywhere with a car on the move.
(b) Messages could not be heard outside the car and, therefore, did not attract attention.
(c) No time was taken with routine 'calling in' messages.
(d) Phonetic errors were unknown and messages were received more accurately.
(e) Signals could only be received on a specially adapted receiver.
(f) The speed of telegraphy was much greater.
(g) Telephony interfered with normal broadcast stations and there was no secrecy.

Comprehensive reports on the tests were compiled by the three policemen involved, Sergeant Henry Giddings of C.O.C.1. Branch, PC Thomas Cole and PC Alfred Stephens. Flight Lieutenant John McDonald of the R.A.F. and Mr. Kenworthy also reported on the trials. As a result the conclusion was that 'Radio Telephony was not a practical proposition at that time' and Lord Trenchard instructed that wireless telegraphy continue as the means of communication with vehicles.

In 1933 ex-Naval Commander Kenneth Barrington Best was appointed as a Chief Inspector to take control of operational communications work. He had transferred from the Admiralty to assist the Force with wireless in which he had a great deal of practical experience. Cole summed up his commitment with the phrase 'Only the best for Mr. Best'.

The Chief Inspector was to oversee some fascinating trials and his enthusiasm and willingness to test and evaluate new equipment operationally did much to prepare the Force for the advanced communications methods which exist today. Although holding a relatively senior rank it appears that Best enjoyed nothing better than to be trying out new devices personally along with Kenworthy and the constables. In June, 1934 he was appointed an associate member of the Wireless Telegraphy Board representing police interests countrywide.

The story of wireless would not be complete without a description

Lord Trenchard, GCB., DSO, DCL, LLD,
Commissioner of Police, 1931 to 1935.

of some of the evaluations and improvements undertaken during the ex-Commander's term of office. On 3rd May 1934, resulting from Best's proposals, approval given by the Home Office allowed modernisation of transmitting equipment in the three Flying Squad vans (Call signs GTB, GTC and GTD). Permission was also given to fit transmitting equipment to two further Squad cars. The approximate total cost amounted to £330. The two experimental cars (call signs GTE and GTF) were left with their existing equipment, one of which had a 'controlled' type of van transmitter and the other a semi portable capable of being removed for use at a temporary ground wireless telegraph station.

An amusing suggestion that vehicles, not fitted with transmitters, should carry message forms for completion by the operator during a pursuit, for instance, to be thrown out in an envelope when passing an officer on foot duty, does not appear to have been implemented. The message would notify the car's activity in order that the information could be passed on to other officers. The foot duty man's attention would be alerted by sounding two 'P's in Morse on the car's horn.

Vans were more suitable for transmitters, the available space allowing aerials to be fitted relatively easily. Transmitting apparatus in cars suited those with fabric bodies and only one vehicle, the Invicta saloon, met this requirement. By 1934 complete fabric bodies were dying out on vehicles and a new Talbot 105, which had half fabric, seemed to meet the requirements for a satisfactory transmitter. In fact, the transmitters were fitted to two Lagonda saloons used by the Flying Squad, although sending messages proved to be less than successful both between the cars or from the car to the headquarters receiving station.

Discussions took place in 1933 into the possible use of 'call up' signals for wireless cars thereby obviating the necessity for operators to wear conspicuous earphones continuously. Kenworthy indicated that the power available from the transmitter existing at that time was insufficient to allow these earphones to be dispensed with.

In 1934 in an attempt to find a less conspicuous earphone an 'in ear' device, of the type used on a deaf aid, was tried. Although the three constables who tested the appliances found reception as good as that over a headset they were bothered by the considerable noise of interference as they were unable to move the earpiece away from the ear.

After the early bedstead aerials on the Crossley tenders aerials consisting of several strands of wire attached to the underside of the soft top hoods of cars were used. Later, in August, 1934, trials were carried out by Chief Inspector Best with an aerial suspended from the running board and a receiver of commercial manufacture, both fitted in a Lagonda motor car borrowed from the Flying Squad. The aerial consisted of a length of copper gauze lashed to wooden blocks under each running board. Comparisons were made during the test with the normal Metropolitan Police receiver and the normal soft top vehicle aerial and, initially, the trial aerial proved to be just as efficient. Later tests with the same equipment, carried out by PC Percy Hughes on a Ford Saloon, found that signal strengths dropped rapidly about 2 miles from the wireless station. The decision was not to pursue the introduction of these aerials at this time. Best also tried the apparatus on his own private Vauxhall and later that year tried a wire aerial under his car.

In November, 1936 a Philco car top aerial, offered to the Force by the Company, was claimed to be far more efficient than the under car aerials and described as 'favourable to the 'Chicken wire' aerial installed under soft top vehicles'. However, Best immediately declined the offer stating that any aerial system on a police car had to be concealed.

A receiver from the Philco Radio and Television Corporation, tested along with the running board aerial, was found to be more noisy than the normal police receiver. The advantages were the smaller size, lighter weight and no requirement for head phones to be worn, which meant that the blinds did not have to be drawn to conceal their use thereby making the car less conspicuous as a police vehicle. The noise of incoming signals and interference could, however, distract the attention of the occupants of the car. There was also concern that the noise may have been heard outside the car. The cost of the Philco set was £14 compared with only £12 for the ordinary police receiver.

The Philco set, tried over a period of months in a car and Thames launches, in a modified form proved to be much more efficient in the former comparing favourably with the normal police equipment. The use in the boats did not reach such a high standard. Tests continued with sets on loan from Philco until March, 1937 when they were returned to the Company.

In June 1934, Best visited Plessey's works at Ilford for a demonstration of short wave wireless telephony equipment fitted on two cars. The experiment, limited to a radius of five miles from the Company's premises, did not have to contend with any significant hills or buildings which may have interfered with reception. The Chief Inspector concluded that the two aerials, each nine feet high located on the rear of the vehicle, were far too conspicuous for police work. He also felt that more tests in the built up area of central London were necessary before the equipment could be considered and, in view of this, the use of short wave in cars was not pursued further at this time.

In May 1935 at New Scotland Yard 5 metre two way short wave telephony equipment produced by the Ardente Company of 309 Oxford Street, London, W1, was examined by Best. The complete apparatus for transmission and reception, contained in a box weighing about thirty pounds, measured 18 inches by 10 inches. The aerial appeared as a telescopic rod on top of the set. The tests were carried out between a set in the roadway outside the Yard, and a moving van, belonging to the company, but, unfortunately communication ceased once the van had passed the centre of Westminster Bridge. The equipment did, however, have potential, particularly for short distant communication, although use on Derby Day at Epsom in 1935 found it to be unsatisfactory. Best wrote to F.C. Johnson of the Home Office in February and, when referring to ultra short wave, commented, 'I am afraid though, that a lot of difficult and tiresome experimental work lies ahead of us in this connection and there is always the possibility we shall have to admit defeat in the end'.

The 1932 Derby saw the use of an autogyro fitted with W/T equipment to assist with traffic control; further experiments with the aircraft followed.   On 4th September, 1934 at Croydon Aerodrome W/T apparatus (modified for telephony), hired from the Marconi Company, was installed in an autogyro, identification G-ACIN, for test purposes.   A Talbot 75 touring car, loaned by Messrs Philco and fitted with transmitting and receiving equipment, provided the ground station.   Best went up in the aircraft and carried out initial tests using Morse to communicate with the Headquarters Wireless Station.   Tests, using telephony, were then carried out between the aircraft and the car before it was driven to Hyde Park where two-way communication was later established between the autogyro flying over Sloane Square and the car in the Park.   On 9th September similar trials were carried out at Hendon and good speech communication took place over a distance of two miles.   Again the aircraft and car went to Hyde Park but there were, on this occasion, problems in communicating from ground to air.

As early as March 1934 Chief Inspector Best attended demonstrations of the Baird television equipment but found it of little practical use for police work.   The Marconi equipment, also examined, had much clearer definition than the Baird when using films.   Direct television pictures were not so good but Mr. Best concluded that television might be of considerable interest for police purposes in the future. The BBC were approaching the Force the following year to discuss the possibility of using television for appeals to the public in respect of wanted criminals.

Facsimile is taken as a device of the present day but in 1929, (before Best joined the Force) Kenworthy was reporting on a demonstration of the Fultograph Picture Transmission attachment to a wireless transmitter along with receiving equipment.   The Marconi Wireless Telegraph Company offered the Chief Engineer attendance at an experimental demonstration in 1930 of their facsimile equipment developed for use in aeroplances and tanks.   On 18th September, Kenworthy attended a remarkable demonstration at the Company's works at Chelmsford between an aircraft in flight and the ground station.

In January, 1935 Best and Kenworthy visited the army signals experimental establishment at Woolwich where they inspected a wireless facsimile apparatus developed by the army and known as the 'Eidograph'. This equipment could be used for both sending and receiving pictures; the police representatives made satisfactory tests in sending fingerprints and Police Gazette photographs.   At that time there was not considered to be sufficient scope for use by the Metropolitan Police of this costly facility.   An article in the 'Daily Telegraph' of 4th March announced the experiment with the headline 'Fingerprints by Radio' but the decision to develop use further was to be delayed until other ogranisations had

Marconi transmitting and receiving equipment installed in
Scotland Yard's Autogyro, 1934.   Morse Key strapped to the
observer's leg.

perfected it. However, Edwin Woodhall states in his book 'The Secrets of Scotland Yard' published in 1936, 'Scotland Yard makes frequent use of radio in transmitting fingerprints to foreign Police departments'.

The Metropolitan were co-operating with other forces by 1935 in respect of wireless and, in fact, were willing to provide and maintain their equipment at a charge. Although Liverpool Police had in mind the equipping of cycle patrols with receivers in that year this does not appear to have been pursued by the Metropolitan Police.

An article in Popular Wireless of 2nd March 1935 refers to the use of receivers on solo motorcycles in the Metropolitan Force in the early years of wireless and highlights the difficulties experienced due to the need for compact aerials on the machines. A 'calling up' device, necessary as wearing headphones proved undesirable when riding, led the Scotland Yard engineers to design an efficient and compact fixed tuned receiver sensitive enough to pick up signals on a yard of aerial. The power supply was produced from a generator driven from the motorcycle accumulator and a light on the handlebar indicated an incoming message. No other documentary references have been located in respect of these experiments.

Even as early as 1932 experiments were being carried out by the Wireless Branch with pocket wireless sets but they were not felt to be of any practical use. Best communicated by letter with the Royal Engineers in 1935 about a pocket transmitter produced in Vienna although it is not clear whether it was ever tried.

Trials were undertaken also on apparatus which could convert messages into a scrambled form to prevent interception. This equipment, and the other facilites described in the preceding paragraphs, are not generally appreciated as devices considered by the Force over 50 years ago.

The organisation for arranging wireless in the Force had gradually developed from the original group set up to carry out experimental work. More constables had been taken on in the section as demand increased until, in 1934, Lord Trenchard drew up his plan for 'D' Department to take over responsibility for the operating of the Headquarter Wireless Station from the Receiver's engineers. Trenchard wrote to the Receiver, 'I want to place on record here and now my appreciation of and gratitude to the Receiver's department and in particular Mr. Wootton and Mr. Kenworthy, for all the valuable work they have done for the wireless of the Metropolitan Police up to now. In fact, without them the present state of efficiency could not have been achieved'. Wootton had succeeded Vittey as Engineer in 1930.

On 19th March 1934 the Wireless School at Scotland House (the South Building of NSY) was formalised under George Abbiss, Deputy Assistant Commissioner, and became part of D.1. (Communications) Branch with instruction carried out by a Station Sergeant assisted by a section sergeant, who were under the direct supervision of the Chief Inspector for W/T Duties (Best). The length of a course normally

Sir George Abbiss, appointed Assistant Commissioner 1936.
Served with Force 1905 to 1946.

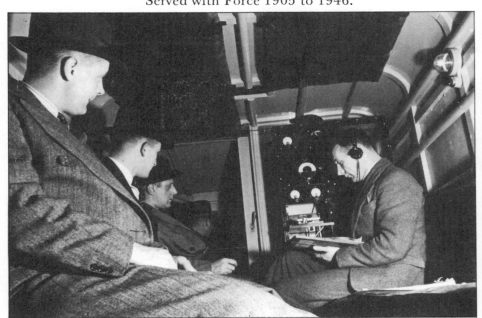

Receiving the Morse message.

amounted to two months but depended upon an individual's ability and could be as long as three. Operators showing efficiency and promise were given advanced instruction and those reaching the required standard became Class A operators. Only operators of this class were employed at the HQ W/T Station or as transmitters of messages on W/T vehicles. Other operators who passed were grade 'B'.

The standard of competence required for Morse reception was 95% at 20 words per minute and transmission 100% at 18 words per minute. A theoretical knowledge of valves, circuits and transformers was required.

Early in 1935 the School was transferred to the Metropolitan Police College at Hendon. As the training commitment increased, later including provincial officers, the instructing staff were increased in number in December, 1936 to one Inspector, one Station Sergeant and two sergeants. The Metropolitan Police charged a provincial force ten shillings each week per man and £5 for a full course of twelve weeks. In September, the following year, six constables from the City of London Force were trained at the Wireless School in preparation for the introduction of their wireless cars on 23rd March, 1937. Wireless training continued at Hendon until 1951 when it was transferred to the four Districts.

In March, 1934 the official establishment of police officers in the wireless section at New Scotland Yard totalled 36 (there were 35 permanent staff and three on loan actually employed). Sixteen operators were on Flying Squad vehicles, eighteen in the Wireless Telegraphy Office, and another four instructing divisional staff and involved in repair of equipment. Prior to 1934 the responsibility for all aspects of wireless rested virtually entirely with the Receiver's engineers. The Wireless Branch police officers were under the Assistant Commissioner 'C' for actual duties but operators' expenses, clothing, discipline, leave and time off were the responsibility of the Chief Constable A.2. Branch.

On 16th April, 1934 'D' Department took over control of operations in the Headquarters Wireless Station from Wootton and Kenworthy. The Receiver's staff continued with the responsibility for the supply and major maintenance of equipment, while the Chief Inspector 'D' Department became responsible for the up-keep of the Wireless Station and the police operators. Experimental work remained with the engineers along with a continued involvement in wireless interception. The long and close association between the police officers and the engineers had ensured that police wireless was established on a sound base.

At this time separate permanent staffs were allocated to the Flying Squad and the HQ Wireless Station. The staff at the Station consisted of two constables performing duties as senior and assistant instructors and three teams of five constables for each tour of duty with one PC in charge at an allowance of 2s.6d. per week. Four other W/T operators were employed on experimental work at Denmark Hill and a further twenty on permanent Flying Squad duties.

In 1934 the wireless section engineering staff were reorganised into 'interior' and 'exterior' maintenance. The former dealt with major repairs

and the latter with outside maintenance. A staffing plan for four assistant engineers, two electrical fitters and two boys was considered. As an
experiment two Commer wireless maintenance vans, carrying engineers
and equipment, were brought into use. One van worked north of the
Thames and the other south between 2pm and 6am. Only one maintenance vehicle operated from 6am to 2pm. These engineers, not engaged
in routine maintenance, carried a wireless receiver in order that they
could be directed to any breakdowns. By 1938 experience proved that
excessive time was being wasted by police crews awaiting the arrival of
maintenance vans, consequently a procedure for the police vehicles
to attend District Garages for W/T maintenance was introduced.

The personnel actually involved in wireless engineering work by
1934 amounted to ten, clearly insufficient in number to meet the
increasing work loads. Experimental and development work, taking up
a great deal of time, led to the fear that the Met would fall behind other
Forces if manpower remained at such a low level. The Commissioner,
Lord Trenchard, took the matter up the following year with the Acting
Receiver, Lionel Fox, expressing serious concern about the situation.
The middle of the year saw agreement to recruit an additional research
staff of one Grade I Technical Assistant, two electricians and six assistant electricians although they do not appear to have been taken on
immediately.

The engineering staff were so busily employed on the maintenance of
existing facilities that, even during 1936 the backlog of equipment to be
manufactured and experiments to be carried out remained undiminished.
This included the modification of the seven existing transmitters, manufacture of four new transmitters for boats and similar equipment for the
autogyro and the Wireless School. Experiments in respect of short wave
were becoming urgent, however, the view of the Engineer was that they
should not be pursued from New Scotland Yard but delayed until the
opening of the new workshops at West Wickham. Employment of more
engineers proved difficult due to the limited accommodation available at
New Scotland Yard. The Coronation created a great deal of work for
engineers including the production of two mobile transmitters and a
number of items of equipment for public address. Loudspeakers on the
roof of traffic cars for public address were becoming a feature by 1936.

The 1930s saw increasing electrical disturbance making it essential
to remove the Wireless Station to a more suitable site than that at New
Scotland Yard. In 1933/34 tests were carried out to ascertain the suitability of Grove Park (Denmark Hill) for this purpose. Although the
tests in transmission and reception were satisfactory the decision was
to use the site as a receiving station only; operation commenced officially
in May 1936. One of the reasons for restricting this station to receiving
was the proposed Police Regional Wireless Scheme which, if the Force
were to take a proper part, would require separate sites to receive and
transmit. The new receiving station, fitted with the most modern
apparatus of the time, established itself as a centre of much sophisticated

Denmark Hill Wireless Receiving Station, 1936.

research and experimental work in connection with wireless. Built to proportions in excess of those actually required at the time it provided accommodation for the foreseeable future. Tests were undertaken there to ascertain the most suitable site for a new transmitting station. Transmitting continued at Scotland Yard pending the opening of a new transmitter site.

Negotiations had begun in 1935 into the purchase of a site at Layhams Farm, West Wickham, an ideal location for the construction of the transmitting station; the purchase was completed in August 1936. The station, located on high ground to the south of London and built with plenty of space to allow for expansion, was finally opened in May 1937. Designed to provide transmission coverage over a radius of about 30 miles it ensured that the whole of the Metropolitan Police area was within range. There were two transmitters one built by Marconi and the other by the Force engineers. The Coronation of George VI in 1937 was actually controlled with the use of a temporary third transmitter at West Wickham.

The station, operating initially for telegraphy, saw control resting with the Information Room operators at Scotland Yard providing them with much improved communications with vehicles. The old Headquarters Wireless Station at the Yard had served well but London's increasing motor traffic, wireless receivers and electrical apparatus had taken their toll on its efficiency. Equipment had been developed gradually as the need arose and the additional accommodation became essential for the system to improve further.

Experiments, continuing at the transmitting and receiving stations, even led Mr. Watson, a Force Engineer, to take a receiver with him on leave to Scarborough in 1937 involving himself while there in tests with Denmark Hill and Banstead at agreed times of the day. Much work on the interception of foreign stations continued at Denmark Hill with countries including Denmark, Norway, Poland, Estonia and Brazil, being received during the experiments with 30 megacycle equipment. Clearly this was to prove of great value during the war years.

A short wave transmitter, on loan from the Royal Navy, was used for experiments by the Force in 1937.

Mr. Lyell Herdman, who later became a Chief Wireless Technician, on joining the section in December, 1937, recollects the development of radio telephony for car to car communications being carried out at West Wickham, prior to use at the Hendon Driving School. Edgar Brown, involved earlier as a constable, had also joined the engineering staff.

In order to examine the developments in police wireless systems, between 15th and 21st October, 1934, Chief Inspector Best visited various provincial forces on behalf of the Commissioner at the request of the Home Office. The reason for the tour was to examine the feasibility of implementing Police Regional Wireless Schemes throughout the country incorporating groups of forces in common wireless facilities. The Chief Inspector visited Nottingham, Wakefield, Newcastle, Liverpool and

Brighton, forces with wireless in operational use.

Nottingham, since 1930, had operated a two-way telegraphy system between at least nine patrol cars and a central police station. The County Force were to be included in an extension of the system in 1934 with a suggestion that Leicestershire could also take part. Liverpool Police had for a few months been using two-way telegraphy with four mobile stations whereas wireless in Wakefield was very much in the experimental stage. The Tyneside system operated from Newcastle with one-way transmission to one car and three motor cycles. A regional scheme using Philco sets, installed in cars operating in the various forces in the North East (Gateshead, South Shields, Tynemouth, Sunderland, Northumberland and Durham), was already being tried.

Brighton were using pocket sets operationally by September, 1933 which comprised of a receiver and earphone weighing together about four pounds. The sets could not transmit but received messages up to about six miles. Normally about twenty sets were in use by uniform officers on foot, four by C.I.D. officers and three in vehicles.

At this time Nottingham was the most advanced of those provincial forces visited in the use of wireless equipment. England, in Best's view, could easily be divided into between five and seven regional areas which could cover the police forces of the whole country. He felt that a scheme covering London and the Home counties could be introduced as soon as the necessary equipment and trained personnel were available. The counties, with their own receivers and transmitters, would have the ability to receive messages from the Metropolitan Police headquarters. He recommended that, in order to ensure a common wireless procedure throughout the country, a Central Police Training School should be set up in the London area where all proposed police operators would be instructed.

The News of the World of 16th June, 1935 announced the proposals as a new Home Office scheme. The article went on 'When the scheme is in full working order "crooks" will have a thin time, Flying squad cars will prowl along the leafy lanes of rural England as well as the busy streets of industrial towns ready to dash to the scene of the latest crime, whether it be at a lonely country house or at a city office'. The newspaper indicated that the regional wireless centres would be located at London, Manchester, Nottingham, Wakefield, Bristol, Birmingham, Liverpool and Newcastle with each station covering an area of at least 40 miles radius. A certain amount of co-operation between forces in respect of wireless did take place over the succeeding years, but a nationwide regional system did not materialise in the form envisaged.

The Commissioner, Lord Trenchard, expressed his concern about each force developing their own radio instruments independently albeit, with Home Office approval, leading to incompatibility of communication between one force and another. Trenchard believed that all police wireless experimental work should be carried out at one centre with all manufacturers working in accordance with the same specifications.

An idea that his engineers in London should design and manufacture apparatus for the Regional Wireless Schemes in provincial forces was welcomed by Trenchard who considered the locally produced equipment poorly finished and less reliable than that used by the Metropolitan Police. These views were not universally accepted by other forces who often wished to maintain their independence.

HM Signal School at Portsmouth assisted Best by producing a specification for a mobile radio transmitter and receiver for regional police purposes. Some alterations to this specification were recommended by Ian Auchterlonie and A.J. Gill of the Post Office Radio Section and Mr. Robert Watson-Watt of the National Physical Laboratory, Teddington provided valuable advice. In late 1936 Marconi wireless, fitted to Wolseley cars and tested in Manchester and London, was considered by Best to be far less efficient than his Force's equipment.

The Commissioner, willing for Best (by then promoted to Superintendent) to continue giving advice to the Home Office, argued, "his main work is for the Metropolitan Police and to keep them the most efficient Force in the world as regards wireless even though communication cannot be maintained outside owing to the disparity of others". In November, 1936 Best's appointment as Home Office adviser on police and fire brigade communication for the whole country ensured that any information and experience filtered through to the service as a whole and chief officers were advised appropriately on all aspects of communications.

The use of police vehicles to provide a response to calls for assistance gradually increased during the 1920s with the introduction of the Flying Squad and divisional transport. The methods adopted to handle serious incidents prior to the widespread use of motor vehicles by the Force, are illustrated by the problems at Epsom on 17th June 1919 when, at 9.40 p.m., PC Hinton and PC Monk, were called to the 'Rifleman' Beer House in the town where they were faced with a disturbance requiring the premises to be cleared of the rowdy customers. Outside they were forced to arrest one of a number of Canadian soldiers from a nearby army camp, who had been taking part in the incident, and escort him to Epsom Police Station. About fifteen to twenty soldiers followed the officers towards the police station, abusing them as they went, until finally dispersed by other police.

About an hour and a half later the Canadian soldiers from the camp gathered together and headed for the police station seeking to release their colleague. Their approach was heralded by the sounding of a bugle. Fearing serious trouble Inspector Pawley had used the station telephone to contact surrounding stations to secure assistance and then waited for the disorderly mob's arrival.

During the subsequent attack on the station the windows were smashed and the doors and railings seriously damaged; the soldiers entered the cell passage releasing the prisoner by 'jemmying' the cell door. Station Sergeant Green was killed while defending the station.

Inspector Pawley's telephone call to Wandsworth Police Station seeking assistance led Superintendent Boxhall, at that station, to direct that messages be immediately sent to Wandsworth Common, Wimbledon, Malden, Surbiton and Kingston for all available cyclists to be sent to the scene. He then drove himself to Epsom followed soon afterwards by about one hundred men all arriving on bicycles. The affray was already over by the time this aid arrived.

A Police Order of September, 1929 authorised the use of official police transport "in order that prompt and efficient action may be taken in circumstances of urgency, when information, or a request for Police assistance, is received at Stations from Police officers or members of the public'. The station officer was responsible for arranging the attendance of a vehicle in appropriate cases and any car used had to be returned 'at the earliest possible moment'. A constable, able to drive, was posted on reserve duty at the station for such purposes. The list of stations where cars were garaged was published in the Police Order and particulars of all applications for their use had to be forwarded each month to A.3. Branch.

The considerable extension of the Force's fleet of wireless vehicles, beyond the sixteen cars and three vans of the Flying Squad, commenced in 1933 when agreement was reached to fit receiving sets to four 'Q' cars (plain clothes crew) on each of the four Districts. This decision meant that an extensive training programme was necessary to instruct sufficient Morse operators to crew the vehicles. There were by then less ex-service personnel available with the necessary skills. Following the 'Q' cars, approval was given by Lord Trenchard for sixteen Traffic Patrol cars to be fitted with receivers and by 27th July the sixteen 'Q' cars and eight of the traffic cars were complete.

A decision as to the way forward was required particularly whether wireless should be extended to divisional vehicles; the views of Districts were sought. The Superintendent of 'Z' Division commented 'It is necessary to guard against too many cars being fitted with wireless until its worth has been definitely proved in connection with crime'. The Superintendent of 'W' Division, also sceptical of the advantages of a divisional scheme, argued, 'I do not think any good purpose would be served by fitting divisional cars (uniform or C.I.D.) with wireless receivers. These cars are continually in touch with stations and telephone boxes and therefore can promptly be informed of any occurrence calling for immediate action'.

The attendance of a wireless operator on divisional cars covering twenty four hours was considered by the Superintendent 'M' Division to be a 'waste of manpower'. The fitting of divisional cars with wireless was in general opposed by the four District Deputy Assistant Commissioners on the grounds that the vehicles were often not on patrol. They did, however, recommend an increase in the number of Traffic Patrol cars to be fitted with the equipment raising opposition from some quarters that this would lead to the cars' crews concentrating on crime rather than traffic matters with their receiving sets. In agreeing to the provision of receivers on sixteen more such vehicles Trenchard directed that the cars must deal primarily with messages connected with traffic.

The total cost of fitting sixteen 'Q' cars and thirty two traffic cars with wireless amounted to £2,830. Annual maintenance was in the region of £1,200.

'Q' cars were marking up their early successes in that year. At 1.30 a.m. on 30th May a 'Q' car observed a vehicle, containing five suspects, which had been circulated over the wireless, and gave chase at high speed through Camden Town. When stopped four of the five occupants were arrested and the proceeds of a recent robbery were found in the vehicle displaying false index plates. The view expressed, 'This valuable result was directly due to the presence of a wireless equipped fast car' would be repeated many times as the system extended.

The 'F' Division 'Q' car received a wireless message on 12th July, at 1.41 a.m. concerning a man seen with a Bentley car in Kensington. Another message followed indicating that it had been seen leaving a shop in Acton. At 2.40 a.m. the 'Q' car spotted the stolen vehicle and arrested the driver, known by the nickname the 'Demon Bentley Driver', who had been operating in the area for some considerable time, always using stolen Bentleys. Various vehicles were used as 'Q' cars in the pioneering days and included MG tourers, Commer vans, Talbot saloons, Hillman saloons and Ford V8 saloons.

By the closing months of 1933 the Commissioner, convinced that the large number of divisional cars were not being used to their fullest extent, was pursuing his Area Wireless Scheme for divisions. An estimated cost involved in supplying and fitting wireless apparatus to 82 cars, incorporating the necessary alterations, amounted to £3,670 with an additional £300 for gongs, blinds and signs. (Depending on their function, vehicles were fitted with gongs and either 'Police' or 'M.P.' signs in 1933). An additional 186 drivers also required training. A total of 34 Ford tourers, suitable for wireless, were available on divisions, and additonal Ford saloons with fabric bodies were also ordered. The annual maintenance cost was estimated at £2,000 and an additional service van, purchased for the purpose, became available.

On 5th March 1934 Home Office approval was given for the Area Wireless Scheme to commence and on 11th June the scheme went into operation incorporating a new central control room — Information Room.

The Area Wireless Scheme involved dividing the Metropolitan Police District into a total of 52 areas by day and 30 areas by night. In each of these a car fitted with a wireless receiver operated continually. Messages received in Information Room by telephone could be passed immediately to the patrolling vehicles by wireless. The patrol cars, named 'Area Cars' as they are today, were fitted with 'receive only' Morse apparatus built by the Force engineers. The organisation was achieved by dividing the inner and semi outer divisions into eight wireless areas. A, B and C divisions shared a car as did G and E. D, F, H, L, M and N had their own Area Car. The outer divisions were divided into 44 wireless areas each comprising of one sub-division. There was concern that the scheme left less cars avail-

Invicta Police Car 1930s — Fabric suitable for an aerial inside.

Early wireless equipment in use.

able for supervision as many previously allocated for this purpose, had been used to form the new fleet.

The Area Cars were only used between 7 a.m. and 11 p.m. During the night other divisional cars operated covering two sub-divisions on the outer divisions and the same wireless areas on the inner and semi outer divisions. After August, 1935 the main operating period changed to 3 p.m. to 7 a.m. Each car was allotted a separate call sign for example, '6X' would have been the 'X' Divisional car patrolling Harlesden subdivision. Although the cars were subject to control from Information Room they formed part of the divisional organisation with the intention that they should patrol where crime was likely to be committed on their own area. The instruction 'Orders for Crews of Wireless Cars Operating in the Area Wireless Scheme' stated, 'The primary duty of these cars is the prevention and detection of crime in the Areas to which they are allotted'.

The cars were crewed initially by a driver and a wireless operator, although experience later proved that an observer was also required as the W/T operator had little time away from his continually busy wireless. All messages were numbered and any missed were obtained by telephoning Information Room. A rota, intended to ensure that at least half of the Force's fleet was on the road all the time, had to be strictly complied with. Information Room had to be kept informed regarding any variations in the refreshment times allocated to the crew. Information received by the cars had also to be passed on to officers patrolling on foot or bicycle. The Commissioner's Report of 1934 reported a total of 821 arrests as a result of the new scheme. Clearly the new Area Cars were proving to be an effective crime fighting force.

The transmitter at the Wireless Station had sent out on average thirty messages each day to vehicles in 1933. Clearly this would be insufficient work to justify the maintenance of a much enlarged wireless fleet. A new arrangement for the dissemination of relevant information and the co-ordination of the fleet was necessary. As indicated above, in conjunction with the new scheme, the Information Room and Operation Map Room were formalised on 11th June. The Daily Herald announced the event with a very short article headed — 'Non-stop Patrol of London — 52 Radio Police cars on duty'.

Initially two additional telephone lines, which were wired into Telegraph Office for use during major operations, were connected up and formed a temporary Information Room. This control room, where information is 'collected, sifted and sent out as necessary', has been relocated and modernised over the years but still retaining the same name and basic function. The Headquarters Wireless Station continued to operate with its own special responsibilities at Scotland Yard and subsequently at Denmark Hill until 1950.

A pamphlet headed 'Dissemination of Information', circulated to the Force, to explain the new system commented, 'Experience has amply proved that the speedy and accurate transmission of information concerning crimes and criminals has become a vital necessity in dealing with the

Early wireless equipment in use.

Harold Charles Kenworthy, (sitting with wireless) Thomas George Cole
(4th. left standing) at Epsom 1930.

modern criminal.

Police may have at their disposal the fastest cars, ablest drivers on the roads, but if our method of forwarding information is defective our efforts are not likely to be successful.'

Instructions for wireless operators were published and took effect from 1st October, 1934. These instructions included an order that messages were to be repeated 15 minutes after the original transmission and, in the case of urgent messages, after five minutes. In vehicles, where wireless transmitters were not carried, the operators had to acknowledge receipt of a message by stopping and telephoning Information Room as soon as possible. The index numbers of outstanding stolen motor vehicles were transmitted to police vehicles at 0715, 1015, 1515 and 2330 daily.

The 'Wireless Telegraph Procedures and Operating Tables' were completely revised and replaced by the 'Wireless Procedure and Code Book' in January, 1935 and a copy issued to each wireless telegraphy operator. This book provided operators with their authorised codes and abbreviations for use when sending and receiving messages. The prefix X followed by a number would be used to convey regularly used phrases and instructions.

Some examples are

X12	Approach with caution
X19	Assistance, foot PC at . . . . requires immediate
X40	Burglar alarm ringing
X64	Counterfeit coins attempting to utter
X108	Escaped from Borstal Institute
X223	Interrogate carefully of friend
X441	H.M. The King
X455	Signals, your, are weak and fading
X460	Smash and grab

The book also gave codes for telephone exchanges and police stations.

A time signal, transmitted to wireless vehicles each hour or half an hour if wireless traffic was light, indicated to operators that they were still receiving. Messages received by vehicles were recorded by the operator in a Telephone Message Book and he included the time of origin and serial number of each. On completion the books were forwarded to the Headquarters Wireless Station for checking and retention.

By 1935 District Commanders were requesting additions to their Area Car fleets with a suggestion that additional crewed cars should be made available centrally to patrol crime black spots. At this time the Force were using Hillman Sixteen tourers, Hillman 20/70 saloons and Ford V-8 Forder saloons.

In February, 1936 a review of the cars operating under the Area Wireless Scheme found the Ford chassis and body unsuitable for the work.

Due to the amount of strain placed upon the cars a large number of mechanical breakdowns were occurring leading to an agreement that the Ford would be substituted by a Hillman 17hp vehicle with a saloon body. Twenty more vehicles were added to the area wireless fleet providing more even coverage throughout the 24 hours.

By 1937 the crew of an Area Wireless Car generally consisted of the driver, an observer sitting in the front and the wireless operator receiving messages, with a headset, on equipment fitted in the back of the car. By the end of that year experiments were underway with loudspeaker units in selected Area Cars on each District. Four of their Model 821 police car loudspeaker receivers, already in use by a number of northern forces, were offered free of charge by Philco Ltd. for evaluation. Although it was suggested that telephony should be used the speakers were in fact evaluated with W/T. Phillips and Marconi were also approached, although a previous trial of Marconi's equipment had proved unsatisfactory.

On 29th September, Superintendent Best and Chief Inspector Fallon tested the Philco and Phillips apparatus. During October/November nine Area Cars were fitted with loudspeakers (four semi-inner and five outer division vehicles). Four vehicles (Call signs 6B, 6M, 7X and 7J) were proposed for installation of the Philco sets, one vehicle (Call sign 7S) for a Phillips set and the Metropolitan Police loudspeakers were recommended for four (Call signs 5D, 6G, 7V and 7R).

The Philco equipment produced far too high a signal and, after being fitted to one car, was removed after two days. The Phillips set also proved unsatisfactory. The loudspeakers built by the Metropolitan Police engineers were the most efficient showing the possible advantages over headsets of improved reception, less outside interference, a unit less obvious to the public, more freedom of movement for the operator and the removal of headset discomfort.

During the evaluation the crews were reduced to a driver and W/T operator which was generally felt to be satisfactory, except during busy periods (4 p.m. to midnight) when the reintroduction of the observer was considered necessary. The trials resulted in a decision not to extend the use of loudspeakers until their suitability for use with radio telephony had been proved.

By 1936 Traffic Patrol were still operating eight wireless cars per District each crewed by a wireless operator and two other officers. The types of messages sent to these vehicles were generally in relation to vehicles being driven in a dangerous manner or where the driver was believed to be under the influence of drink in addition to accidents, traffic obstruction and stolen vehicle messages.

The Thames Division fleet consisted in 1933 of three large boats used by the Chief Inspector and the sub divisional Inspectors at Wapping and Blackwall. There were a total of twenty-eight open motor boats of three varieties based at the five stations. Albeit without W/T, communication from boat crews to the police stations proved relatively easy during the day time when officers could land at a wharf or pier and request the use of private telephones. At night, however, landing places were fewer and telephones not so readily available. The biggest problem, communicating from the police station to the boats, placed reliance upon the goodwill of the wharf managers and pier masters to intercept the boats and ask the officer in charge to telephone the station. This assistance did not always prevail. A police boat could often be patrolling in the vicinity of a serious incident and, due to lack of adequate communication, the crew would have no knowledge of it.

Chief Inspector Dalton, in charge of the Thames Division at Wapping, set out a clear requirement for W/T to be installed in his report submitted in January 1933, and in June boats with temporary equipment were used at the Greenwich Pageant. Although wireless communication with the boats had been considered as early as 1927 the equipment at that time turned out to be insufficiently well developed to be suitable. The Chief Inspector's report stated that the area between Barking Creek and Wandsworth Bridge required efficient communication as a priority being the busiest part of the River.

In 1933, two new cabin boats were under construction with Home Office approval given in January, the following year, for the installation of transmitting and receiving equipment on these two vessels. In addition authority was given to fit receiving sets on four of the existing supervision boats. The total estimated expenditure reached £480. The installation of the equipment, built by Metropolitan Police engineers, saw completion in one of the cabin boats on 24th October, 1934 and the other on 23rd January 1935. Four receiving sets were built and six small launches were wired to take the equipment. After an expression of concern about the weight of the transmitting apparatus it was agreed that, in one of the boats, the framework for mounting the equipment would be of Duralumin instead of the normal brass. Although not liable to corrosion the brass fitting weighed seventy pounds.

The noise from the engine created difficulty in reception of messages and the fumes caused a great deal of discomfort for operators. On the open boats with receiving sets only the weather and spray caused problems only overcome to a degree by fitting canopies.

The wireless operator, also employed as deck hand on the boat, could not use headphones and relied upon the loudspeaker reception which proved difficult due to the engine noise. Breakdowns in equipment were prevalent in the early days as a result of the vibration and bumping to which the boats were subjected; they were regularly out of service for repair, placing a strain on efficiency.

Between February and October 1935, 28 messages were transmitted by Thames boats and 150 concerning Thames Division only were received. The following year approval was given for the fitting of two way equipment in four additional large launches and receive only sets in two smaller launches. Wireless communication with boats, gradually extended to cover the section from Wandsworth Bridge to Teddington Lock, avoiding the necessity for a police officer, patrolling by the river, to call the boat

Receiving the 999 calls in Information Room.

to the river bank to pass an important message to the crew.

The Information Room proper, replacing the temporary arrangement, was to be accommodated in Room 210A linked by four separate telephone lines wired from the exchange. (Ex-Police Constable Harold Langton remembers working in this second floor room). Once completed the lines in Telegraph Office reverted to their original use. Before the Area Wireless Scheme commenced a remote control circuit, for transmission and reception from the Wireless Station in Scotland House, was connected to Room 211. Chief Inspector Best expressed his concern that the batteries supplying the existing transmitter would not be able to cope with the increase in 'transmitting time'. The solution was either the installation of a duplicate battery or adaption to AC mains.

The new Force control room required an adequate staffing structure to meet the anticipated demand for the service from police stations, the public and the vastly increased wireless fleet. The telephone was to be the important feature in the receipt of information and in early June the following officers were transferred to D1 Branch to prepare for operating the new system:-

PC.118795 REGAN	(458A — 167 'CO')
PC.119219 EGERTON	(612A — 170 'CO')
PC.116694 PAULL	(579B — 171 'CO')
PC.116342 PUCKEY	(403C — 172 'CO')
PC.107722 BATCH	(227L — 173 'CO')
PC.107228 RANDS	(551M — 174 'CO')
PC.114581 COOK	(701M — 176 'CO')
PC.109803 CARTER	(— 180 'CO') (not confirmed)

Inspector Tom Fallon, posted to the Communications Branch on 4th June, took command of the new unit and an authorised establishment of four 1st Class Detective Sergeants to supervise the reliefs. The first four to take up these positions appear to have been PS (1st Class CID) Gillan, PS (2nd Class CID) Stevens, PS (1st Class CID) Barratt and PS (2nd Class CID) Tarr who were transferred to D.1. Branch on 1st June. On 16th July the initial team of one Inspector, four C.I.D. sergeants and eight constables were transferred onto the establishment of A.2. Branch.

Throughout 1934 and 1935 the staffing levels in the Branch increased and PC Fletcher, currently serving at Edmonton, recollects being told by his grandfather, PC 109219 Frank Jacob, that he received his posting to Information Room in November, 1934 due to his skills in clear handwriting. In May 1935 the number of constables totalled forty three employed as follows:-

HQ Wireless Station	—	19 W/T operators
Information Room	—	8 W/T operators
Information Room	—	10 telephonists

Telegraph Office   —   6 operators

Of the nineteen W/T operators attached to the HQ Wireless Station eleven were engaged on special monitoring work also carried out at Denmark Hill.

The W/T operators on the Flying Squad vehicles and divisional 'Q' cars were financially better off, with five shillings each week commuted overtime and a further five shillings plain clothes allowance, than their counterparts in the Wireless Stations and Information Room.   This anomaly was put right in October when the Home Office gave approval to pay the aggrieved the five shillings allowance.   Additionally the telephone operators in Information Room and Telegraph Office were granted a three shilling per week allowance.

Harold Langton, employed as a constable in Information Room in 1935, recollects four reliefs (Early, Late, Night and Relieving) each under a detective sergeant.   He remembers that such officers as Reg Spooner, Guy Mahon, Tom Hayward and Jim Callaghan, who later rose to senior ranks in the C.I.D., were involved in the early years.   Langton states that each of the four reliefs provided three telephonists to receive incoming information and deal with other telephone matters and two W/T operators one of whom acted as a telephonist when not on the 'key'.   Constables Banfield, Livett, Filkin, Stevens, Smith and Henry are recollected by him as being some of the early W/T operators in the Information Room.

The status of the officers in charge of reliefs had changed from C.I.D. sergeants to uniform Inspectors by 1937.   At one stage there was a short lived inter-change scheme and as a result C.I.D. sergeants on promotion became uniformed Inspectors.

Information Room's incoming and outgoing messages were recorded in manuscript in the large Telegraph Book and on the first day at 8.52 in the evening an Armstrong Siddeley, which had been circulated as a suspect vehicle, was stopped after a chase in Peckham by a 'Q' car.   The following day the crew of 'Q' car call sign Z'Q' arrested a thief in possession of an MG tourer stolen from Chichele Road, NW2 after circulation by wireless to all cars.   On 20th June an early Area Car success was clocked up by 7'T' with the detention of a man for the abduction of a five year old girl following the circulation over the W/T of his description.

The four separate table top maps, initially covered with cellophane paper, soon required hard wearing celluloid.   The fifty two Area Cars, signified by circular plotting marking pieces, the sixteen 'Q' cars by square markers and the thirty two traffic cars by triangular markers were moved around the maps of London indicating their availability.   In 1937 further shaped tokens were introduced to signify the seven Thames vessels and the City Police vehicle.

Plotting involved selecting the following indications of vehicle status:-

| a. | Normal Patrol | — Token lying flat, call sign uppermost, |
| b. | On 'assignment' | — As above with red ring surrounding token. |

c.	At Refreshment	— Token lying flat white bar uppermost.
d.	Out of Action (available by telephone)	— Token lying flat surrounded by white ring.
e.	Out of Action (Not available for assignment owing to mechanical fault or other causes)	— Token lying flat surrounded by black ring.

Langton describes the early days in Information Room. "It was the duty of one of the telephonists who ran the daily log to keep the tables up to date by adding tokens representing wireless cars as they came on duty, by turning them over during 'refreshments', etc."

In January, 1935 Best reported that the telephone communications in Information Room were not at all satisfactory with the operators being unable to differentiate between the calling buzzers which identified the line being called. A revision of the equipment incorporated four lines for normal information purposes and additional separate single lines for the sergeant and the supervising Inspector. Three of the normal lines were fitted with headphones and breast transmitters and the remainder with hand microphones. 'Light' calling signals ensured that the line being called could be easily identified. The lines also appeared on the sergeant's switchboard allowing him to supervise properly and cut in on any line if he wished.

In January, 1936 Information Room featured in the BBC radio programme 'Let's go somewhere'. The script for this broadcast, which took place in the Room, describes, 'the long desk containing telephones above which a light appears and one of the police operators answers the call. The police operator receiving the call writes it down as shortly as possible and then takes it across to the wireless operator who sends it out by Morse'. It goes on to describe how the messages also go out by teleprinter to twenty two divisional stations.

The script continues 'the Information Room has four low tables which contain a map of the whole of the MPD. There are passageways between the tables to allow access to any part of the map in order that tokens of different shapes signalling different types of police car on patrol can be placed thereon. Police launches fitted with wireless are also represented by tokens'.

The introduction of the Information Room, with access to far more vehicles by wireless, clearly required a more efficient method for the public to pass urgent information to the police.

A Police Order of 13th March, 1929 had instructed officers to telephone to C.1. Branch at Scotland Yard any information which led them to suspect that persons using motor vehicles had committed crimes. This enabled wireless messages to be sent to Flying Squad vehicles from the Wireless Station. Observed more widely than anticipated a variety of messages were passed to the Yard for transmission by this method.

The first permanent Information Room, New Scotland Yard, 1934 — Map tables in the foreground.

The receipt of information from the public generally centred on the police stations. A variety of methods were available for gaining assistance in respect of crime and suspects or other urgent matters. A person could call at the station personally or notify the constable on the beat of the problem, methods used since 1829, or possibly use one of the new police boxes to make contact with the police station by telephone.

With the great increases in the number of private subscribers and public kiosks the telephone became the more popular and efficient means of communication. As the number of automatic telephone exchanges increased the public were advised, through the telephone directories, from November 1927, that to gain the assistance of the emergency services they should — 'Dial 'O'. When the Exchange Operator answers give your telephone number and ask for the Fire Brigade, Ambulance or Police as the case may be'. A request for the police would be connected to a police station. In a high percentage of instances calls would be made by the member of the public dialling the station telephone number direct; often police stations would for ease of memory be allocated the number '1111' following the code. A change, in the mid-1930s, to '1113' proved necessary for technical reasons.

When Information Room commenced operation in 1934 the public were not encouraged to telephone there direct. A person who required the police continued to contact the local station where the information would be carefully considered and, if suitable, passed on to the new control room normally by use of the renowned number 'WHItehall' 1212. Consideration had initially been given to advising the public to telephone Information Room direct but a fear that the centre would be flooded with 'useless information' led to the decision against this. Officers at police stations were directed to forward any matters which 'might be useful to officers patrolling elsewhere: either in motor cars, on cycles or on foot'. 'Scanty or vague details of an alleged crime which could not possibly be used with success' were viewed as unsuitable for Information Room.

By early 1935 three important observations became clear —

'a. the public did not readily ring their nearest police station because they had not been educated to do so or they did not know the number and made little effort to find it out.

b. Valuable time was lost by the public telephoning the police station as the information had to be passed on from there to Information Room.

c. That practically all information given by the public to the police stations was, in fact, passed on to Information Room. This clearly meant that direct contact by the public would not place any higher workload on the Room.'

The feeling of senior officers that more arrests would be made for crime if the public were encouraged to ring direct led to a new procedure being adopted.

In October, a pamphlet entitled "Use the Telephone to Help the Police Help You', was distributed with telephone accounts to all subscribers in the London Telephone Area. It advised them to report urgent information in respect of crimes direct to Information Room using 'WHItehall 1212'. After circulation of the notice direct calls increased with November, December 1935 and January 1936 experiencing 258, 288 and 207 respectively, compared with August and September 1935 when such calls only reached 72 and 85.

The press announced the new system with enthusiasm. The Times of 5th October headed its article 'New scheme to combat crime' — 'Use the Telephone to Help the Police' and the Evening News report of 7th October, stated 'If you see a Crime, Telephone to the 'Yard' — a police car will soon be there'. The article went on, 'Someone may ring up and say that a smash and grab raid is taking place in, say, Shaftesbury Avenue. Within a few seconds Information Room has sent the nearest police car racing to the scene'. Certainly this direct and much more immediate contact by the public with Information Room reduced those valuable minutes wasted previously in passing the information, albeit through a normal exchange line.

A more efficient means of contacting the emergency services rapidly rather than using an exchange number or dialling 'O' through the operator needed to be found. Could 'Nine, Nine, Nine' finally achieve John Fielding's plan of 1753 for his Thief taker's at Bow Street — 'quick notice and sudden pursuit'? Certainly it would provide the public with a sense of security, knowing that obtaining the assistance of the Police, Fire Brigade and Ambulance only required those three dialled digits.

As is normal a disaster of some description was needed before the authorities would be prompted into actually improving the method for the public to summon assistance. This duly occurred in Wimpole Street during a night in November, 1935 when five women died in a fire at a doctor's house; the brigade arrived before an answer could be obtained by a neighbour attempting to contact the telephone exchange operator. Although an enquiry revealed that the small number of operators on duty at the exchange were actually tied up dealing with a number of similar calls about the incident, and had, in fact, called the fire brigade, a requirement for the operators to be able to identify immediately an urgent incoming call was identified. A system, whereby such a call would go to the 'top of the queue' as a priority over normal dialled 'O' calls, seemed to be the answer.

The incident led to the setting up of a Parliamentary Committee, the Belgrave Committee, to examine the problem and come up with a solution. During 1936 the Post Office, in co-operation with police, experimented in London with 'emergency' calls into the exchanges from various parts of the capital. A test caller dialling 'O' would ask for the police and thereby secure a connection with the local police station. In the same year the Post Office made their proposals for the introduction of a special three figure number to be dialled when the emergency services were required urgently. The exchange operator would be made aware by a special signal that the incoming call required emergency action.

The Post Office were of the view that members of the public making calls on the new number should be connected to the local police station. They indicated this would prove quicker than directing calls to 'WHItehall' 1212 by not involving the operator in dialling and possible intermediate switching. In addition the Post Office expressed concern that a sudden rush of calls to the WHItehall automatic exchange on 1212 would result in other subscribers with numbers commencing with '12' receiving the engaged signal.

The views of the Force were contrary to those of the Post Office with Superintendent Best indicating why all urgent calls should be connected to Information Room. Switchboards at police stations were not always staffed by full time professional operators which Best considered could lead to delays in answering. In the case of a station, other than a divisional headquarters station, no direct line to Scotland Yard existed to easily pass a call on to Information Room for the wireless car. Many stations only had one exchange line which, if engaged, would delay the exchange operator connecting the caller.

There was an unaccepted suggestion that calls for police received from the public dialling 'O' should be connected to the station and those on the emergency line to Information Room. One problem which confronted the Force involved the City of London Police as it would often not be possible for the Post Office operators to distinguish between those calls for the City and those for the Metropolitan Force area. This required discussion between the two Forces.

The Superintendent, opposed to discarding the number, WHItehall 1212, recommended that five new exchange lines should be fitted direct into Information Room for the emergency calls from exchanges. He suggested that some of the seven extensions from the Scotland Yard switchboard into the Information Room could then be surrendered. Concern expressed about the ability of existing staff to handle the anticipated rise in telephone calls led Best to seek an increase in the number of telephonists from sixteen officers to twenty eight. The Commissioner, Sir Philip Game, concerned about cost, did not receive the request favourably.

Before deciding upon the procedure to be adopted by the Force in respect of the new system the Commissioner asked for further information about the number of emergency calls at that time being made by the public. During a period of six months in 1936, 91,604 calls had been made, 56, 724 of which were for the police and the remainder for the ambulance or fire brigade. (4569 of these calls were directed to WHItehall 1212). Information Room, was, at that time, receiving an average overall total of 8,000 calls each month.

A great deal of discussion took place between the Home Office, Post Office and police in connection with the emergency lines. The Commissioner originally favoured a system whereby the caller who dialled the

999 attracted many press articles in 1937.

SHE IS FIRST TO DIAL 999

Arrest Follows

Mr. Stanley Beard, of Elsworthy-road, Hampstead, heard a noise outside his house at 4.20 a.m., and, on looking out, saw a man's foot.

His wife immediately dialled the new emergency number "999" and asked for "police." Seconds later radio patrol cars raced to the spot. Four minutes later a man was detained by the police near Primrose Hill.

Later in the day Thomas Duffy (24), labourer, was charged at Marylebone Police Court with attempting to break into the house, and was remanded in custody.

Dial- 999 If Your Call Is Urgent

SIR WALTER WOMERSLEY, the Assistant Postmaster-general, announced in the House of Commons to-day that technical arrangements are complete, so far as London is concerned, by which a telephone subscriber or a call office user may dial 999 as a special signal indicating to the exchange operator that the call must receive immediate attention.

Such a call might be made free of charge from a call office.

"I would strongly emphasise," Sir Walter said, "that the No. 999 should be dialled only when the fire brigade, police or ambulance' is needed in circumstances of real emergency, otherwise the whole purpose of the arrangement may be defeated.

"It will, until further experience has been gained, be in operation in London only."

Sir Walter added that the arrangement related to all automatic exchanges in London except those few where the telephones did not bear letters as well as figures on the dials.

EMERGENCY TELEPHONE CALLS

"999" IN OPERATION

The new emergency telephone call "999" came into operation yesterday. Until some experience has been gained it will be operative only in London, where it applies only to automatic telephones of subscribers and in public call offices which have letters as well as figures on the dial.

Special equipment that has been installed at automatic exchanges in London ensures that when 999 is dialled an emergency lamp and buzzer at the exchange indicate to the operator that the call is specially urgent. In each exchange the telephone numbers of the Fire Brigade, Police Station, and Ambulance station are prominently displayed. The exchange operator answers the 999 call by saying "Emergency—which service, please?" The caller should then reply "Fire," "Police," or "Ambulance" as the case may be, and will be connected with the service required.

WHEN CALLER IS SILENT

If the operator receives no reply from a caller who has dialled 999, the police station will be notified of the call. This will be done on the assumption that the call has been made by someone who has been able to dial 999 but can manage nothing more, as, for example, in the case of a caller overcome by the fumes of a fire, the violence of a burglar, or unconsciousness in sudden illness.

The number 999 has been selected as the only practicable number after careful examination of technical and other considerations. It must, of course, only be dialled in circumstances of real emergency when the Fire Brigade, Police, or ambulance is needed. The average number of emergency calls received in a week in London is 2,400 police calls, 1,200 ambulance calls, and 250 fire calls.

RAILWAY RELICS

BOY OF 13 DIALS "999" & SAVES FACTORY

A HUNDRED firemen and 20 fire engines raced to answer the call of a 13-year-old boy who dialled "999" last night.

His prompt action saved what might have been a serious fire—houses surrounded the factory involved.

He was Gordon Sims, of Burghley Road, Tufnell Park. When he was going to bed he saw a light in the factory of Acme Productions, Ltd., furniture manufacturers, of Fortess Road.

Jumping out of bed, he dashed to the nearest telephone and dialled "999."

When the brigade arrived the whole of the premises were ablaze. Gordon told the News Chronicle: "I just saw a little point of light at first. It then burst up quickly, till it was like a bonfire."

999 TAKES 2d. ON ACCOUNT

MR. HARRY DAY, M.P., hasn't finished with the Postmaster-General yet. He returns to the charge to-day about people trying to call the fire brigade on the phone and finding they have to put 2d. in the slot.

On Monday Major Tryon laughed Mr. Day's question off, hoped that publicity would "prevent any similar disaster"—such as emergency callers being unable to find two pennies at the crucial moment. Press the emergency button, he said, or dial 999.

But the last laugh is going to be with Mr. Day.

"Is the Postmaster-General aware," he is going to ask, "that notices have been erected recently in public telephone kiosks in the Post Office in Great Cumberland-place, W.1, with the following wording appearing:

"Emergency Calls; place two pennies in the slot; ask Exchange for FIRE, POLICE, AMBULANCE; No number required.

"And in view of the fact that it is impossible to obtain any reply until the coins have been placed in the coin box, will he consider having the telephone kiosks and other similar telephone boxes, in thickly populated and important areas, fitted with emergency buttons?"

When this matter was brought to the attention of the Post Office by the "Daily Herald," the only answer was: "We don't believe any such notice exists. . . . Why not go and see for yourself?"

A "Daily Herald" reporter did go and see for himself and found Mr. Day is quite right.

The notices are there—and there are no emergency buttons.

three figure number would either say to the operator 'Police' or 'Police Urgent'. With the former he would be connected to the station and the latter to Information Room. The Post Office opposed this as the service provided an urgent call facility only.

The emergency number finally agreed, '999', operated initially only as a trial in London, the first service of this kind in the world. The dialling of the number caused an alarm to sound in the exchange and lights to flash leading the operator to handle the call immediately. A decision on three figures was purely for technical reasons in London. Using the same digits meant they were easily remembered and, situated at one end of the dial they could be located readily in smoke for instance. Although '111' would have taken less time to dial it was liable to be set off accidently by faulty equipment or persons tapping the handset. '222' could not be used being identical to the code for the ABBey Exchange and '000' would have achieved a connection by the normal method 'O'. The new 'Button A and B' coin boxes, introduced in 1936, were relatively simple technically to convert to allow the dialling of '999' without requiring coins to be inserted.

The Post Office considered that once the new emergency system came into operation members of the public attempting to contact the police by dialling '0' should be given the telephone number of the police station to call themselves. However, the public using this code continued to be passed direct to police for some considerable time. The cost of emergency calls from outer areas (which could be up to four pence) to Scotland Yard required consideration and a flat rate of a penny throughout London was agreed. Calls from public kiosks were free. The service, opened initially at 91 automatic exchanges, soon became permanent. It did not operate outside London until 1938 when Glasgow adopted the system.

By December, 1936 the Commissioner of the City of London Police had agreed that all calls in his Force area would be passed to Information Room. The Forces also agreed wireless co-operation, implemented in March, 1937.

The Assistant Postmaster General, Sir Walter Womersley, announced in the House of Commons on 30th June that the technical arrangements were complete for the introduction of the new system saying, 'I would strongly emphasise that the number 999 should be dialled only when the fire brigade, police or ambulance are needed in circumstances of real emergency, otherwise the whole purpose of the arrangement may be defeated'.

The Times announced the arrival of 999 on 1st July, 1937 which, for technical reasons, could not initially be routed to Information Room. Calls on this number and those from members of the public dialling 'O' continued to be passed to police stations. An article in the Daily Sketch of 8th July claimed the first 999 call to be at 4.20 a.m. from 33 Elsworthy Road, Hampstead where a burglar, Thomas Duffy, had been disturbed by John Stanley Beard, the occupier. While Mrs. Beard dialled

EMERGENCY CALLS FOR "FIRE", "POLICE", "AMBULANCE", DIAL "999"

Dear Sir/Madam,

A new procedure is being introduced at your exchange to enable you, by dialling "999," to secure the special attention of the operator for calls to the Fire Service, Police or Ambulance Authorities on occasions of emergency. For this purpose, special equipment has been installed at the exchange so that, when "999" is dialled, an emergency lamp and loud buzzer will indicate to the operator that the call is specially urgent. The telephone numbers of the Fire, Police and Ambulance Authorities are prominently displayed for the information of the operators and connection with these authorities will be secured by simply asking the exchange operator for "Fire!", "Police!" or "Ambulance!" as the case may be.

In your own and in the public interest you are asked to make yourself and regular users of your telephone installation familiar with the new arrangement.

The number "999" has been chosen for this purpose as the only practicable number after very careful examination of the technical and other considerations involved.

You can of course still obtain the operator by dialling "0." Instead of "999" if you so choose, but the operator will have no means of knowing that the call relates to an emergency and, in time of pressure, would not therefore give it precedence over other calls which might be claiming attention.

It cannot be too strongly emphasised that the number "999" should be dialled only when the Fire, Police or Ambulance Service is needed in circumstances of real emergency and never for any other purpose whatsoever.

Information about the "999" service will be included in the telephone directory in due course. Meanwhile, you are advised to place this letter inside the cover of your directory. Perhaps you will also be so good as to insert the number "999" instead of "0" in any records which you may now be showing that "0" should be dialled to call the public exchange for emergency calls to the Fire Service, etc.

A Post Office representative will call on existing subscribers as soon as the labour position permits for the purpose of replacing the paper label on the telephone dial by a new label drawing prominent attention to the new "999" service.

TO CALL FIRE! POLICE! AMBULANCE - BY DIALLING "999"

1. Lift Receiver.
2. Listen for Dialling Tone.
3. Dial "999." The receiver rest must not be touched after dialling. A method of dialling "999" in darkness or in smoke is shown below.
4. When the operator answers say "Fire," "Police," or "Ambulance," as the case may be.
5. Give the operator the number of the telephone from which you are speaking.
6. Remain at the telephone until the Fire, Police or Ambulance Authority replies.
7. Give the precise address at which its services are needed and any other necessary particulars.

On receipt of the demand "Fire" the operator will effect connection with the appropriate Fire Station. On calls to "Police" and "Ambulance" the operator may ask you for the name of the Authority serving your premises and if this information can readily be given it will greatly assist in the speedy connection of your call. You are advised therefore to ascertain these particulars and to display them prominently near your telephone.

If you are using a dial telephone with which a coin box is associated you should not insert coins in respect of a call obtained by dialling "999."

HOW TO DIAL "999" IN DARKNESS OR IN SMOKE

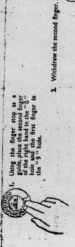

1. Using the finger stop as a guide, place the second finger of the right hand in the "0" hole and the first finger in the "9" hole.
2. Withdraw the second finger.
3. Then dial "9" with the first finger.
4. Then lift finger and let the dial return to normal position.
5. Repeat these operations twice more.

Figures only are shown against the holes in the telephone dial illustrated above. The instructions apply equally however to subscribers with telephone dials showing letters as well as figures.

A595

Information to telephone subscribers.

999 the husband gave chase. The rapidly connected call to the local police led, within five minutes, to Duffy's arrest.

Letters from readers disputed the Beards' claim to being the first 999 callers. Mrs. Wheal of Berkeley Street, W1, stated that she had used the number after a burglary on the 3rd July and another quoted instance described a subscriber using the system on 2nd July at 11.30 p.m. It will never be definitely ascertained who made the first call, but during the first week, 1336 people dialled 999 of which 1073 calls were genuine. Some subscribers were alleged to have abused the system for merely obtaining the services of the operator quickly.

Further meetings were held between representatives from the City and Metropolitan Forces and the Post Office to finalise the introduction of the routing of all emergency calls to Information Room. There was agreement that the introduction should be immediately preceded by pamphlets delivered to all subscribers. Five new exchange lines (WHItehall 4321), the number of which would not be published, for incoming traffic were installed in Information Room to replace five existing extensions from the Scotland Yard Private Branch Exchange (PBX). The five remaining extensions were left as 'overflow' lines. Four additional extensions from the PBX were installed at the Inspector's table, the loggist's table and the remaining two at telephonist positions for outgoing calls.

The Post Office were concerned that the new emergency system should only be implemented if sufficient equipment and staff were available to deal with the calls as delays in answering would result in some blame being attached to them. In the case of calls from outer areas a delay of 30 seconds was likely anyway.

The 29th November, 1937 at 8 a.m. heralded the arrival of routing 999 calls to Information Room (whether the caller asked for the local

lated to all subscribers. Initially the emergency number operated only within 12½ miles of Oxford Circus. On the first day of operation Information Room was overwhelmed with calls and, as a temporary measure, the Post Office agreed to interrogate callers to ascertain the urgency of their information. The Evening News of 30th November advised callers "Only dial 999 if the matter is urgent; if, for instance, the man in the flat next to yours is murdering his wife or you have seen a heavily masked cat burglar feeling round the stack pipe of the local bank building. If the matter is less urgent, if you have lost little Towser or a lorry has come to rest in your front garden, just call up the local police".

999 continued to attract numerous press articles praising its efficiency or advising the public against abuse. The Daily Express of 30th November announcing the direct routing to Scotland Yard stated that on the first day there were '100 facetious and minor complaints such as 'There's a man playing bagpipes outside the house', and 'There's a cat up a tree and it can't get down'. Unfortunately fifty years on many members of the public still view their minor problems as an emergency

for 999 to handle.

The number of calls received in Information Room in 1937 totalled 130,898 compared with 102,130 in 1936. The number of arrests by crews of wireless vehicles in 1937 reached 3,477 which included 671 motor car thieves and 320 for house or shop breaking.

The exchange operators were still vetting calls in 1938 and of 836 received over the 999 system during one week in January only 65.8% were passed to Information Room. Emergency calls were still being received from subscribers dialling '0' of which 28.5% were passed to Information Room. The 999 system remained unavailable for connection to the manual exchanges from where a high percentage of calls were received.

The Post Office soon became concerned about their staff filtering calls which they felt merely caused delay. The Information Room shift of four telephonists, clearly unable to cope then with the increased telephone traffic, would have an even greater problem when the Post Office stopped interrogating callers. The work load meant that police staff had to forego their refreshments or ate their meals whilst handling incoming calls. To quote Chief Inspector Fallon when writing about his men, 'A keener body of men than the Information Room staff would be difficult to find'.

The total establishment of four Inspectors, eight wireless telegraphy operators and sixteen telephonists divided into three working reliefs 8 a.m. to 4 p.m., 4 p.m. to midnight and midnight to 8 a.m. needed review. The additional Inspector, two telegraphists and four telephonists then available merely provided relieving capacity. To cover the busy period between 10 p.m. to midnight two of the night duty telephonists were brought on early. The Commissioner finally agreed to increase the establishment by four constables and a clerical assistant.

In May, 1938 the exchanges ceased interrogating persons making calls on the 999 system but they continued to vet calls received via the code '0' until the following year. These changes resulted in the feared greater work load for the police operators. Information Room and its association with the receipt of emergency calls remains today. In the fifty years that have passed 999s have continued to be received 24 hours a day in ever increasing numbers.

Co-operation with the Essex County Constabulary in respect of wireless commenced in 1936 when a number of their vehicles were fitted with receiving equipment purchased from the Metropolitan Police. The call sign GWZ was issued to Essex cars followed by an individual number for each, and messages for transmission to these vehicles were intially telephoned to WHItehall 1212 — Information Room. Log Books, supplied by the Met for use by the County operators, were returned on completion to the officer in charge of communications at New Scotland Yard for checking and subsequent return to the Essex Police. A number of constables from that Force were trained at the Hendon Wireless School.

On occasions, cases involving motor vehicles concerned in crime, occurred outside the Metropolitan Police District where it was suspected that the criminals were heading for London. Lack of publicity found county forces unaware of the existence of Information Room, consequently Police Gazette of 29th May, 1936 drew attention to the value of passing appropriate information to WHItehall 1212 for transmission to patrolling cars.

In April 1936 the Assistant Commissioner 'D' Department wrote to the Chief Officer of the London Fire Brigade agreeing to provide a wireless service via Information Room to the senior officers of the brigade. In the event of a senior fire officer being required at the scene of a fire the brigade would telephone Information Room and ask for a special call to be transmitted. The message, a series of long and short Morse signals, would be sent out over the Force W/T and when received by the senior officer of the brigade in his car he telephoned the brigade headquarters. In August 1936 apparatus, which sent the signal automatically, was installed at the Denmark Hill Wireless Station followed in 1937 by two separate signals depending upon which senior fire officer was required. During their training courses Leading Watchroom Attendants of the brigade visited Information Room.

The introduction of improved communication facilities ensured the more efficient control of public events. Wireless vans were, by 1934, in regular use during any events attracting large crowds or those likely to result in public disorder. The vans, normally accompanied by two motorcyclists responsible for liaison, provided information to and from officers in charge of the operation or those commanding sections of a route. The vans normally took up the rear of a procession reporting back to Scotland Yard information regarding its size and progress and the temper of the crowd. During fixed operations one would take up the most advantageous position for liaison with senior officers.

In the case of Royal processions a van would be positioned at the point of departure and, by a pre-determined wireless message operators in other vans along the route would be informed of the commencement of the procession. The gongs on these vans would be sounded to alert officers on the route that the procession had started. The despatch riders were also available for the dissemination of the information. A small room leading off Information Room, with a W/T key, provided an experimental operations room for ceremonials.

The funeral arrangements for King George V had resulted in severe criticism of the new Commissioner, Sir Philip Game, in respect of crowd control. This was not to be the case with the Coronation of George VI on 12th May, 1937 for, although there was some delay in guests departing from Westminster Abbey, he was praised generally for the efficient organisation. Good communications played their part in ensuring that the event went smoothly.

A Route Control, with complete exchange line equipment separate from the Scotland Yard exchange, involved installing ten lines multiplied to eleven positions.   This equipment, also available for use during future events at short notice, required control staff of twelve constables and three supervising officers with direct communication to the headquarters of each of the fourteen sectors of the processional route.   A wireless receiving car was allocated to each control area.   Telephones installed at some of the more important crowd barriers were supported by arrangements with the G.P.O. for the exclusive use by police some thirty telephone kiosks.

In addition to the Route Control traffic regulation, under a Central Traffic Control also set up at Scotland Yard, required manning by six constables and two supervising officers along with a representative from London Transport.   Traffic officers were responsible for sending half hourly reports by code to the control room in respect of pedestrian and vehicular traffic.   Loudspeakers mounted on cars and fixed loudspeaker points were used to give directions to the crowds.   Each control room had its own separate wireless transmission facilities over and above Information Room's function.   The policing of a ceremonial had moved a long way since Wellington's Funeral in 1852.

Even the implementation 999 left the Force with the old Morse key for transmitting messages to cars.   However, in 1936, experiments with radio telephony were well under way on vehicles at the Motor Driving School, Hendon, initially on a Lagonda and a vehicle, named in records as a 'Snawk'.   There were problems in mounting this equipment, supplied by the Ardente Company, which suffered damage during fast speed driving.   Heavy maintenance costs were incurred.

Certainly by September, 1936 the police forces of Lancashire, Nottingham, Derby County and Derby Borough were well advanced in their experiments with radio transmissions.   They did not, however, have to contend with the traffic and building congestion of the Metropolis. The telephony used exclusively by some American police forces proved to be much more reliable.   Detroit, for example, had a total of 86 cars receiving speech by 1935 including four with transmitting facilities. Similarly New York Police were operating 366 cars with receiving apparatus but, as two way transmissions had not been perfected, only one with sending facilities.   In 1937 Inspector Fallon proposed that further experiments should be pursued into the operational use of telephony by the Force.   The Inspector emphasised the saving that would be made by not requiring the skills of highly trained Morse operators.   Similarly savings could be made by transferring the transmission of All Station messages from the high cost rental of the Creed teleprinters to that of radio communication with stations.

In the attempt to find more satisfactory equipment the Lancashire Constabulary loaned three transmitters and receivers to the Force for tests at the Driving School.   Three cars, delivered to Preston in April, were fitted with the equipment and later returned, along with a wireless mechanic, to Hendon.   The transmitter in one of the cars, an Alvis, occupied the whole of the boot leaving no room for tools.   Overheating occurred after four hours of use to such a degree that some of the parts melted. The tests overall were however reported as satisfactory.

Due to defects in equipment, training in telephony on the Advanced Wing of the Driving School was suspended in June, 1937. Talbot and Chevrolet cars, fitted with Ardente transceivers, had proved unsuccessful. Maintenance of R/T was difficult due to the engineers being located at Denmark Hill. Consequently arrangements were made for the wireless maintenance van to visit the School each day.

The Commissioner had to decide the way forward in respect of R/T in view of the continued unreliability of the Ardente sets. The whole value of advanced driving instruction would be restricted without R/T; the decision for the Force engineers to manufacture their own equipment answered his dilemma. By early 1938 four out of the nine Advanced Wing cars were fitted with R/T sets, far superior to any sets previously used. The weight, however, still caused serious problems with the vehicle springs affecting steering.

Mr. C.N. MacDermott and A.A.L. Collis were to follow Wootton as Engineer from 1935 and Kenworthy, with his team, did not rest but continued the work to improve the efficiency of their systems. Although radio telephony was not generally introduced onto the Force fleet until after the Second World War agreement in principle to convert vehicles to this form of communication was reached by the late 1930s.

It is appropriate to sum up this chapter with a description of early experiences provided by John Trendall who joined the Force in 1935 and retired as the Superintendent in the Communications Branch some thirty years later —

"In I.R. messages were received from the public either by 999 or through Whitehall 1212 switch board; from police through direct lines from stations or again through 1212. As received, messages were written down on pads in triplicate; the first copy being taken by the telephonist by hand to the W/T operator, second to the Log and the third to a clip board for temporary reference for queries, etc. There was only one channel throughout my service and messages were transmitted to cars (or boats) twice through, except during times when traffic was very heavy, when delays started to build up. Then transmission was at a slower speed and once only. Abbreviations were used as much as possible — Aust for Austin, blk for black, o/ct for overocat, etc and we had a book of codes although they were discontinued when R/T took over after the war. These started at X01 = found abandoned and as far as possible tried to cover every eventuality. X295 for example meant 'Lost or stolen', X17 meant 'assault' and so on. There was also a 'D' code for personnel. D62 was 'driver', D99 was 'Flying Squad Office', and individual officers on the Squad had their own D codes. The code books were jealously guarded and woe betide any operator who lost his.

Each message by radio was numbered, starting from midnight, and operators were expected to log everything that referred to their car, in full and just the call sign and number of those that did not affect them.

Nearly all operators took a pride in maintaining a perfect log as far as it was possible and would phone I.R. for messages that they had missed for one reason or another. Some parts of inner London were notorious "black-spots" for reception — Oxford street, for example which we patrolled from Marble Arch to Oxford Circus, north side, was dead country for the operator. During the war, our W/T would shut down as soon as the first warning was received of enemy action and cars would go to stations where I.R. could contact them by phone.

My own service in police communications started in 1937 when I worked as W/T operator on 'D' Division Area Car, 5D, which patrolled between Oxford Street in the south to Swiss Cottage in the north, from Queensway in the west to Kings Cross in the east. We had a crew of three at first — driver, operator and plain clothes observer who usually sat in front with the driver. The set was in the back alongside the operator, who wore headphones. Later, when manpower fell off during the war, the observer was dropped and a loudspeaker was fitted to the dashboard of the car and the operator beside the driver. Before the war, police used a variety of cars for divisional purposes but these were replaced finally by Wolseley 14s.

Our car was reckoned to be one of the busiest but we were never averse to poaching on calls to neighbouring cars if there was a chance of making an arrest. This was pretty general practice throughout the Force. There were six operators on 'D' Division so those not posted to the car would either perform normal duties on the street or fill in for other Area Cars whose crews were undermanned. In this way I frequently worked as operator on the Flying Squad which operated a variety of fast cars of well-known makes — Bentley, Lagonda and Railton, etc. These cars, like all divisional radio cars were one-way reception only, but the Squad did have a few non-descript vans with transmitters."

By 1937 the system for the public to obtain a rapid response to their calls for assistance operated in basically the same form as it does today. Since the 1930s the Information Room has been moved and modernised on a number of occasions. 999 has given the public easy access to the police standing the test of time, and providing confidence to the caller knowing that help is only three digits away. It can be described as the most successful method of raising the 'Hue and Cry'.

The years following the War were to see the Morse 'key' rapidly give way to the 'microphone' creating Information Room's 'stars' of the R/T (like the clear, calm and unflappable North American accent of 'Canada Bill' (PC Bill Rutherford)) whose voices became so reassuring to wireless vehicle crews whatever the emergency. The future may well witness the R/T itself decline substantially in favour of the impersonal, yet more secure, mobile computer terminal in the Area Car for receiving and trans-mitting messages by data and utilising an automatic vehicle location system constantly plotting the vehicle's movements on a computerised map.

CHAPTER VI

BRINGING IT UP TO DATE

Although this detailed study of communications in the Metropolitan Police was completed with the introduction of the 999 emergency system into Information Room on 29 November 1937 it was felt appropriate, in this final chapter, to briefly examine the major developments made since that date. Comparisons have been made which will enable the reader to appreciate the value of good communications whether in the past or present.

The threat of the Second World War led the Force to reconsider its policies in respect of communications as the priorities had inevitably changed. A safer location for Information Room was required; consequently early in 1940 it was moved to the basement of the partially completed northern extension of New Scotland Yard along with the telephone switchboard, Telegraph Office and the Urgent Communications Room. The siting of air raid sirens at police stations and police boxes became essential. Initially they were activated locally but later simultaneous control was carried out centrally from the Urgent Communications Room.

The radio communication between headquarters and stations became more important than the vehicle telephony programme as there was a fear that telephone and teleprinter networks could be disrupted by bombing. Radio, installed at a total of eighty seven police stations, provided a service which was successfully maintained throughout the 'blitz'.

The planning for a VHF R/T system to replace Morse transmissions with vehicles continued during the war and from 1946 onwards the Force's fleet was gradually fitted with the new equipment and by 1950 two hundred vehicles and thirteen Thames launches were provided with two-way telephony. Whereas the Force was to experience during the Great Exhibition of 1851 the earliest use of an internal electric telegraph, radio equipped motorcycles were operating at the Festival of Britain in 1951 where they were used for crowd and traffic control for the first time. The Grey Velocette lightweight motorcycle was to become a feature of policing in the late 1950s and 1960s. Given the affectionate nickname of 'Noddy Bike' a number were fitted with Cossor receiver/transmitters. The 'Noddies' on beat patrol were able to find their way into places where a car could never reach and could well provide a useful crime fighting service today.

The vehicle fleet initially operated on one full R/T channel but by the early 1950s three extra channels had been incorporated into the system. Eleven main R/T channels are now being used to control the Force's ever increasing number of vehicles amounting to over 3100 cars, boats and motorcycles with fitted radio facilities. Many famous companies, including E.K. Cole, Cossor, Marconi and Pye, have provided

Police cyclist — Air Raid Warning — World War II.

Sergeant 19D/114775 Frederick Bunker (the author's father) at St. Johns Wood Station during World War II.

the Force with equipment since the war and to a great extent Met 'produced' equipment was discontinued.

A site at Forest Hill was initially chosen as a headquarters' station to cater for telephony and, as the Force's requirements increased in the 1950s, three additional sites were developed.

As early as 1946 portable radio transmitters were purchased from the Cossor Company, but it was not until 1966 that personal radios were successfully introduced operationally, over 30 years after Chief Inspector Best had considered the concept. Stornophone VHF equipment was selected and by 1969 the installation of the divisional personal radio system was complete which, over the years, has been improved substantially. Each of the seventy five divisions (except two which share) have their own personal radio system giving almost every officer patrolling the beat or in a car immediate contact with his Divisional Control Room. In addition there are a number of personal radio channels which can be allocated for use during the policing of public disorder or major events. Even some Traffic Wardens have the benefit of a personal radio.

The extensive and sophisticated equipment available today is often stretched to the limit to meet the demand of a modern Police Force as the Broadwater Farm disturbance of 1985 highlighted. Lessons in the most effective use of communication facilities are learned today by experience as they were at the Trafalgar Square Riots one hundred years earlier when the Committee of Enquiry called attention to the inadequate telegraphic facilities existing in the Force.

Despite the improvements in passing information rapidly crime statistics continue to rise every year. One of the reasons for the introduction of the Police Box in 1929 was to help stem the ever increasing crime figures. The Morning Post of 30th November 1929 reported, 'The new system, which, it is hoped, will play an important part in the capture of elusive motor thieves, is still in an experimental stage, and its success will depend on the intelligent co-operation of the public'. Whether the very extensive network of police boxes actually assisted in slowing the increase in crime to any great degree is doubtful.

The Commissioner, Sir Philip Game, states in his Annual Report of 1938, "The use made by the public of the telephone in boxes shows a steady improvement, but in spite of extensive publicity there is still a noticeable reluctance to make full use of this service. From the point of view of facilitating communication between stations and police on patrol these boxes are a great improvement on the old system, but the public have not yet acquired the habit of regarding them as a normal means of getting into touch with the local police'. After all by the time the system was Forcewide the 999 facility had been established and a much more effective means of calling the police was available to the victims of crimes.

Unfortunately in many respects 999 has been too successful with the public as they regularly communicate information and requests for assistance of a less than urgent nature over the system. Often it is

Radio telephony on a Metropolitan Police Motorcycle.

Air raid siren — World War II.

wrongly used to report the loss of 'poor Towser' or similar 'emergencies' which may, at busy times, hold up the genuine urgent call for help. However, what one person may consider a frivolous request for assistance is another's emergency.

The provision of a central communication point with direct access from the public has inevitably led to more and more demands on the police service. However, the Commissioners who opposed the introduction of the telephone in the early part of the century have been proved wrong in their assessment, 'Cranks of all kinds will be ringing up Scotland Yard all day long'. Wide-spread increases in the sources of incoming information have taken a toll on the ability of the Force to respond rapidly over the past fifty years. The majority of homes now have telephones as do business premises and the new Cellnet mobile units and the private Mercury systems are likely, in the future, to have an impact on the number of messages received in Information Room.

The development of burglar alarms is not covered in any detail in this book although there are references to the alarm bell system at the Geological Museum, and that installed at the Houses of Parliament by the Exchange Telegraph Company. Burglar alarms were well established in the United States by the end of the Century, having been developed from fire alarm systems, but prior to the Second World War in this country they were generally simple audible devices on premises alerting the attention of the beat constable. The proliferation of Central Stations operated by large private companies did not occur until the 1960s although a company, Rely-a-Bell, operated such a station at Wilson Street, EC2 in the 1930s. Autocall and Ideal also provided early facilities. The Burgot automatic call gramaphone record to police had been developed on a small scale in the early years of Information Room to raise the alarm to a burglary.

The majority of applications for alarms into police stations in the last century were refused. Such a request to connect Warren House, Coombe Wood to Kingston Police Station was not approved although in 1896, permission was given for Lord Roseberry's house to be connected by electric alarm to Epsom Police Station. There are now in excess of seventy Central Station Burglar Alarm companies passing information to the Information Room about activated alarms in addition to numerous other recorded connections in corner shops and similar premises.

In the year 1987 an average in excess of 2450 '999' calls were received each day in Information Room coupled with an average of over 750 burglar alarm calls of which about 97% were false. If we compare this with 1956 when emergency calls averaged 428 each day it is clear that the workload is continually rising beyond anything ever envisaged in 1937. Even between 1985 and 1986 the number of emergency calls to the Metropolitan Police increased by 6½ percent.

Rising workloads have led to the need for staff increases over the years. In 1938 there were 24 constables employed in Information Room

218

Changing from Morse to Speech after the War.

Public address on the motorcycle.

compared with 140 and 20 civilian operators today. Staff alone cannot solve the problems and the pressure of work dictated the need to find more effective methods of handling messages. By 1956 the procedure of delivering messages received on the telephone to the radio despatcher by hand was clearly inefficient, bearing in mind the high number of calls received. In that year, with the move of Information Room to a new room on the first floor of New Scotland Yard, a new conveyor belt system was introduced to enable written paper messages to be passed rapidly from the telephonist to the radio despatcher at the other end of the room. A more advanced belt operated successfully when the centre was transferred to the 1st Floor of the new New Scotland Yard in Broadway, SW1 in 1967. This belt delivered direct to despatchers or direct to Telegraph Office for passing messages to division by teleprinter.

Whereas in the early years the direct telephone and telegraph connections from premises for which police had a special responsibility or those which required regular communication with the Force tended to be connected to local police stations such lines are now normally linked to Information Room. The Fire Brigade, Ambulance Service, British Transport Police and similar organisations are in regular contact with the Force over direct lines. This is a far cry from the numerous connections between police stations and fire stations in the last century.

Even 'the belt' and paper could not cope with the increased demand on the Force communications and in July, 1984 the new Command and Control Computer Aided Despatch system was introduced after a successful pilot scheme on 'Y' District. A new Central Communications Complex was opened, and no longer are messages written onto paper, but are entered directly onto a VDU screen. Once the system is completely operational there will be 75 Divisional Control Rooms in direct communication with Information Room on Computer Aided Despatch. Messages can now be rapidly passed by computer terminals throughout the Force. This is a revolution which must match the introduction of the Force electric telegraph in 1867 and the system will eventually accommodate in excess of 800 terminals throughout the Force linked to a computerised internal Network.

The 999 facility is an expensive service to provide in terms of manpower and equipment. Training of staff is extensive and the police officers are well paid today. It is likely that future years will see more civilian staff employed in this field thereby releasing valuable police officers onto the streets where their special skills are in demand. This civilianisation programme, desirable though it may be, cannot be carried out rapidly as many of the qualities required on the streets are required by the officer handling a victim of crime on the telephone. The response must be correct and graded to meet the requirement. The loss of 'poor Towser' type of message can be sent direct to the station to handle; the more serious incidents need a fast Area Car.

The computer provides access to detailed contingency plans which are put into effect in the event of a terrorist attack or similar incident.

Information Room in the 1940s/50s — Tables and tokens.

Information Room in the 1950s/60s — The first 'belt' supplied
by Lamson Engineering Co.Ltd.

All radio channels, including the seventy five divisional systems, can be accessed from one computerised switching panel at every operator positon in the Central Command Complex which incorporates Information Room. The Automatic Call Distribution telephone system ensures that incoming calls are answered by police in the order in which they are made. Priorities can be given to emergency lines over other types of calls. 999 is the first, and sometimes the only contact the citizen of London has with the police, and for this reason, if no other, it must be ensured that the service is beyond criticism. The quote made by Chief Inspector Fallon after the introduction of the emergency system, 'A keener body of men than the Information Room staff would be difficult to find' , must continue to apply whether it is police officers or civil staff performing the important task.

The 1930s saw the speeding up of the circulation of stolen motor vehicles by sending details to divisions by teleprinter, which were then passed to the officers patrolling their beats. For officers to retain lists of stolen vehicles these days would serve little useful purpose with the huge proportions of traffic on our streets. Easy access is all that is needed so that when a constable is suspicious he can obtain the information quickly. The Police National Computer (PNC) introduced in 1974 now does this for policemen throughout the country. PNC also provides rapid up-to-date information about criminals and wanted persons. It even gives the constable immediate access to details of the registered owner of a motor vehicle. As a method of broadcasting important messages relating to crime to all Forces in the country it is of untold value. PNC is far removed from the direct telephone line installed in the Convict Supervision Office in 1905 to allow communication between Scotland Yard and division in respect of criminal matters.

A vehicle pursuit now involves a detailed commentary over the radio by the R/T operator all of which is tape recorded and can be played back later and analysed. No such luxury was available with Morse and the suggestion that an operator should throw a message out of the window when passing a policeman on foot informing him of what was happening really made a great deal of sense. Even if the vehicle was one of the few with a transmitter one can imagine the difficulties in passing information during a chase in Morse.

The movement of London's traffic is now one of the biggest headaches of the Metropolitan Police and since the war traffic control has relied more and more on efficient communications. Whereas in 1937 a traffic control room was set up specifically for the Coronation it is now a permanent feature of the Force's communication network operating effectively from the Central Command Complex at Scotland Yard along with Information Room. It has three dedicated radio channels for exclusive use in respect of traffic matters and controls a large fleet of vehicles. Accidents, removals, clamping of vehicles, transfer of heavy loads and providing traffic information to the media all place a tremendous burden on the Traffic Controllers. The early experiments in

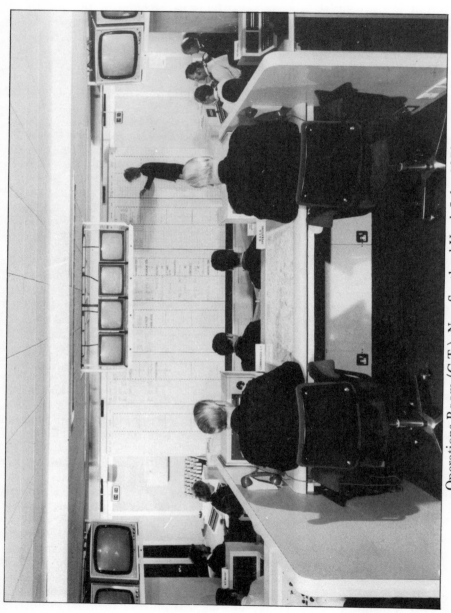

Operations Room (G.T.), New Scotland Yard, July, 1973 – Plot boards and CCTV.

observing and controlling traffic congestion at Epsom during the races in the 1920s, with the aid of a Superintendent up in a balloon, Morse operators and motorcyclists, are now difficult to imagine in these days of Closed Circuit Television and computerised traffic lights. However, some traffic officers would no doubt argue that the best place for the Superintendent is up in a balloon and maybe much could be done today with this method of surveillance. The Force helicopters can today provide 'helitele' pictures from the sky.

A specialised section of Traffic Control now supervises over 1400 computerised traffic lights and associated CCTV installations at major junctions. Traffic information is regularly passed by direct lines, and in some cases a computer link, to the motoring organisations and the main public broadcasting stations. Central Traffic Control which developed from humble beginnings in 1958 in a small room at Wellington Arch, to a purpose built room at Scotland Yard, is now using all the computerised technology of Information Room. The specialist Urban Traffic Control Unit (known to the Force as Area Traffic Control (ATC)) now controls the traffic light junctions working alongside the other communication sections having commenced operation in a small back room at New Scotland Yard in 1968.

The inner and outer circle of wires introduced after the 1886 riots to provide a better method of communicating between one division and another inevitably led to a demand in excess of that which the system could cope with. A computerised Message Switching System replaced the Force teleprinter network in mid 1984 allowing a direct and immediate method of passing routine messages anywhere in the MPD. Fortunately this system is able to cope with the unexpected demand which has been placed upon it. Whereas in the past information would be passed by means of written report through the despatch service it is now often sent by the Message Switch System. The constable standing in front of the ABC machine recording the incoming message on his slate is long forgotten. A 'space age' Message Switch Office and a small number of staff are able to monitor the whole network by means of VDUs.

Telex traffic has increased beyond belief between the Met and other forces throughout the country. Between 1956 and 1962 messages rose from 3,800 to 62,500 and have now reached over 200,000. Criminals are more mobile and disorder, such as the Miners Strike of 1984, requires co-ordination of resources. The Chartist troubles of 1848 and the message traffic which they generated between forces over the electric telegraph bear many resemblances to some of today's Telex usage.

International communication is now a regular feature of the work of the Metropolitan Police over the International Criminal Police Organisation (ICPO) Network using the most up to date radio teleprinters and Telex to transmit to and receive messages from 142 member countries. The service has been completely transformed over a relatively short period of thirty years from an entirely Morse operation with two operators to a

The teleprinter switchboard, New Scotland Yard until 1967.

control room which provides a communication centre for all United Kingdom police forces and has the ability to transmit photographs and fingerprints rapidly across the world. Morse has almost died out as a means of passing messages, but this is the one area where it still survives giving us a constant reminder of the past. The Quaker, Tawell, made good his escape from Slough to Paddington, and Crippen travelled slowly by ship to Canada but today's criminal can quickly travel by air from one side of the world to another. The Interpol network must keep up with him as the needle telegraph did with the Slough murderer and the Marconigram with the Cellar killer.

Public disorder and major ceremonial events occurring in the Metropolis have been controlled in many instances since November 1986 from a new Special Operations Room with up to date computer facilities and radio communication. Whereas in the last century control of police resources was of necessity carried out from the ground this can now be done more effectively by a senior officer in a modern control room who has an overall picture of manpower deployments and incidents which are occurring throughout the whole area of a demonstration. Much, however, still depends on the discipline of the men and the ability of ground commanders to direct them properly without overstretching communications facilities beyond their limit.

With the aid of Territorial Support Groups and a Mobilisation Plan the Force is today able to muster up large numbers of officers to handle disorder which may break out spontaneously. This plan's success obviously relies very much on good communications by way of radio, computer and telephone. It is not unlike the method of mobilising a force of some 1,942 men to deal with sudden Chartist troubles in 1848 with the use of a messenger travelling in a cab. The Section House always had a ready supply of off duty officers who could be gathered together quickly.

Whereas in the past the public had less expectations of the service the Force should provide they now turn to the police when there is no other organisation responsible for a particular duty. The Lewisham Train crash in 1957 led to the realisation that a Central Casualty Bureau was necessary to handle enquiries from members of the public concerning casualties in the event of a major incident. This enabled those enquiries to be removed from the hospitals and local police stations and dealt with efficiently by a central unit unhindered with the operational problems at the scene. Fortunately the facility is not used to any great degree for this purpose but has proved its worth at such tragedies as the Harrods bomb and the recent King's Cross station disaster when over 10,000 calls were received during a period of about five days. The value of the Bureau as a Police Information Centre at the time of public disorder was highlighted during the well remembered Tottenham disturbances.

It can only be assumed that no similar facilities were available in the last century. Today the public are aware, through television and radio, as soon as a major incident or terrorist outrage occurs whereas the Fenian

Central Command Complex, New Scotland Yard, July, 1984.

attack on Clerkenwell Prison in 1867, resulting in death and injury to innocent residents nearby, would only be known to local people or those in the vicinity for some considerable time as would the deaths in the crowd crushes at the lying in state of the Duke of Wellington in 1852. A disaster in London now attracts enquiries from anxious relatives throughout the world.

The hesitance of the Force to adopt 'this new fangled instrument' the telephone in 1900 was soon overcome at police stations and like every other organisation it became a feature of day to day work. By the 1960s the old station switchboards were unable to cope efficiently with the workloads and the new Switching Centres serving two police divisions (later known as Districts) were introduced in an effort to improve the situation. The first such centre was opened at Paddington in 1973. The Switching Centres have not proved popular with the public as they are remote from the neighbourhood police station and connections with the correct person to handle an enquiry often proves difficult. It has been recognised that a more personal service is required and the future holds in store a return to the concept of local switchboards accompanied by some of the better features of the Switching Centre.

Howard Vincent's Police Code in 1882 instructed that on no account must police give information to the 'Gentlemen of the press'. This view has been completely reversed over the past twenty years particularly under Sir Robert Mark who encouraged openness with the press which benefitted both parties and the Force even employs ex-editors and journalists in the Public Information Department. Police use of television in obtaining the assistance of the public in solving crimes has moved a long way since Shaw Taylor's first 'Police Five' programme. There is no comparison between the BBC radio appeals of the 1920s and the professional co-operation between police and the television company which produces a popular programme like 'Crimewatch UK'. Television provides the 'Wanted Notice' of the late 20th century although the poster still appears outside today's police station in the attempt to track down the criminal. The Metropolitan Police now uses all means of communication at its disposal in the fight against ever increasing crime.

This Chapter is not intended to give anything more than a taste of the Metropolitan Police communications today which will provide the reader with 'food for thought' in his observations of the years up to 1937. The position previously taken by the rattle has now been taken by the personal radio and we can now truly say that the constable on the beat has moved from 'Rattle to Radio' although the whistle still lurks in his pocket should everything else fail.

ABBREVIATIONS AND TERMS USED IN THE TEXT

ABC Machine	= Wheatstone Alphabetical Telegraph Instrument
AC 'A')	= Assistant Commissioner 'A' Department (Force Administration etc). No longer exists.
AC 'B') Instituted 1909	= Assistant Commissioner 'B' Department (Traffic etc). No longer exists
AC 'C')	= Assistant Commissioner 'C' Department (Crime). No longer exists.
AC 'D')	= Assistant Commissioner 'D' Department (organisation). No longer exists.
AS	= All Station Message.
Area Car	= A divisional wireless vehicle with the primary role of providing a fast response to calls from the public.
A2 Branch	= Personnel records etc.
A3 Branch	= Back Hall
Back Hall	= Reception and administrative section at Scotland Yard
Beat	= A designated area patrolled by a Police Constable
Call signs	= Codes used on the W/T to identify vehicles.
CID	= Criminal Investigation Department
CO	= Commissioner's Office. A term used for the Force headquarters at Scotland Yard
Commissioner's Orders	= Regular instructions and notification to the Force of staff information. Normally referred to as Police Orders.
CRO	= Criminal Record Office
Districts	= During the period covered by this book four territorial areas of the MPD containing a group of divisions. Implemented in 1869 under the command of District Superintendents. From 1886 known as Chief Constables. In recent years the old divisions became Districts.
Division	= During the period covered by this book a territorial area of the MPD containing a head-quarters station under the command of a

Superintendent. In recent years became known as Districts which also no longer exist.

Divisional Station	=	The headquarters or chief station of a division
D1 Branch	=	Responsible for Force communications in 1934
D4 Branch	=	Centralised communications including Information Room. After the war designation changed in 1968 to A2(3), then A9, B6 and finally TO25.
ETC	=	Electric Telegraph Company.
Executive Branch	=	Administrative centre at Scotland Yard absorbed by A.3. Branch during McCready's Commissionership.
Fixed Point	=	Set position where a Constable performed all or part of his tour of duty.
General Orders (GO)	=	Book of Force instructions and Regulations.
GPO	=	General Post Office.
HQ Wireless Station	=	Transmitting and receiving station at Scotland Yard, later at Denmark Hill and West Wickham.
Hue and Cry	=	Proclamation for the capture of a criminal. The original name for Police Gazette.
Informations	=	A circular providing information in respect of crimes etc.
IR	=	Information Room - the centre at New Scotland Yard for the receipt of urgent information and circulation by wireless.
Instruction Book	=	A manual issued to police constables setting out Force instructions.
Morning Reports	=	Divisional Superintendents reports to the Commissioner.
MPD	=	The Metropolitan Police District.
MPO	=	Metropolitan Police Office - Scotland Yard
NSY	=	New Scotland Yard
NTC	=	National Telephone Company incorporated in 1881 and in 1889 merged with UTC retaining its own name.
PS	=	Police Sergeant
PBX	=	Private Branch Exchange
Police Gazette	=	A publication for circulating information concerning crime and suspects

Police Orders	= Also known in early years as Commissioner's Orders. Instructions to the Force published daily. In later years published twice each week.
Private Wire	= An internal telephone or telegraph wire not on the public network.
Q Car	= Plain clothes Crime Car
Receiver	= Person responsible for Force finance etc.
Route	= A despatch route covering a series of police stations where orders, messages and correspondence are delivered.
R/T	= Radio Telephony - voice radio.
Scotland House	= Receiver's Office adjoining the New Scotland Yard building on the Embankment.
Section	= A station area which is part of a sub-division. Known as sectional stations. In recent years became Sub Divisions.
Section Sergeant	= Responsible for supervision of beat constables.
Station Codes	= Codes consisting of two letters designed to identify a police station clearly and concisely over the telegraph and wireless.
Sub Division	= A territorial part of a division with a main police station. In recent years became known as division.
TO	= Telegraph Office at Scotland Yard.
UTC	= United Telephone Company formed in 1878.
UPTC	= Universal Private Telegraph Company incorporated in 1861.
W/T	= Wireless Telegraphy = Morse.

PLACES OF PARTICULAR VALUE TO THE RESEARCHER

British Telecom Technology Showcase, Blackfriars
British Telecom Museum, Oxford
Commissioner's Library, New Scotland Yard (not open to the public)
Metropolitan Police Archives Section (not open to the public)
Metropolitan Police Museum (not open to the public)
Post Office Archives, St. Martin Le Grand
Public Record Office, Kew
Science Museum, South Kensington
Thames Division Museum, Wapping (not open to the public)

BIBLIOGRAPHY

The majority of the research for this book was carried out from the Metropolitan Police files now retained at the Public Record Office, Kew.

I have not attempted to itemise all my sources of information but detailed below are a few of particular interest or significance.

PUBLIC RECORD OFFICE

Manuscript Metropolitan Police Orders from 1829 to 1856	MEPO 7/1 to 7/17
Commissioner's Telegraph 1852	MEPO 5/33
Introduction of the Force Telegraph system and extensions	MEPO 5/33
The Telegraph 1878 to 1883	MEPO 5/50
Printing Telegraphs	MEPO 5/82
Rattles and Whistles	MEPO 5/54
Fixed Point Boxes	MEPO 5/86 5/87 2/8827
Islington and Brixton Telephone Boxes	MEPO 5/72 2/8827
Telephone lines to Division	MEPO 2/618 5/86
Connection to the Public Exchanges	MEPO 2/903 2/921
Creed teleprinters	MEPO 2/6554
Police Boxes	MEPO 5/347 2/9488 2/2576
Wireless	MEPO 2/1992
Emergency Calls experiments	MEPO 2/3891
Area Wireless Scheme and Information Room	MEPO 2/3851 2/6134
Arrest of Crippen	MEPO 3/198
Letter from Thomas Home, Licensee of the GWR Telegraph	RAIL 1014/17
There are numerous Home Office files containing information on communications in the PRO	HO45
Post Office Records	
Electric Telegraph Company Order Book 1849	POST 18/70

OFFICIAL DOCUMENTS

Beat Books and Ringing in Schedules

Commissioner's Annual Reports.

Contracts between the Post Office and Metropolitan Police.

Dissemination of Information — 1934 circular.

Metropolitan Police Accounts.

Metropolitan Police Instruction Book various 19th Century issues.

Minutes of evidence taken before a committee appointed to inquire into the system of Police. 11 February to 16 March 1868.

Police arrangements for the Coronation of Their Majesties King George VI and Queen Elizabeth, 12th May, 1937.

Police Orders.

Report of the Commissioner appointed to inquire as to the best means of establishing an efficient Constabulary Force in the counties of England and Wales — W. Clowes & Sons, 1839.

Report of a committee to enquiry into the origin and character of the Disturbances in the Metropolis on 8th February 1886 and as to the conduct of Police authorities.

Telegraph Book from Information Room commencing 11 June, 1934.

SUGGESTED FURTHER READING

BELL J and
WILSON S

Practical Telephone.
(S Rentell & Co.Ltd., London 1906).

BROWN Douglas G

The Rise of Scotland Yard (George Harrap & Co.Ltd. 1956)

CAVANAGH T.A.

Scotland Yard Past and Present Experiences of Thirty Seven Years (Chatto and Windus 1893).

CLARKSON C.T. and
RICHARDSON J.H.

Police!
(Field and Tuer, London 1889).

COX Ronald

Oh, Captain Shaw.
(Victor Green Publications Ltd. London 1984).

DILNOT George

Scotland Yard
History and Organisation 1829-1929.
(Geoffrey Bles 1929).

DURHAM John

Telegraphs in Victorian London.
(Golden Head Press 1959)

EVANS Peter

The Police Revolution.
(George Allen and Unwin 1974).

FABIAN Robert
Ex Det Supt

The Boys book of Scotland Yard Chapter 16 — Dial 999 (Clerke & Cockerman London).

FROST George

Flying Squad (Rockliff 1948)

GOODMAN Jonathan and
WADDELL Bill

The Black Museum
(Harrap, London 1987).

GRIFFITHS Arthur

Mysteries of Police and Crime.
(Cassell and Co.Ltd. 1920).

HERBERT T.E.

The Telephone System of the British Post Office - A Practical Handbook.
(Page and Pratt, London 1898).

HERBERT T.E.

Telegraphy - A Detailed Exposition of the Telegraph system of the British Post Office.
(Isaac Pitman, London 1926).

HOLOWAY Sally

London's Noble Fire Brigades 1833-1904. (Cassell, London 1973).

IVIMEY Alan

Robert of London (Hutchinson & Co. 1939).

KIEVE Jeffrey	The Electric Telegraph. A Social and Economic History. (David and Charles 1973).
LARDNER D.	The Electric Telegraph Popularised (Walton and Maberley 1855).
LUCAS Norman and SCARLETT Bernard	The Flying Squad (Arthur Baker Ltd., 1968).
MOYLAN J.F.	Scotland Yard and the Metropolitan Police (G.P. Putnam's Sons Ltd. 1929)
OVERMAN Michael	Understanding Telecommunications. (Latterwerth Press 1974).
PULLING Christopher	Mr. Punch and the Police (Butterworths 1964).
RIVERS Kenneth	History of the Traffic Department of the Metropolitan Police.
SCOTT Sir Harold	Scotland Yard (Andre Deutsh Ltd. 1954).
SMITH Philip Thurmond	Policing Victorian London (Greenwood Press, 1985).
VINCENT Sir Howard	A Police Code and Manual of Criminal Law. (Cassell Petter, Galpin & Co. London 1882).
WILLIAMS Guy	The Hidden World of Scotland Yard. (Hutchinson of London 1972).
WILKES John	The London Police in the 19th Century. (Cambridge University Press 1977).
WOODHALL Edwin T.	Secrets of Scotland Yard (John Lane, The Bodley Head, London).

ARTICLES IN PERIODICALS, JOURNALS ETC.

ABBOTT F.W.	'Printing Telegraphs for Police', Police Journal Vol. IV.
BACK John	Unpublished article 'The Blue Lamp' c.1979.
BACK John	Unpublished article 'Early Days of Wireless in the Metropolitan Police', c. 1977.
BOYES Anthony	Police Communications. A Brief History (unpublished by Police Sergeant of Thames Valley Police 1976).
BRITISH TELECOM	Booklet 'Britain's Public Payphones' (1984).
BROWN E.C.	'The Metropolitan Police Radio Communication System', Electronic Engineering, August 1950.
CREED & CO.LTD.	The Creed "Start Stop" Telegraph System Sales brochure, early 1930s.
FAIRFAX Norman	'From quills to computers' - The History of the Metropolitan Police Civil Staff, 1829-1979. (Manuscript not published 1979).
FAIRFAX Norman and WILKINSON Victor	A history of Metropolitan Police Uniforms and Equipment. Unpublished. c. 1971.
FRIEDERICI Otto	A paper headed Electrical Appliances, to the Civil & Mechanical Engineers Society, 1891.
GRANT T.D. Detective Sergeant	Printed extract from 'A Fragmented History of the Flying Squad' - source not known.
HACKNEY Bruce	'The History and Development of Wireless Branch in the Metropolitan Police Scotland Yard', Clearway Met Police Traffic Magazine Autumn 1970
ILLUSTRATED LONDON NEWS	'The Murder at Salt Hill The Electro-Magnetic Telegraph at Slough'. 11.1. 1845.
ILLUSTRATED LONDON NEWS	'Riots in the West End of London'. 13.2.1886.

ILLUSTRATED LONDON NEWS	'Sketches by Telegraph'. 20.2.1886
ILLUSTRATED LONDON NEWS	'The Metropolitan Preventive and Detective Police'. 29.9.1883.
INSTITUTE OF TELEGRAPHIC ENGINEERS Journal of	'The Present State of Fire Telegraphy' Vol.17 1888.
JOHANNESSEN N	'Half a Century of Saving Lives' British Telecom Journal, Autumn 1986.
LUXTON James	Various articles under heading Cranks Corner between June 1972 and Dec. 1978. 'Intercom' Home Office Directorate of Telecoms Journal.
MATHER F.C.	'The Railways, The Electric Telegraph and Public Order during the Chartist period 1837-48' History, Vol.38, 1953.
MORRIS T.C.	'Police Telephone Systems' Journal of Post Office Electrical Engineers, Oct. 1937.
NATIONAL TELEPHONE COMPANY	Directory of 1898-1899.
NATIONAL TELEPHONE COMPANY	Directory of 1901-1902.
NATIONAL TELEPHONE COMPANY LTD	Telephone and Telegraph Apparatus Sales Catalogue, 1903.
PICTORIAL WEEKLY	Policemen take the Air, No. 49 Vol. 4, 6 October 1934.
POPULAR WIRELESS	'Calling All Cars' 2 March 1935.
POST OFFICE	Publicity Brochure for the Creed Teleprinter 'Typewriting over the Telephone Wires'.
PUNCH	'New Police Regulations' and 'The Whistling Bobby' Vol.84 1883.
QUARTERLY REVIEW	'The Electric Telegraph' Vol.95 June 1854.
UNITED TELEPHONE COMPANY	List of subscribers, Issue 8, 30 September 1881.
UNITED TELEPHONE COMPANY	Professional and Trades Classified Directory 1885.

WIRELESS WORLD

WIRELESS WORLD AND
RADIO REVIEW, The

'Police Wireless - The Radio Link
between Scotland Yard and Patrol
Cars', 29 Oct. 1937.

'How wireless helped in controlling
the Derby Traffic', 16 June 1923.

NEWSPAPERS - A SELECTION OF ARTICLES CONSULTED ON MAJOR MILESTONES

Pressure on the Force to connect to the telephone exchange —

Daily Mail	—	15.11.1898
		3.12.1898
		5.12.1898
		23. 2. 1899
		22. 2. 1906

Capture of Crippen —

Morning Advertiser	—	1. 8.1910
Weekly Dispatch	—	31. 7.1910

Police Boxes

The Star	—	29.11.1929
Daily Express	—	30.11.1929
Daily Mail	—	17. 1.1930
Daily News and Westminster Gazette	—	30.11.1929
Daily Telegraph	—	29. 1.1930
Morning Post	—	30.11.1929
Richmond Herald	—	30.11.1929
Richmond and Twickenham Times	—	30.11.1929 - 14.1.1930
The Times		30.11.1929
		17. 1.1930
Evening Standard	—	13. 1.1930

Creed Printers

The Star	—	21. 2.1931

Opening of Information Room

Daily Herald		12. 6.1934

The Auto Gyro

The Times	—	10. 8.1934

Facsimile

Daily Telegraph	—	4. 3.1935

Proposed National Police Radio System

News of the World	—	16. 6.1935

Use of Whitehall 1212 by the public to contact Information Room

Daily Herald	—	5.10.1935
Daily Mail	—	5.10.1935
Daily Mirror	—	5.10.1935

Daily Sketch	—	5.10.1935
Daily Telegraph	—	5.10.1935
Evening Standard	—	5.10.1935
Liverpool Post	—	5.10.1935
Morning Post	—	5.10.1935
The Times	—	5.10.1935
Evening News	—	7.10.1935

Denmark Hill Wireless Station

| The Times | — | 28. 4.1936 |

Loudspeaker on Vehicle

| The Times | — | 9.10.1936 |

The 999 system

Daily Mail	—	22.10.1937
Evening News	—	30.11.1937
Daily Sketch	—	8. 7.1937
Evening Standard	—	2. 7.1937
Daily Mail	—	3. 7.1937
Evening News	—	1. 7.1937
The Times	—	1. 7.1937
The Times	—	2. 7.1937
Daily Herald	—	6. 1.1938
Evening Standard	—	13. 7.1937
Daily Mail	—	26.11.1937
Daily Express	—	30.11.1937
Daily Herald	—	2.12.1937
Observer	—	11. 7.1937
Daily Herald	—	29. 7.1937
Sunday Pictorial	—	8. 8.1937
Daily Mail	—	11. 9.1937
Evening Standard	—	24. 7.1937

A SELECTION OF SIGNIFICANT POLICE ORDERS

28.10.1829	—	Attendance at CO for orders.
30.11.1829	—	Method of Patrolling the Beat
27.11.1830	—	Winter supply of lanterns.
31.12.1832	—	Formation of Fire Engine Establishment.
5. 2.1845	—	Mention of Whistles.
25. 5.1851	—	Great Exhibition - Use of Telegraph.
7. 2.1852	—	Circulation of Police Gazette.
2. 9.1865	—	100 new pattern rattles to Divisions.
30. 9.1867	—	Telegraphic Communication Established.
5. 8.1868	—	Duties at Fires.
1. 4.1869	—	Routes of Mounted Messengers.
22. 9.1869	—	Routes of Mounted Messengers.
19.12.1871	—	List of Code Signals for Stations etc.
2.10.1872	—	Telegraphy a qualification for promotion.
30.10.1873	—	List of Fixed Points.
14.11.1872	—	Despatch Cart on T Division.
9.11.1882	—	Telegraph to Fire Stations.
8.1883	—	Use of Telegraph to call ambulances.
7. 2.1884	—	Issue of whistles.
20. 2.1886	—	Demonstrations at Hyde Park instructions re messages.
18. 3.1886	—	GPO system connected to Met Police Telegraph.
16. 4.1887	—	All rattles withdrawn.
5. 6.1888	—	List of locations on telegraph and telephone. Station codes.
3. 4.1889	—	Introduction of Type Printing system.
23. 2.1907	—	List of Telephone and Telegraph connections.
9. 8.1907	—	List of Stations on Public Telephone.
24. 8.1908	—	List of Telephone and Telegraph connections.
7. 2.1916	—	List of Telephone and Telegraph connections.
7. 2.1916	—	Instructions for use of Column Printers.
13. 3.1929	—	Communication of Information to COCI Branch
7. 3.1934	—	Formation of Wireless School.
11. 3.1936	—	Station Code Signals.
26.11.1937	—	Introduction of 999 to Information Room Announced.

COMMISSIONERS OF POLICE OF THE METROPOLIS

* Colonel Sir Charles Rowan, K.C.B., July 7th, 1829 - January 5th, 1850.

* Sir Richard Mayne, K.C.B., July 7th, 1829 - December 26th, 1868.

*/- Captain William Hay, C.B. January 6th, 1850 - August 29th, 1855.

Colonel D.W. Labalmondiere, C.B., Acting Commissioner.
  December 30th, 1868 - February 12th, 1869.

Colonel Sir Edmund Henderson, K.C.B., R.E., February 13th, 1869 - March 26th, 1886.

General Sir Charles Warren, G.C.M.G., K.C.B., R.E., F.R.S.,
  March 29th, 1886 - December 1st, 1888.

James Monro, Esq., C.B., December 3rd, 1888 - June 21st, 1890.

Colonel Sir Edward Bradford, Bt., G.C.B., G.C.V.O., K.C.S.I.,
  June 23rd, 1890 - March 4th, 1903.

Sir Edward Henry Bt., G.C.V.O., K.C.B., C.S.I., March 5th, 1903 - September 2nd, 1918.

General the Rt. Hon. Sir Nevil Macready, Bt., G.C.M.G., K.C.B.,
  September 3rd, 1918 - April 14th, 1920.

Brigadier-General Sir William Horwood, G.B.E., K.C.B., D.S.O.,
  April 20th, 1920 - November 7th, 1928.

General (Subsequently Field-Marshal) the Rt.Hon. the Viscount Byng
  of Vimy, G.C.B., G.C.M.G., M.V.O., LL.D., November 8th, 1928 - September 30th, 1931.

Marshal of the Royal Air Force the Lord Trenchard, G.C.B., D.S.O.,
  D.C.L., LL.D., November 2nd, 1931 - November 11th, 1935.

Air Vice Marshal Sir Philip W. Game, G.C.B., G.C.V.O., November 29th,
  1935 - May 31st, 1945.

Sir Harold R. Scott, K.C.B., K.B.E., June 1st, 1945 - August 13th, 1953.

Sir John R.H. Nott-Bower, K.C.V.O., August 14th, 1953 - August 31st,
  1958.

Joseph Simpson Esq., O.B.E., (afterwards Sir Joseph Simpson K.B.E.)
  September 1st, 1958 - March 20th, 1968.

Sir John Waldron, K.C.V.O., April 5th, 1968 - April 16th, 1972.

Robert Mark Esq., Q.P.M. (afterwards Sir Robert Mark, G.B.E., Q.P.M.)
  April 17th, 1972 - March 12th, 1977.

David McNee Esq., Q.P.M., (afterwards Sir David McNee, Q.P.M.)
  March 13th, 1977 - October 1st, 1982.

Sir Kenneth Newman, Q.P.M., October 2nd, 1982 - July 31st, 1987.

Peter Imbert, Q.P.M. August 1st, 1987 -
  (afterwards Sir Peter Imbert).

* Sir Charles Rowan and Sir Richard Mayne were joint Commissioners 1829 - 1850, and Sir Richard Mayne and Captain Hay 1850 - 1855.

/- Inspecting Superintendent from September, 1839 - January, 1850.

RECEIVERS FOR THE METROPOLITAN POLICE DISTRICT

John Wray, Esq. July 7th 1829 - April 30th. 1860.
Maurice Drummond, Esq., C.B., May 1st 1860 - August 31st. 1883.
Sir Richard Pennefather, C.B., September 1st. 1883 - December 31st. 1909.
George H. Tripp, Esq., C.B., January 1st. 1910 - December 31st. 1918.
John Moylan, Esq. (afterwards Sir John Moylan, C.B., C.B.E.)
    January 1st.1919 - April 30th. 1945.
(Lionel W.Fox, Esq., Acting Receiver July 1940 - April 12th 1942).

Frederic C. Johnson, Esq., (afterwards Sir Frederic Johnson, C.B.)
    Acting Receiver 13th. April 1942 - 30th. April, 1945.
    Receiver May 1st. 1945 - October 31st, 1952.
(Stanislaus) Joseph Baker, Esq. C.B., (afterwards Sir Joseph Baker C.B.)
    November 1st 1952 - December 31st. 1960.
William H. Cornish, Esq. C.B., January 1st. 1961 - April 30th. 1967.
Kenneth A.L. Parker, Esq., C.B., May 1st. 1967 - September 1st. 1974.
Ronald Guppy, Esq., C.B., September 2nd. 1974 - December 31st. 1976.
Richard James, Esq. C.B., M.C., January 1st. 1977 - August 31st. 1980.
Alexander Douglas Gordon-Brown, Esq., September 1st. 1980 - 5th. March, 1987.
David Henry Jephson Hilary, Esq. 9th. March, 1987 -

It is taken for granted today that everybody knows how to use the telephone but in the early days of the Exchange clear instructions were circulated by the Executive Branch at Commissioner's Office throughout the Force —

TELEPHONES — DIRECTIONS AS TO USE OF

TO MAKE A CALL
See that the receiver is resting correctly on its supports, turn the handle quickly twice, take off the receiver and listen for an answer. In the case of Chief Stations which are in direct communication with CO no ringing is necessary, the mere insertion of the plug for CO and removal of the receiver from its rest calls attention of CO operator.

TO ANSWER A CALL
Take off the receiver and reply by stating who you are, or the name of your station, e.g. "Cannon Row" "Walton Street" etc. (not codes such as "AD" "RD" etc., owing to liability to error) the caller will then reply by giving his name, or name of station, thus ensuring that both are acquainted with whom they are connected.

THROUGH CONNECTIONS
If a through connection be required, caller will acquaint the operator with whom he first speaks of the destination he desires and each successive intermediate operator will pass the call on to the operator at the next connection, leaving the original caller through. The original caller is not to ring again until he has reached his destination and finished conversation. Where the connection is through CO the operator there will ask the Division concerned to get the station required and when informed by the Chief Station that the station required is at the telephone, will connect the division making the call. In cases where plugs are inserted to make connections, operators are to hold the plug itself by the shoulder and drive it well home in the switch hole, on no account holding the cords either when inserting or withdrawing pegs; where turnover switches are in use the turn over to be carefully and fully made.

SPEAKING
Speak directly into but a few inches off the transmitter, not loudly, but in the highest pitch of your voice (deep base does not carry well), take care

also to articulate every syallable distinctly; spell figures, if queried; and any names or difficult words. Important messages should be called back or the most important point of a message so verified. When speaking with a table set, take care to press the spring marked "press this while speaking" into its bed, not excessively, but without relaxation while speaking, as any variation of pressure upon the spring prevents carrying clearly. When using wall sets see that the rest correctly springs up up to its full extent as any failure of the spring to assume perfect position, will cause faint or imperfect conversation.

DIS- CONNECTIONS
When conversation has ended the receiver should be restored to its rest and if a through connection has been established, both ends should give a ring to indicate to intermediate operators that disconnection is to be made, such disconnections to be immediately made by officers concerned. The mere withdrawal of the plug and placing of receiver to its rest at Chief Stations in direct communication with CO will give a clearing signal to CO operator who will at once disconnect, leaving lines clear.

EXCHANGE CALL
As soon as the Exchange operator speaks in reply to your call, give the name of the Exchange and the number of the subscriber wanted and wait until the subscriber speaks, an intermittent buzzing sound indicates that the subscriber's line is engaged. When the subscriber answers, ascertain with whom you are speaking and inform him who you are before proceeding with conversation. In answering an Exchange call ascertain with whom you are speaking (including exchange and number) before conversing.

TRUNK CALLS
Acquaint Exchange operator that you require "Trunks" and when Trunk operator replies give him the name of your Exchange and number (City 400 if obtaining the trunk through CO) and ask for the town, name of Exchange and number you require. If through CO acquaint CO operator.

MARCONI'S WIRELESS TELEGRAPH COMPANY Ltd.

Marconi House,
Strand.
London. W.C.2.
10th Jan. 1924

The Engineer,
New Scotland Yard, S.W.1.

QUOTATION

1 (One) SET OF APPARATUS, as per Schedule No. 18282 herewith — At a total price of £160. 0. 0 (One hundred & sixty pounds) packed and delivered to Scotland Yard.

For MARCONI'S WIRELESS TELEGRAPH
Co. Ltd.
(ltd.)   A.A.Kift
Sales & Enquiries Dept.

Delivery:—
Already in your possession
Terms:—
Encl. — Schedule No. 18282

SCHEDULE OF APPARATUS

Item	Qty.	Msr	Article and Description
1.	1	—	TRANSMITTER, Type AD.1.
2.	1	—	MICROPHONE, Type AD.1. complete.
3.	3	prs.	TELEPHONES L.R.
4.	4	—	SPARKING PLUGS, Type KLG. with screens
5.	16	ft.	CABLE for ditto.
6.	2	—	VALVES, Type MT. 3 F.
7.	1	—	SWITCH, 5-amp. Tumbler.
8.	1	—	AMMETER in ebonite case, Type AD.2.
9.	1	—	AMPLIFIER, Type 55A. No. 201590.
10.	250	ft.	CABLE, No. 100.
11.	1	—	GENERATOR, 100-watt, Type YB. No.1106.
12.	2	prs.	SUSPENSION BRACKETS.
13.	14	ft.	ELASTIC, suspension.
14.	1	—	CONDENSER, smoothing.
15.	1	—	INSULATOR, leading-in.
16.	24	—	INSULATORS, small, porcelain.
17.	1	—	SUB-CONTROL UNIT, No. 239227
18.	6	—	VALVES, Type V. 24.
19.	1	—	VALVE, Type "Q".
20.	1	—	SWITCH, C.O. 4-way, barrel.
21.	2	—	VALVES, Type MT.3.
22.	1	—	SOCKET, 4-way.
23.	16	ft.	CABLE, H.T.
	2	—	M.T. 5 valve.
	1	—	H.T. Batty.

PERMANENT WIRELESS STAFFS FOR THE FLYING SQUAD
AND THE HEADQUARTER WIRELESS STATION
AS FROM MONDAY 16 APRIL 1934

HQ W/T STATION

FLYING SQUAD

PC.348 'CO' WORSFOLD — Senior Instructor

PC.370 'CO' COLE — In charge of Station
and Assistant Instructor

PC.349 'CO' JANES — in charge of tour PC.344 'CO' STEPHENS
PC.334 'CO' FRANCIS   PC.396 'CO' HARRISON
PC.345 'CO' LOVEMAN   PC.312 'CO' GREEN
PC.372 'CO' CHALLONS   PC.314 'CO' BEALCH
PC.346 'CO' MACHIN   PC.323 'CO' ALDRIDGE
                                                 PC.320 'CO' MORRISON
                                                 PC.350 'CO' DAVIS
                                                 PC.393 'CO' ABEL
                                                 PC.371 'CO' LAYZELL
PC.387 'CO' GRIFFIN — in charge of tour PC.392 'CO' WOOLVEN
PC.356 'CO' HOLLAND   PC.391 'CO' HEATH
PC.317 'CO' DAWKINS   PC.352 'CO' CONWAY
PC.330 'CO' WALKER   PC.366 'CO' HUGHES
PC.336 'CO' STROUD   PC.332 'CO' COE
                                                 PC.333 'CO' PROSS
                                                 PC.328 'CO' JOHNSON K
                                                 PC.365 'CO' GUNTRIP
                                                 PC.327 'CO' BAILEY
PC.319 'CO' SIDLE — in charge of tour PC.395 'CO' JOHNSON A
PC.360 'CO' CROFTS
PC.311 'CO' HOBSON
PC.373 'CO' GUNNER   PERKINS (229 'L')
PC.374 'CO' WILLIAMS

Officers underlined to receive
"Charge" allowance of 2/6d a week.

NB PC PERKINS to be
transferred permanently to
CO.

POLICE WIRELESS MID 1930s
CALL SIGNS

GSX 1, 2, 3	Metropolitan
GSY	Metropolitan HQ Station
GSZ 1, 2, 3	Metropolitan
GTA	Metropolitan 2 Way Car
GTB	Metropolitan Flying Squad Vans
GTC	
GTD	
GTE	Metropolitan HQ Wireless Vans
GTF	
GTG	Metropolitan General Group Call (Vans and Cars)
GTH	Edinburgh
GTI	Metropolitan 2 way car
GTJ	Metropolitan HQ Wireless Van
GTK	Glasgow
GTL 1, 2, 3	Lancashire
GTM	Liverpool (transmission and reception). Bootle (reception only)
GTN	Brighton
GTO	Nottinghamshire 2 way vehicles
GTP	Nottingham City 2 way vehicles
GTQ	Metropolitan Flying Squad Van
GTR 1, 2, 3	Rochdale (Fire Bridgade)
GTS	Stockport
GTT	Newcastle on Tyne
GTU	Nottingham (Headquarters Stations)
GTV	Metropolitan Vans Group Call
GTW	Wigan
GTX	Metropolitan HQ Wireless Van
GTY	West Riding
GTZ	Metropolitan, Denmark Hill Station
GWA	Aberdeen
GWB	Manchester
GWC	Salford
GWD	Oldham

GWE		Ashton-under-Lyne
GWF		Hyde
GWG		Stalybridge
GWH		Bolton
GWI		Rochdale
GWJ		Macclesfield
GWK)		
)		Metropolitan Thames Launches 2 way
GWL)		
GWM		Metropolitan HQ Wireless Van
GWN		Cheshire
GWO		Manchester regional group call
GWP		Boston
GWQ		Chesterfield
GWR		Metropolitan HQ Wireless Van
GWS		Metropolitan 2 way car
GWT		Grantham
GWU		Leicester City
GWV		Newark
GWW		Metropolitan, West Wickham Station
GWX		Rutland
GWY 1, 2, 3		Reigate Borough
GWZ 1, 2, 3		Essex County
MVA		Northampton Borough
MVB		Preston Borough
MVC		Congleton Borough
MVD		Glossop Borough
MVE		Bacup Borough
MVF		Blackburn Borough
MVG		Brecon County
MVH		Metropolitan Police (Hyde Park Observation Box)
MVI		Swansea Borough
MVJ		Grimsby Borough
MVK		Chester City
MVL		City of London
MVM		Wallasey
MVN		Metropolitan Police (Boat)
MVO		Liverpool Region Group Call Sign
MVP		Metropolitan Police (W/T School)
MVT)		
)		
MVU)		Metropolitan Police (Boat)
)		
MVW)		

CALL SIGNS (AREA WIRELESS SCHEME)
11th. June, 1934.

District	DAY Area	Call Sign	NIGHT Area	Call Sign
	A,B & C Divisions	5C	A,B & C Divisions	5C
	F Division	5F	F Division	5F
	Acton Sub Division	5G	Acton and Ealing	
	Ealing Sub Division	6T	Sub Divisions	5T
	Twickenham Sub Division	7T	Twickenham and Staines	
1.	Staines Sub Division	8T	Sub Divisions	7T
	Wandsworth Sub Division	5V	Wandsworth and	
	Richmond Sub Division	6V	Richmond Sub Divns.	5V
	Wimbledon Sub Division	7V	Wimbledon and Kingston	
	Kingston Sub Division	8V	Sub Divisions	7V
	D Division	5D	D Division	5D
	N Division	5N	N Division	5N
	Hampstead Sub Division	5S	Hamstead and Golders	
	Golders Green Sub Divn.	8S	Green Sub Divisions	5S
	Edgware Sub Division	7S	Edgware and Barnet	
	Barnet Sub Division	9S	Sub Divisions	7S
2.	Harrow Road Sub Divn.	5X	Harrow Road and	
	Harlesden Sub Division	6X	Harlesden Sub Divns.	5X
	Harrow Sub Division	7X	Harrow and Uxbridge	
	Uxbridge Sub Division	8X	Sub Divisions	7X
	Hornsey Sub Division	5Y	Hornsey and Wood	
	Wood Green Sub Divn.	6Y	Green Sub Divisions	5Y
	Tottenham Sub Divn.	7Y	Tottenham and Enfield	
	Enfield Town Sub Divn.	8Y	Town Sub Divisions	7Y
	E & G Divisions	5G	E & G Divisions	5G
	H Division	6H	H Division	6H
	Hackney Sub Division	5J	Hackney and Leyton	
	Leyton Sub Division	6J	Sub Divisions	5J
	Walthamstow Sub Divn.	7J	Walthamstow and	
3.	Woodford Sub Division	8J	Woodford Sub Divn.	7J
	West Ham Sub Division	5K	West Ham and Ilford	
	Ilford Sub Division	6K	Sub Divisions	5K

Plaistow Sub Division	7K	Plaistow and East Ham		
East Ham Sub Division	8K	Sub Divisions	7K	
L Division	5L	L Division	5L	
M Division	6M	M Division	6M	
E Dulwich Sub Divn.	5P	Lewisham and E.		
Lewisham Sub Division	6P	Dulwich Sub Divns.	5P	
Southend Village Sub		Southend Village and		
Division	7P	Bromley Sub Divns.	7P	
Bromley Sub Division	8P			
Blackheath Rd.Sub Divn.	5R	Blackheath Road and		
Eltham Sub Division	6R	Eltham Sub Divisions	5R	
Woolwich Sub Division	7R	Woolwich and Bexley		
Bexley Heath Sub Divn.	8R	Heath Sub Divisions	7R	
Lavender Hill Sub Divn.	5W	Lavender Hill and		
Balham Sub Division	6W	Balham Sub Divisions	5W	
Tooting Sub Division	7W	Tooting and Sutton		
Sutton Sub Division	8W	Sub Divisions	7W	
Streatham Sub Division	5Z	Streatham and Norbury		
Norbury Sub Division	6Z	Sub Divisions	5Z	
Croydon Sub Division	7Z	Croydon and Wallington		
Wallington Sub Division	8Z	Sub Divisions	7Z	

4.

CALL SIGNS
TRAFFIC PATROL CARS FITTED WITH W/T

No.1 District	No. 2 District	No.3 District	No. 4 District
1G	2A	3A	4A
1H	2C	3B	4B
1J	2F	3C	4C
1K	2G	3F	4F
1L	2J	3L	4G
1M	2K	3M	4H
1P	2L	3P	4J
1R	2P	3R	4K

"Q" VEHICLES

No. 1 District	No.2 District	No.3 District	No.4 District
1Q	2Q	3Q	4Q
5Q	6Q	7Q	8Q
9Q	2U	3U	4U
9U	6U	7U	8U

The above to be allocated by Officers I/C Districts to the vehicles performing the duties concerned, irrespective of the actual individual vehicle which may be employed, i.e. if a spare Q vehicle is brought out it will take over the call sign of the duty on which it is employed. The allocation made should be reported to D.1. Branch.

INDEX

N.B.   Due to the extensive reference to divisions, police stations and other premises these have not generally been included in the index.   Many junior ranks have been mentioned and are not indexed in every case.   The ranks shown for police officers are not always the highest rank they finally achieved.

ILLUSTRATIONS

John Bunker has for the past three years held the rank of Superintendent in the Metropolitan Police where he is deputy to the officer in charge of the Central Command Complex at New Scotland Yard.

Born in Kilburn, north west London, his father also spent thirty years in the Force retiring as a sergeant.

In April 1957, at the age of nineteen, on joining the Metropolitan Police as a constable, the author served his first two years at Cannon Row Police Station, the division then responsible for policing the Royal Palaces and many Government Buildings. He later saw service in this rank at Hyde Park and Southall Police Stations.

On promotion to sergeant he was posted to the busy Paddington Division followed by five hectic years in the rank of Station Sergeant at Wembley and Harlesden.

In 1974, achieving the rank of Inspector, he found himself at Hammersmith Police Station continuing in an active operational role.

By 1981 the Force was moving rapidly towards computerisation of its message handling systems and he took up a post of Chief Inspector on the Command and Control Project Team becoming involved in the successful commissioning of this new technology in July 1984. After the opening of the new communications complex by the Duke of Gloucester that year he remained in the field of Force communications.

'From Rattle to Radio', researched over six years, is his first book; although he has subscribed short articles on communications history to the Metropolitan Police History Society Magazine and the Force newspaper 'The Job'. 'On Line', an in house magazine produced to promote the new Command and Control, was organised by the author prior to the introduction of the new system.

His off duty interests, apart from history, include photography and genealogy, having traced his family back to 1691 in Plymstock, Devon.

John is married and lives with his wife, Audrey, and daughter, Michelle, at Ickenham in Middlesex.

BRITISH POLICE HISTORY SERIES

Other titles in our Police History Series are as follow:

Policing Shropshire 1836-1967 by Douglas J. Elliott

A year by year account of the police forces of the Shropshire Constabulary and the police forces of the Boroughs of Bridgenorth, Ludlow, Oswestry, Shrewsbury and Wenlock.

Fully illustrated. 288 pages   **Hardback ISBN 0 947731 00 8   £10.95**
                                Paperback ISBN 0 947731 01 6   £ 5.40

Policing Northamptonshire 1836-1986 by Richard Cowley

A comprehensive history of Northamptonshire Police and of the police forces of the boroughs of Northampton, Daventry and Higham Ferrers to commemorate 150 years of service to the county.

Fully illustrated. 248 pages.   **Paperback ISBN 0 947731 21 0   £ 8.40**

Policing West Mercia 1967-1988 by David J. Smith

An illustrated review containing over 400 photographs of the work of The West Mercia Constabulary in Shropshire, Staffordshire and Worcestershire. The photographs cover the force at work and recreation with illustrations of people, equipment and vehicles. The book also deals with the major crimes and events handled by the force from establishment to coming of age in 1988.

Fully illustrated. Over 200 pages Large A4 Format.

Paperback ISBN 0 947731 46 6   £10.95

The above titles are available from good bookshops or, in case of difficulty, direct from the publishers (adding 10% towards postage).

BREWIN BOOKS,
Doric House, Church Street, Studley, Warwickshire. B80 7LG.